DISCARD

D1403411

{ HALLELUJAH LADS AND LASSES }

DISCARD

HALLELUJAH LADS & LASSES

{ **Remaking the Salvation Army in America, 1880-1930** }

LILLIAN TAIZ

The University of North Carolina Press
Chapel Hill and London

© 2001 The University of North Carolina Press
All rights reserved

Designed by April Leidig-Higgins
Set in New Baskerville by Keystone Typesetting, Inc.
Manufactured in the United States of America

The paper in this book meets the guidelines for
permanence and durability of the Committee on
Production Guidelines for Book Longevity of the
Council on Library Resources.

Library of Congress Cataloging-in-Publication Data
Taiz, Lillian. Hallelujah lads and lasses: remaking the
Salvation Army in America, 1880–1930 / Lillian Taiz.
p.   cm. Includes bibliographical references and index.
ISBN 0-8078-2621-9 (hardcover: alk. paper)
ISBN 0-8078-4935-9 (pbk.: alk. paper)
1. Salvation Army—United States—History—19th
century. 2. Salvation Army—United States—History
—20th century. I. Title.
BX9716.T35 2001   287.9'6'0973—dc21   00-047950

05 04 03 02 01   5 4 3 2 1

To my mother, Malvena Taiz,
who showed me the way

{ CONTENTS }

{ ILLUSTRATIONS }

{ TABLES }

{ ACKNOWLEDGMENTS }

As so many have said before, in the course of completing a project like this, one incurs many debts. First, I would like to acknowledge the intellectual nurturing of Paul Goodman and Roland Marchand of the University of California–Davis history department, both of whom have, sadly, passed away. I am also grateful for the unflagging support provided by Ruth Rosen and Mary Felstiner, both of whom had profound effects on my development as a historian.

Early in my research I received vital economic assistance from the University of California–Davis and its Humanities Institute, as well as the Center for the Study of Philanthropy in the Graduate Center of the City University of New York. More recently I benefited from a Research, Scholarship and Creative Activity Award from the California State University, Los Angeles (1995–96); a Faculty Fellowship from the Pew Program in Religion and American History (1997–98); and supplementary support provided by the Dean of Natural and Social Sciences, California State University–Los Angeles, David Soltz.

At the Salvation Army Archives and Research Center, I was assisted by an able team of archivists and administrators. I would like to thank all of the staff whom I have come to regard as friends. Connie Hagood always responded quickly and efficiently to my endless, nagging inquiries. Scott Bedio provided valuable assistance in gathering the photographs that informed my work. Finally, I am very grateful to Susan M. Mitchem for not only facilitating all my work at the archives but putting me up in her home during my last visit.

On each of my trips to the archives I was assisted by Deena Belikoff. A skilled auto mechanic, Deena turned her formidable abilities to intellectual work and demonstrated that only her distaste for sitting still for long stretches of time and not smoking prevented her from becoming a professional scholar. She brought new meaning to the word *friendship*. I would also like to thank Kit and Jules Timmerman, as well as Carol Lourea Black, who at various times put me up in their homes while I worked on the East Coast. I also owe a debt of gratitude to Nikki Mandel, who repeatedly helped me pull out of analytical dead-ends and corners. I could not possibly have completed the project without her help, literally, to the end. I would also like to thank my longtime friend Carol Seigel, who always provided perspective. In addition, my project was improved by feedback from Carole Srole, Phil Goff, Pamela J. Walker, Ann Taves, and Colleen McDannell, each of whom read all or parts of the manuscript. I must also acknowledge the extremely helpful comments provided by the readers selected by the University of North Carolina Press, which greatly enriched my discussion of the Salvation Army.

Finally, I would like to thank all of my family. My mother, Malvena Taiz, provided unconditional love while teaching me to respect power and question authority. Paul and Christine Washington, my mom and dad, provided models of lives lived through courage, honor, and integrity. My husband, Chris Toomey, has consistently respected and supported my goals; I am overjoyed by the fact that we still love each other after so many years and so very many adventures. Finally, my children, Jason West (and his family, Angela and Joseph) and Kampala Taiz-Rancifer (and her family, Mark and Jordan), have been my other life project. If this book turns out half as well as they have, then I can, indeed, be proud.

{ ABBREVIATIONS }

CDO	Chief Divisional Officer
CUS	Christian Undenominational Society
DO	District Officer
HQ	Headquarters
IHQ	International Headquarters
NHQ	National Headquarters
PCHA	Pacific Coast Holiness Association
PO	Provisional Officer
UMW	United Mine Workers

{ HALLELUJAH LADS AND LASSES }

The washerwoman is a member of the Salvation Army.
And over the tub of suds rubbing underwear clean
She sings that Jesus will wash her sins away,
And the red wrongs she has done God and man
Shall be white as driven snow.
Rubbing underwear she sings of the Last Great Washday.
— CARL SANDBERG, *Cornhuskers*

As it has for most Americans, the Salvation Army skirted along the periphery of my consciousness all of my life. In the early 1950s I lived in a section of Philadelphia that today is dominated by oceans of row homes. In those days, however, there was just a handful of houses around the corner from Five Points Cafe, a local bar. For the few children in the area, the duckpond and hillside sledding at Children's Heart Hospital, the Fairmont Riding Academy, Woodside Amusement Park, and the Salvation Army's orphanage distinguished the neighborhood. I lived down the street in one of two huge, nearly identical three-story brick mansions each of which that had, by this time, been broken up into apartments. Although the neighborhood children played a made-up game called "orphanage," none of us ever visited or played with the kids at the Salvation Army home. Perhaps the large, gray stone building seemed too forbidding or the idea of meeting real orphans too disquieting for the many of us who lived in single-parent households.[1]

Over the decade during which I lived in that neighborhood, it changed radically; the other brick apartment building was torn down along with Woodside Park and the Riding Academy. The area quickly overflowed with block after block of new row homes. Even the Salvation Army tore down its building in 1962 and replaced it with a series of individual "bungalows" reflecting the latest ideas about caring for children in smaller familial-style groupings by the 1960s.[2]

Except for their ubiquitous Thrift Stores and Christmas-time bell ringers, I never gave the Salvation Army another thought until 1971 when my obstetrician moved his practice to Booth Memorial Hospital on City Line Avenue in Philadelphia. First opened in 1896 as a "rescue home" for "fallen women," by the 1920s the hospital had evolved into a "Home and Hospital for Unmarried Mothers."[3] By the 1970s, in a world in which young single women increasingly chose to keep their children, the home once again transformed itself into a "birthing center" where married and single women could have their children in a less hospital-like setting.

In the 1980s I was searching for a dissertation topic that would somehow resonate with my own lengthy experience living on the economic margins as a single mother of two. In the course of that hunt I attended a meeting of the Organization of American Historians in Reno, Nevada. During his commentary at a session on the settlement house movement, Clark Chambers elder statesman of social welfare history, reiterated some of the points that he raised in his 1986 article, "Toward a Redefinition of Welfare History." Most welfare history, he suggested, has focused on middle-class social workers and philanthropists. But "[w]hat of the networks, informal and formal, of reciprocal assistance . . . [that] defined the lives of those millions who were not middle class either in objective condition or in subjective self-perception." Furthermore, other aspects of voluntary associationalism in American life also need study. "Mainline, respectable Protestant charities have received dutiful attention," he wrote, "but the welfare programs of evangelistic crusades — the Salvation Army, Volunteers of America, Goodwill Industries of America — have yet to be taken seriously."[4]

In retrospect, it seems somehow appropriate that I would write about this organization with which I'd had periodic contact but about which I knew absolutely nothing. I must confess that (perhaps because I am not a Christian) never once in my contact with the orphanage, thrift stores, bell-ringers, and hospital did it occur to me that the Salvation Army was a Christian religious organization. Indeed, I am now embarrassed to say that I imagined the "salvation" in Salvation Army referred to the salvaged goods they sold in their second hand stores! Why, I wondered as I began my research, had I never realized that this was an evangelical Christian group?

I discovered, to my surprise, that in 1978 the Salvation Army organized and funded a sophisticated Archive and Research Center initially located in New York City but now housed in their National Headquarters building in Alexandria, Virginia.[5] The archive has a number of strengths, not the least of which is its team of professionally trained archivists who, with resources provided by the organization, have ensured the preservation of historical materials. The number of documents is staggering and includes thousands of photographs, hundreds of films, audio recordings, reports, correspondence, personal papers, memoirs, personnel or career files, birth records from the maternity hospitals, and much more. The staff has carefully cataloged the materials to which they constantly add new documents.[6] I found the resources rich and largely untapped by outside researchers. Typically the archive serves Salvation Army members who are writing histories of the organization and individuals who, armed with court orders, are seeking information about their birth parents.[7]

While the archival resources are quite rich, they also have serious limitations. When I began the project I expected to focus more on the Salvation Army's rank-and-file members (also known as soldiers). Unfortunately, data for soldiers is very difficult to find. Not only did corps (mission stations or churches) move frequently, but Salvationists often lacked the educational skills needed to maintain accurate written records. Of the few Soldiers' Roll Books that survive, most date from the early twentieth century and provide very little information beyond a name and address. Geographical mobility made tracking these men and women through the census virtually impossible; the books regularly show four or five addresses for a single soldier and do not indicate when he or she lived at any one particular location. There may be other materials out there, but they are probably in the attics and basements of Salvationist families.

In addition to the dearth of materials on the rank and file, the Salvation Army exercises considerable control over their holdings. For example, the organization restricts access to the founding family's papers including those of Evangeline Booth, commander of the Salvation Army forces in the United States from 1904 until 1934. While they did provide access to previously restricted officer career files, the archivists established strict written guidelines that allowed me to "record only non-identifying information for the sole purpose of compiling aggregate statistics," which I then used to draw a portrait of male and female officers. Moreover, although the group kept their own aggregate statistics in the nineteenth and early twentieth centuries explaining why officers left the organization, they still do not permit these data to be published.

Even without the limitations imposed by the archive, it would be difficult for me to provide information about the number of participants, their movements in and out of the organization, where they came from, and where they went. The very nature of Salvation Army religious activities makes even defining who qualifies as a "participant" difficult. Although thousands of Americans attended Salvation Army events, much smaller numbers actually became soldiers. Who, then, should be considered a "participant"? I decided to limit my focus to the men and women who committed themselves to the rigors of officer or soldiership (those for whom data is available).[8]

Salvation Army: Working-Class Religion

In 1865 William and Catherine Booth organized what would eventually become the Salvation Army in Britain. During the 1870s the group evolved from a loosely organized nondenominational urban home mission to a more structured revivalist movement. In 1878, the organization adopted military symbolism and discipline and renamed itself the Salvation Army. This book investigates the Salvation Army in the United States from its earliest days as an evangelical Christian holiness mission advertising salvation with its peculiarly working-class form of experiential religion. It also examines the group's developing style of evangelical-social Christianity and the concomitant "refinement" of its religious culture beginning at the turn of the century. These discussions reveal ongoing tensions between autonomy and hierarchy, independence and subordination, local innovation and centralization that characterized the group's evolution.

The Salvation Army is a colorful but understudied religious movement. Historians of American religion, urban poverty, and reform movements regarded the Salvation Army in the United States as part of the Protestant response to urban life. As a consequence, their discussion of the organization focused exclusively on its welfare work in city slums and its influence on the emerging social gospel movement. I would argue, however, that representing the Army solely as a "Gospel Welfare" movement obscures its role as a working-class religious institution.[9] Studying the Salvation Army as an evangelical Christian organization, on the other hand, provides a unique opportunity to examine the character of working-class religiosity in the late nineteenth century.

Scholars do not agree on the nature and meaning of religious experience among the working class in the United States. The few labor historians who have addressed the issue argue that Christianity provided organized labor with a language to critique capitalism and justify trade unionism. Religion, they suggest, was an area of contested terrain where labor and capital "each . . . [made] claims upon Christianity for justification and legitimacy." Others have stressed the role of religion in dividing the working class. "The most visible sign of the importance of religion in working-class communities," wrote one historian, "was its divisiveness." These cleavages have at various times pitted revivalists against traditionalists, Protestants against Catholics, Christians against Jews, and the religious against the irreligious. Finally, immigration historians have studied working-class religion by examining the ways in which immigrant churches sometimes helped their communities hold onto traditions and sustain "mutual assistance" but at other times divided them.[10] This rich body of research sought to explain the inability of the American working class to gain meaningful political power in the United States. As a result, religion appears primarily as an obstacle to working-class solidarity. None of this work provides insight into the nature of working-class religion and how working men and women experienced, performed, and represented their spirituality.[11]

Between 1879 and 1896, American Salvationists created a working class–dominated cross-class organization.[12] *Hallelujah Lads and Lasses* (as young Salvationists were often known) addresses Salvation Army members, their relationship to the organization, and the American religious marketplace.[13] When the group entered the United States in 1879, it immediately located its "market niche" among young, single, working-class men and women. The Army and its constituency constructed a religious culture that attracted attention, or, as one leader described it, "advertised salvation," by combining individual holiness as the true sign of faith with an intensely experiential, autonomous working-class religious culture. In its crowded daily schedule of services, the Army institutionalized frontier camp-meeting religious enthusiasm by encouraging members to follow up the initial euphoria of conversion with a continuous "revival of feeling."[14]

At these sanctioned, intense, emotional religious performances, audiences prayed, testified, and exhorted not only with their voices but also with their bodies, hands, and feet. The evidence also describes religious services that absorbed and reinvented patterns of working-class popular culture modeled on the saloon and theater. Salvationist spiritual expression in the late nineteenth century resembled an urban version of the old-time frontier camp meeting combined with working-class forms of popular culture. This approach to working-class religion provides insight into evangelical Christianity at the end of the nineteenth century. As historian Richard Wightman Fox has pointed out, we need "to know much more than we do about the development of evangelical Christianity since 1875, especially its paradoxical mixture of modern and anti-modern commitments. . . ."[15] Moreover, the Salvation Army offers a *unique* opportunity to consider how new ideas about the sources of poverty affected an historic shift within a revivalist organization in the late nineteenth century from a highly experiential Christian evangelicalism to an evangelical-social Christian hybrid religion.

Hallelujah Lads and Lasses demonstrates that, in addition to an autonomous experiential religion, the Salvation Army provided its pioneering generation of young, working-class male and female Salvationists with a variety of rewards for their commitment to the movement. Youthful officers found remarkable levels of independence and adventure as they set off to share the keys to the Kingdom with others like themselves. In return for their efforts, the Army provided an organizational hierarchy that offered them new opportunities for religious and administrative leadership, moral authority (regardless of gender), and membership in a sacred community.

Although the Salvation Army drew most of its membership from the working class, the group also attracted much smaller numbers of middle-class men and women with college education and business and/or civil service experience. While their numbers were small, their training facilitated the implementation of the group's social service program for the poor at the turn of the century. Like the many working-class members, the intensity of religious feeling, the communal solidarity, and opportunities for usefulness and leadership drew them to the organization.[16] Unlike their working-class comrades, however, many middle-class Salvationists shared the concern of "respectable" Americans that the democracy of the group's experiential religious practice revealed spiritual shallowness in rank-and-file members. As a result, for some of them, a desire to teach holiness to rank-and-file Salvationists took priority even over the conversion of sinners. Furthermore, in contrast to working-class members, these middle-class men and women apparently regarded their mission as *service* to others quite *unlike* themselves. Their reservations about experiential religion as well as their understanding of religious service facilitated the development of a Salvationism in which they preached to the already converted (Salvationists) and performed Christian service through social work to the "heathen masses."

As *Hallelujah Lads and Lasses* explains, the Salvation Army experienced several significant changes between 1879 and 1934. In the early years, tensions between centralized hierarchical authority and local autonomy sparked two near-fatal confrontations between the British and American administrations. Within the United States, at the same time, similar conflict generally resolved itself peacefully in favor of democracy giving local corps and soldiers significant levels of autonomy. The introduction of the Army's social Christian work in the United States, as well as the growing numbers of second-generation and upwardly mobile Salvationists, changed the organization at the turn of the century. Democracy and local autonomy declined as bureaucratic authority shifted upward. Increasingly, instead of "advertising salvation" with highly experiential religious performance, the Army attempted to attract souls by addressing the physical needs of the masses.

Finally, long-time opponents of the Army's expressive religious culture found new allies among the Army's second generation and bureaucrats promoting the social work. Together they successfully tamed the group's once boisterous services. Increasingly the group replaced its adaptations of working-class leisure culture with the new technologies of mass commercial culture. Like the transformed world of the nineteenth-century theater and variety shows, once rowdy and highly participatory religious meetings now featured formalized religious rituals, sedate stereopticon slide shows, and films. Similarly, spontaneous and boisterous street parades representing the religious fervor of the Salvationists became highly structured, occasional grand parades down main city boulevards promoting the redemptive nature of the Army's social work. In the early decades of the twentieth century, older Salvationists and new converts alike had to either adapt to the organization's now more decorous expression of religion or select another path.

In addition to the contribution *Hallelujah Lads and Lasses* makes to the understanding of working-class religion, it is also important because the Army has been so thoroughly ignored by scholars. There have been only two other histories of the Salvation Army in the United States written by academics since 1980. Edward McKinley's *Marching to Glory* (1980) is an institutional history. While his book does not engage current debates in gender, social, and cultural history, it makes an important contribution to our understanding of the organization's growth and development. Diane Winston's *Red Hot and Righteous* (1999) combines the history of ideas with an American studies approach. Because she relies almost exclusively on published sources, however, her research fails to engage archival evidence of Salvation Army membership. As a result, we learn nothing about the men and women who joined the movement, nor do we discover anything about the group's working-class nature. Winston does, however, provide insight into the impact of New York City's urban middle-class culture of commerce and consumption on the images that the Salvation Army used to promote itself.[17]

Conversion Narratives as Sources

In addition to organizational publications, memoirs, diaries, personal and business correspondence, and internal and external reports, I have used Salvationists' published and unpublished testimony or conversion narratives. In her book, *From Sin to Salvation: Stories of Women's Conversions, 1800 to the Present*, Virginia Lieson Brereton warned that, due to their formulaic quality, conversion narratives not only fail to document the "emergence of self," but they should not be read "as direct accounts" or "accurate historical testimony." What the narratives do reveal, she argues, is that "something important happened, something of a distinctly religious character."[18] Regenia Gagnier, on the other hand, classifies working-class conversion narratives as "the most highly structured pole of working-class autobiography." In these narratives even though she continues to face obstacles, the subject describes a life in which she "is all bad until her conversion, then she is all good." As a result, Gagnier argues, the working-class person is "granted subjectivity (self-importance and the attention of readers) through personal salvation in conversion." The conversion experience gave the working-class person selfhood by making her life story significant.[19]

While Susan Juster agrees that the "often pseudonymous testimonies" found in religious publications provide little biographical information beyond "sex and, occasionally . . . age and marital status," she argues that their formulaic quality makes conversion narratives "useful as a reflection of cultural norms" and "an instrument by which a sociocultural reality is created." According to Juster, early-nineteenth-century conversion narratives reveal that while women and men had gender-specific conceptions of authority and the self which they took with them to the conversion experience, in the end both experienced a restoration of moral agency. "Converted men and women," she says, "stood before God in the same position: as moral agents, integrated into the Christian community."[20]

Similarly, in her discussion of pardon tales, Natalie Zemon Davis believes that there is a great deal to be gained by putting the fictional elements of the documents at the center of her discussion. Indeed, she argues that the fictive aspects of the tales do not necessarily make them false but, instead, "might well bring verisimilitude or a moral truth."[21]

Although both formulaic and fictive, I believe that Salvation Army conversion narratives provide insight in a number of ways. First, they clearly served a pedagogical and prescriptive role by defining sin and explaining how to achieve salvation.[22] Furthermore, the narratives also furnish the means to explore class and gender distinctions among Salvationists before and after conversion by revealing that working- and middle-class men and women defined sin (resistance to God's authority) and agency (gained through regeneration) differently.[23] Finally, the conversion narratives give us some insight into what motivated these working- and middle-class men and women to join an organization that in the late nineteenth century not only exposed them publicly to ridicule but demanded so many personal sacrifices.

In the chapters that follow, I have attempted to explore the evolution of the Salvation Army's bureaucracy and religious culture. Chapter 1 explains why it is instructive to study what began as a British organization in its American context. "Missionaries to America: The Americanization of the Salvation Army" discusses the transformation of the organization from a British missionary effort in the United States to an American evangelical movement with clear but uneasy ties to its British parent. The second and third chapters draw a portrait of the Salvation Army and its members in the late nineteenth century. Chapter 2, "Red Hot Men and Women in the Salvation Army, 1879–1896," looks at the large numbers of working-class people (and much smaller numbers of the middle class) with whom the Salvation Army proved most successful. For these men and women, Salvationism was more than a religion; it provided them with a sacred community within which they created new definitions of manhood and womanhood, gained meaningful careers, found marriage partners, and accrued moral and administrative authority. Chapter 3, "The World Salvationists Made: Democracy and Autonomy in the Salvation Army, 1878–1896," explores the nature of Salvationism and argues that, although the organization represented itself as rigidly hierarchical, the bureaucratic and religious culture it created allowed surprising levels of democratic participation.

Chapter 4, " 'A New Message of Temporal Salvation': Reinventing the Army at the Turn of the Century," examines the impact of the Salvation Army's decision to advertise salvation through social as well as spiritual service. I suggest that it created dramatic changes in the group's administrative structure and bureaucratic culture by centralizing authority and dividing the organization into specialized branches, one for spiritual and the other for social service. Most significant, the changes challenged the older style of democratic participation among the rank and file. Chapter 5, "Salvationism at the Turn of the Century: Refining Religious Culture, Reconceiving a Religious Market," argues that by the turn of the century long-time opponents of expressive religious culture, many newly created Salvation Army bureaucrats, and an upwardly mobile second generation facilitated the evolution of Salvationism from a democratic and highly experiential religion to a much more orderly and decorous style of religious expression. Its new religious form combined carefully scripted or choreographed Salvationist rituals, judicious uses of the emerging technologies of mass culture, the "refinement of spectacle," and audience restraint.

MISSIONARIES TO AMERICA

The Americanization of the Salvation Army

The spiritual tide is rising every hour. It is only a question of time. It is the chance of a generation. — GEORGE SCOTT RAILTON

I n 1885, the *Chicago Tribune* reported on a religious service led by three officials of the Salvation Army. In addition to testimonies by members of the group and a short sermon by Captain Evans, the service featured singing by Mrs. Evans to the less than euphonious accompaniment provided by Captain Gay on the concertina. According to the article, Captain Evans accounted for his colleague's musical inadequacy by explaining, " 'Hi wish to hobserve that the Captain has been compelled to use hanother and hinferior hinstrument tonight. Now hits really a shame, for Capt. Gay saved enough out of his salary of $6 a week to buy that horgan, and devoted it to the service of the Lord. But we forgive the young man as took it, hand 'ope 'e'll be converted.' "[1]

Dialects have always played an important role in American discourse on class, race, and ethnic diversity. Throughout the nineteenth century, minstrel shows used dialects to construct distinct racial and ethnic caricatures.[2] Moreover, American writers like William Dean Howells purposefully used dialect because they believed that it allowed their characters to "reveal not only their motives, personality, range of interests, and habits of thought, but also their origins, social class, and degree of refinement."[3] When the *Tribune* reporter intentionally used a dialect to quote Captain Evans, he both revealed and reinforced American public perceptions about the national origins, class character, and "degree of refinement" of the Salvation Army in the late nineteenth century. The dropped "h" in "'ope 'e'll be converted" clearly established the captain as a cockney or "mongrelized" member of the English working class;[4] the exaggerated and inappropriate use of the aspirate, or "h," as in "Hi wish to hobserve" and "hanother hinferior hinstrument," suggested an un-educated lower-class man's pretensions to a higher class.[5]

Historically speaking, the *Tribune* reporter was accurate; the Salvation Army was, indeed, of British origin and its members were largely working class.[6] By 1885, however, the American branch of the organization strug-gled to redefine itself in relation to both the British parent organization and the American population from which it needed to draw support. Marketing the Army in this country not only required that the organiza-tion conform to American laws but encouraged it to incorporate Ameri-can symbols and cultural styles with which potential members could iden-tify. At the same time, however, this process of Americanization created serious tensions with the British founders who had increasing difficulty exerting control over the American branch of the Salvation Army. This chapter will examine the British evolution of the organization, its entry into the North American religious marketplace, and, most important, its transition from a British missionary effort in the United States to an American evangelical movement with clear but uneasy ties to its British parent.

The Salvation Army emerged in an era of heightened concern about the religious life of the urban working class in both Britain and the United States. When the group entered this country in the late nineteenth century, it confronted a rapidly changing religious landscape in which churches grappled with the transformations caused by large-scale indus-trialization, urbanization, and immigration. Protestant church member-ship grew dramatically in this period as mainstream Protestant churches followed their middle-class and well-to-do congregations into new class-segregated suburbs.[7]

The movement of Protestant churches out of city centers, however, left many religious leaders deeply concerned about the spiritual health of the rapidly changing urban population. In the United States, middle-class Protestants like Samuel Loomis worried that " '[t]he faith on which the nation was founded . . . has almost no place among the working class.' "[8] Indeed, an investigation by the pastor of a Chicago Baptist church re-vealed that church-alienated workingmen in Chicago believed main-stream churches were, at best, not interested in workingmen and, at worst, opposed to them.[9] As they fretted about the spread of "vice," "alien" faiths (Catholicism and Judaism), and ideologies (anarchy and socialism) among the urban working class, the cultural-imperialist im-pulse of these leaders unleashed a wave of activities through which they hoped to safeguard and restore "traditional" Anglo-American values.[10] Wrote the Presbyterian Board of Home Missions in 1894, " 'what the cities are, the country will be in all the phases of national life. Our safety lies, in a great measure, in the evangelization of the foreign elements in our great centres of population.' "[11]

The response included innovations like institutional churches that some liberal Protestants believed provided the best hope of regaining moral authority among the masses in American cities. The key, they believed, "was to de-emphasize the doctrinal elements that rendered Protestantism unacceptable to the newcomers," while providing a variety of community programs ranging "from soup kitchens to banks to gymnasium classes."[12] Although they claimed inordinate success for their efforts, as Paul Boyer has pointed out, very few programs actually existed by 1894.[13]

In addition to institutional churches, Protestants also borrowed from earlier techniques including Sunday schools, revivals, and city missions. In the 1870s, for example, Chicago businessman B. F. Jacobs orchestrated the creation of a network of church Sunday schools, each teaching the same religious curriculum. By the turn of the century, 120 Sunday schools operated in Chicago slum areas alone.[14] Another familiar religious technique, the revival, became mass spectacle in the hands of Dwight Moody in the 1870s. His application of business techniques and innovative preaching practices established the model for "nondenominational professional revivals."[15] Finally, the cultural imperialist impulse also expressed itself in an array of missionary and rescue operations that sprang up in urban districts. City missions opened under the auspices of denominational churches, holiness advocates, and Pentecostals, as well as nondenominational groups.[16]

The Salvation Army was one of the growing numbers of nondenominational movements established in order to bring the Gospel to the "heathen masses."[17] Like other missionary efforts, the cultural imperialist impulse encouraged Salvationists to expand their reach so that by the 1880s the group could be found in the United States, France, India, and Australia.[18] In contrast to most home missions, however, the Salvation Army developed a relatively unique approach to working-class irreligion; in a process of cultural adaptation, working-class Army converts used working-class cultural forms to promote and market Salvationism to men and women like themselves. Wrote the *Christian at Work* in 1883, "[i]t ought not to be forgotten that the Army is composed of a very peculiar class, drawn from the lower strata of society, and that it is on this same class they are striving to operate. The methods they use and the language they employ may not command themselves to more refined and intellectual Christian minds, but they are just such as seem to be appreciated and to reach the class they are intended for."[19] The Army's reliance on cultural adaptation to "market" the organization made Americanization essential.[20] As we will see, however, when confronted by its cultural imperialist impulse, the complicated nature of Americanization created tensions with the British parent organization that plagued the group into the twentieth century.

The Salvation Army fit rather loosely into a larger holiness revival that swept through the Methodist church in the late nineteenth century.[21] The Army's most direct connection to a Holiness Association came in the western part of the United States. In this region the Army did not descend directly from the 1879 pioneering efforts in Philadelphia discussed below. Instead, it evolved from the Pacific Coast Holiness Association (PCHA) in 1883 under the leadership of Reverend George Newton, a Methodist minister. After seeing an issue of *The War Cry* (London), the PCHA initiated its own "Salvation Army" without the British organization's knowledge or sanction. Later that year "the Association drifted away from the 'army'" and Newton wrote to General William Booth "to take into the Salvation Army of the world, the 'army' of the Pacific Coast." Soon after receiving this notice Booth sent his representative, Major Alfred Wells, to take command.[22]

The theological roots of the nineteenth-century holiness movement lay in the eighteenth-century perfectionism of John Wesley. According to Wesley, God believed men and women were capable of achieving perfection in this life. By defining sin as "a voluntary act of will," Wesley suggested that God could free them "not only from particular sinful acts, but also from the disease of sinful motives and the 'power' of sin."[23] In the nineteenth century, Phoebe Worral Palmer helped to revive holiness teaching among Methodists. Her work deeply influenced "the beginnings and temper of the Salvation Army movement."[24] Palmer suggested that the experience of holiness was both an "event in time" and "a way of life." The event took place when a person gave her heart to Christ by "placing all on the altar" with the faith that God would provide "freedom from any inclination [that] did not spring from love." The way of life consisted of "continued exercise of faith and obedience" to God.[25]

Salvationism bears the imprint of Palmer's understanding of perfectionism because it stresses the immediacy of the event, the two stages of religious experience: conversion and sanctification, and the centrality of faith in achieving the second blessing. The Army also embraced Palmer's insistence on public testimony as "not only essential to the promulgation of Christian holiness but even more essential to the personal retention of grace." Furthermore, as it had in Palmer's day, the importance of public testimony created a critical place in the Salvation Army for both women and laymen who, led by the Holy Spirit, asserted significant levels of spiritual authority.[26] Palmer also influenced the Army with her understanding of obedience to God as a life of Christian service. Her own dedication to Christian service led Palmer and other nineteenth-century evangelical Christians to become involved in home missionary enterprises in city slums.[27]

By the late nineteenth century the largely middle-class holiness community increasingly identified sanctification's "inward purity" with "decorous conduct."[28] Truly sanctified Christians did not swear or use other "foul speech . . . bywords and exaggerated forms of expression," nor did they gamble, wear feathers and gold and fashionable clothing, read novels, or attend "frivolous entertainments." They rejected tobacco and alcohol as part of a regime that " 'does away with all that is hurtful to the soul, body or influence, and places before us the highest ideal of perfect manhood and womanhood.' "[29] Similarly, the Salvation Army advocated abstention from sinful behaviors, including consuming alcohol and to a lesser degree smoking tobacco, as a "witness" to potential converts of their submission to a holy life. "The purity and uprightness of [one's] outward conduct," wrote the group's leader, was a public demonstration of one's salvation. "People will say, 'let us see the proofs of it [salvation] in his daily life'; and if they do not, they will conclude that he is either mistaken, or a willful deceiver."[30]

While it may be tempting to regard this working-class organization's advocacy of sober self-control as an effort to achieve a middle-class standard of respectability, it would be a mistake to do so. Said the *New York Times* in 1892, "Whoever joins the Salvation Army . . . bids good-bye to respectability as much as if he went upon the stage of a variety show."[31] As we will see, although Salvationists rejected the sins of the flesh characteristic of working-class saloons and music halls, in order to express religious experience and market Salvationism they adapted the boisterous camaraderie, "atmosphere of conviviality . . . relaxed sociability, comfort and leisure" that characterized these secular spaces.[32]

The Army differed from late-nineteenth-century evangelicals in other ways as well. Premillennial revivalists like Moody believed that the world was hopelessly corrupt and would continue growing worse until the millennium. For these men and women, the establishment of Christ's kingdom on earth could only happen in the future in a period "discontinuous with the history of this era." Moody regarded premillennialism as an impetus to evangelism. He said, "I look upon this world as a wrecked vessel. . . . God has given me a lifeboat and said to me, 'Moody, save all you can.' "[33] In contrast, the Army embraced a postmillennialist outlook which argued that the millennium could be achieved during the present era when "the Holy Spirit would be poured out and the Gospel spread around the world. Christ would return after this millennial age . . . and would bring history to an end."[34] Salvationists served Christ as nineteenth-century heralds and foot soldiers of the millennium; they saw themselves as God's vanguard.

Finally, unlike other evangelicals, the Army applied the concept of sanctification or holiness to the organization itself.[35] Extending the logic of perfection into an institutional category, corporate holiness legitimated the movement by suggesting that its mission of subduing the world for Christ reflected the Holy Spirit's complete, sanctifying control of the organization.[36] Only a truly sanctified movement, they said, could carry out a holy work. Since the role of the Salvation Army, like that of Jesus Christ, was to preach the Gospel, save souls, and be the instrument through which to redeem society, it followed that the organization was a divine creation. "[Y]ou will find," William Booth told his supporters, "a very remarkable resemblance to the coming of the Lord Jesus Christ 1,800 years ago and the coming of the Lord Jesus Christ in this marvelous manifestation of the Salvation Army today. I believe this movement is of God; I am sure it is; I know it is."[37]

The Salvation Army evolved from the religious work of William and Catherine Booth. William Booth was born on April 10, 1829, to a working-class family in a suburb of Nottingham.[38] After his father's death, his mother supported her four surviving children by keeping a small shop in a poor part of Nottingham, where she sold "toys, tape, needles, cotton, and small household wares." After completing six years of school, the thirteen-year-old William was apprenticed to a pawnbroker in the Nottingham slums.[39] During his apprenticeship Booth was swept up in a revival led by an American evangelist, James Caughey, who was touring England between 1841 and 1846.[40] Caughey's revivals were Booth's first exposure to the "new measures" revivalism associated with Charles Finney. Like Finney, Caughey's preaching rejected reasoned argument and instead relied on "a vast store of anecdotes and real-life illustrations." His sermons vividly described the horrors that awaited sinners in Hell and demanded immediate decisions for salvation. Caughey also followed each sermon with a prayer meeting, or "knee work," in which he called sinners to the Communion rail.[41] Booth was not only converted by Caughey's revival but inspired to take up the ministry himself. Over the next twenty years he shifted from one religious sect to another trying establish himself as a minister.[42]

Salvation Army cofounder Catherine Mumford Booth was born on January 17, 1829, to John Mumford and Sarah Milward. Her father was a coach builder and itinerant preacher; her mother was "an ardent and devoted Methodist." Catherine was educated at home by her mother, where, according to her biographers, her chief textbook "was the Bible, which she had read from Genesis to Revelation eight times before she was twelve."[43] As a young woman she became involved in the temperance movement, serving as secretary of the Juvenile Temperance Society. This position provided her with the opportunity to develop her writing skills, and she became "a most ardent propagandist of her cause."[44] Like other women who were influenced by their experience in reform movements, Catherine Mumford soon began to articulate her belief that women were the intellectual equals of men.[45] Some years after her marriage to William Booth, she developed her defense of women preaching the Gospel by arguing that, in the natural order created by God, women had the *right* to preach.[46]

By 1861, six years after her marriage to William Booth, Catherine put her theories of female ministry into practice and began an unusually successful career as an evangelist in Britain. In 1880 reports of her preaching reached the pages of the *New York Evangelist*, a Presbyterian newspaper. The paper called her "earnest," her style "pithy, pointed and sententious," and her "method of treating her themes" reminiscent of Charles Finney. A letter to the paper the following month added "that for simple effectiveness [of preaching] . . . I have never heard her superior and rarely her equal."[47]

Between 1861 and 1864 the Booths and their children lived the nomadic and economically unstable life of nondenominational itinerant evangelists.[48] Then, in 1865 while Catherine supported the family by preaching in a number of chapels in and around London, William was offered a position as a temporary replacement revivalist at an East London tent mission. Backed and advised by a " 'Council of gentlemen,' " the Booths established their own nondenominational Christian mission in

William and Catherine Booth, cofounders of the Salvation Army.
(Courtesy of the Salvation Army National Archives)

the East End.[49] In short order, however, William Booth manifested his characteristic impatience with any authority other than his own. In 1870, chafing under the council's criticism of his leadership, the Booths decided to dispense with the committee altogether.[50] Over the next eight years the Booths pushed their group, the Christian Mission, through a series of changes that transformed the organization from a loosely organized urban home mission to a more tightly structured institution with power and authority officially centralized in William's hands.[51]

MISSIONARIES TO AMERICA

During this period the Booths institutionalized Catherine's advocacy and example of female ministry by giving equal opportunity to women who wished to preach and lead. Well in advance of British Wesleyan churches and mainline American churches, Christian Mission policy provided that, "godly women possessing the necessary gifts and qualifications, shall be employed as preachers itinerant or otherwise and class leaders and as such shall have appointments given to them on the preacher's plan; and they shall be eligible for any office, and to speak and vote at all official meetings."[52]

Beginning in 1877, the Booths wedded revivalist methods to military imagery. The martial ideal had grown quite popular in Britain and the United States in the late nineteenth century. By the 1890s a "full fledged cult of military training" appeared under the auspices of patriotic societies, churches, schools, and fraternal organizations.[53] Idealization of militarism grew, in part, out of a concern that the citizenry had become "debilitat[ed by the] materialism of the city" and that young men and women were becoming "soft." The heroic sacrifices of the Civil War generation in the United States and Britain's increasing imperial power seemed to suggest that the military was a means of regenerating manliness.[54]

Both the foreign mission and social gospel movements embraced militarism by using what one scholar has called " 'conquest' rhetoric." Leaders of the mission movement, for example, talked about its " 'crusader spirit' " and rallied its "growing missionary army," to " 'conquer this modern world of ours.' " Similarly, social gospelers like Josiah Strong relied on military metaphors to describe his hopes for a Christian conquest of the world, calling Christ "the Captain of our salvation" who relies on "his church militant" to bring about the Millennium.[55] In using military imagery the Salvation Army not only associated itself with an extremely popular movement, but balanced the prominent role of women in the organization by establishing the group as advocates of a very "muscular" or aggressive and "manly" form of Christianity.

In the year between 1878 and 1879, the Christian Mission officially became the Salvation Army and made military imagery the standard means of representing the group's organizational structure, its lines of authority, religious practices, and the life cycles of its membership. At the local level, for example, Salvation Army mission stations or churches were called "corps." Regional headquarters were known at various points as divisions, districts, provinces, or territories. Men and women working at headquarters were considered "staff" officers, while those at the corps were "field" officers. All Army officers (i.e., clergy) held ranks that ranged from "Cadet" (an officer-in-training) to the one and only "General." Rank-and-file members were referred to as soldiers, and new converts were "captives."[56]

Salvationists also described their religious practices using military jargon. Planned revival meetings, for example, were "sieges," daily Bible readings were called "rations," short testimonies were "small shot," and donations were "cartridges." In the 1880s one officer employed military imagery to describe an open-air service, the procession to the corps, the indoor service, and conversions. He wrote, "A well fought battle . . . Massing of troops . . . knee drill; preparing for three mile forced march. Reconnaissance corps with fire and blood colors to the front. The noble corps of troops return; masses of counterbands follow the troops into the temple; heavenly time on our ramparts; heavy firing all along the line, battle field covered with smoke, two deserters captured and many wounded."[57] Military jargon even reached beyond religious matters and institutional structure to address phases of an individual's life cycle. Birth indicated the "arrival of reinforcements," going on vacation was a "furlough," and when one died one was "promoted to glory."[58]

The Booths' movement spread rapidly even before it took on its identity as the Salvation Army. As early as 1871, James and Ann Jermy, along with their five children, emigrated to Canada where they tentatively began a branch of the Christian Mission in North America. James (a carpenter) and his wife, Ann, had joined the movement in Britain at its very early stages in 1868.[59] By 1870, however, the needs of their large family combined with "bad trade and force of circumstances" led the Jermys to emigrate first to Canada and, a year later, to Cleveland, Ohio.[60] In both Canada and the United States the Jermys tried to carry on missionary work and, according to Army sources, found their most responsive audience among blacks. Indeed, according to Army sources, James Jermy "was known in Canada as the nigger preacher, because he preached to Negroes" apparently as a lay helper at a black Methodist church.[61]

When Jermy wrote to William Booth about his efforts, he drew clear parallels between East London and urban Cleveland, where, he said, he had discovered a part of town that reminded him of the Whitechapel section of the East London slums.[62] There he found a hall with a sign that read, "Christian Chapel. The Poor have the Gospel preached unto them," and inside "a few coloured people" apparently awaiting the arrival of their minister. Jermy claimed the congregation asked him to stand in for the regular preacher, James Fackler.[63] Upon Fackler's return, the two men joined forces and established the first branch of the Christian Mission in the United States.[64] Jermy wrote home in glowing terms about the work he and his colleague were doing in Cleveland. "[C]onverting work is going on gloriously. . . . Canada and America are full of backsliders. The churches are ornamented and long-steepled, but there is little soul-converting power." Again emphasizing the similarities between missionary work in the United States and Britain, he said, "[i]t is for all the world like being home in England again."[65]

During its first year, Jermy and Fackler's Christian Mission experienced a period of rapid growth; by the end of 1872 they claimed to "have six or seven preachers belonging to The [*sic*] Mission and four indoor preaching stations." By the end of 1873, however, the Mission fell on hard times. First, James Fackler's health declined and he left Cleveland to return home to the South. Then personal financial difficulties, a consequence of the 1873 depression, began to plague Jermy; late in 1875 he returned to England with his family.[66] The Cleveland Christian Mission did not last long after the departure of its two leaders. The five mission stations Jermy and Fackler had opened between 1871 and 1875 lasted only a year after Jermy's return to England.[67]

Why did Jermy's Christian Mission fail to take root in Cleveland? The evidence suggests that the organization spread in Britain (and later in the United States) largely by "developing lay leadership from within." Growth came primarily from converts moving from one neighborhood to another "taking the Mission with them."[68] There is no indication that Jermy's African American converts went on to open mission stations in other areas. This was, most likely, a result of restraints on the ability of blacks to find living arrangements outside of the developing ghetto in Cleveland. Any new missions had to wait for the commitment of preachers who joined from the outside.

Another reason for the group's decline could be Jermy's motives for establishing the mission, which reflected not only a desire to save the "heathen masses" but also the yearning, common among immigrants, to hold on to familiar traditions in a strange land. Engaging in missionary work in Cleveland according to Jermy felt like being "home in England again."[69] Without a critical mass of British-immigrant Salvationists in Cleveland, however, the mission fell into decline. Finally, Jermy's attempt probably failed because he lacked financial support from the British parent organization. As we will see, the work of the first "official" contingent to the United States would be wholly financed by the Booths.[70]

Over the five years following the Jermys' return to England, the few Christian Mission members who had emigrated to various parts of the

United States repeatedly petitioned William Booth to officially extend the Christian Mission into the United States.[71] At the time, however, Booth lacked the financial and human resources to advance his organization so far from home. Moreover, he also demonstrated considerable reluctance to allow anyone to establish a branch so far from his personal control.

Like the Jermys' effort, on October 5, 1879, the "pioneer" corps of the Salvation Army in the United States opened without the official sanction of William Booth.[72] Amos Shirley, a weaver, emigrated to the United States from England in April 1878, where he secured a job as a foreman at the Adams & Company silk mill in Kensington near Philadelphia. Both Amos and his wife, Annie, had been members of the Salvation Army Coventry corps in England, while their seventeen-year-old daughter Eliza had served as a lieutenant at the Bishop Aukland corps.[73] Soon after he found employment in the United States, Amos sent for his wife and daughter, hoping that they might "start a work in America something like the Salvation Army."[74] According to historians of the movement, William Booth was reluctant to allow young Eliza to "transfer" to Philadelphia, citing "the great need for workers in England." Unable to prevent her from leaving, however, he gave her permission to use the name Salvation Army for the Philadelphia effort but promised no financial support. "If it is a success," said Booth, "we may see our way clear to take it over."[75]

The Shirleys settled in Kensington, a working-class suburb that had, in the 1840s, been the scene of ferocious nativist rioting.[76] Using part of his wages, Amos Shirley and his family rented an abandoned chair factory at Sixth and Oxford Streets and opened their Salvation Factory or meetinghouse. While the Jermys had preached to African Americans, the Shirleys sought to market Salvationism to the working-class native-born Americans and Irish Catholics who lived in their Kensington neighborhood. A newspaperman reported that the group's rag-tag parades through neighborhood streets were "followed by almost everything that had legs." Bringing the crowd back to their meetinghouse, the Shirleys preached to a room that was "literally packed" mostly with men "of whom nearly all claimed to have led a life steeped over head and ears in crime and debauchery, but who had been rescued by the 'Army.' "[77]

By the end of 1879 the Shirley family in Philadelphia and Booth's secretary general, George Scott Railton, in Britain were pressuring the leader to absorb the infant American movement. Eliza Shirley forwarded newspaper articles to the general describing their activities and positive public reaction to their work. Railton, meanwhile, urgently argued in favor of bringing the American effort under the supervision of British headquarters. In a letter to Catherine Booth he explained, "I feel sure that our affair in Philadelphia will go with such a sweep that unless we get hold of it, and lead, and go in at full speed at once, I doubt if we should ever be able to get the reins at all. Then it will be a wild affair with no competent direction, and there will be after a while as complete a lull as follows almost all such things."[78] Railton believed that unless they acted quickly the movement in America might never come under the Booths' control. Moreover, he worried that without the direction of the British Salvation Army, the mission in Philadelphia would be neither systematic nor long lived. Finally persuaded that he had to act, William Booth decided to send an official contingent to absorb the American movement. In an article titled "The Salvation Army in America" that appeared in *The War Cry* (London), boldface print announced, "WE MUST GO! This news has come upon us like a voice from Heaven and leaves us NO CHOICE!"[79] Providence officially called the Salvation Army to the United States.

The Salvation Army's marketing of itself in the United States proved fairly successful in the late nineteenth century, and the organization experienced a significant rate of growth throughout this period. Beginning with the pioneer corps opened by the Shirley family in 1879, the Army grew to 735 corps by 1898.[80] New corps opened at an average rate of 29 per year between 1879 and 1899.[81] The geographical distribution of the corps also broadened in this period. In 1880 only three eastern cities (Philadelphia, New York, and Newark) hosted 12 Salvation Army corps; eight years later, however, 246 corps could be found in twenty-seven states around the nation. Most of these corps were located in the Northeast, Mid-Atlantic, and Great Lakes regions of the United States. There were only a scattering of corps in the Midwest and West and none in the Deep South.

According to a 1908 "Brief" — an internal report — the Salvation Army succeeded in cities with a thriving manufacturing base. Nearly three decades of experience demonstrated that a town like Gettysburg, Pennsylvania, with its economy based on agriculture and tourism, was unsuitable for Army work. Oil City, Pennsylvania, on the other hand, with its thriving oil-drilling, refining, and shipping businesses, provided the Army with "a most remarkable work." Army dependence on working-class support was especially clear in towns where manufacturing plants had become highly mechanized and workers' wages cut drastically. In Kane, Pennsylvania, a city of glass factories, the inability to raise sufficient monies from workers in the city had, by 1908, made Salvation Army work there nearly impossible.[82]

Like the growing number of corps, increases in the numbers of rank-and-file members also reflected a pattern of growth. In 1880, the Army reported 412 "privates" in the United States. By 1884 that number increased to 5,000, and by 1896 the Salvation Army claimed 25,000 soldiers across the nation.[83] While the Army's rate of growth reflected significant expansion in the late nineteenth century, the group never really became a mass movement. Thousands reportedly attended its special services, but much smaller numbers actually joined the organization.[84] Moreover, the overall growth figures hide periods of boom and bust. In early 1884, for example, the Salvation Army reported that 250–300 men and women were officers in the organization, while the following year there were only 50 officers.[85]

The Army's erratic growth may be explained, in part, by shifts in American leadership that plagued the group throughout the late nineteenth century. Between 1880 and 1904 there were five changes in national leadership. Two changes resulted in schisms, one of which nearly destroyed the movement in this country.[86] These shifts in leadership revealed an ongoing struggle for power and authority between the center (William Booth and the Salvation Army in Britain) and the periphery (Salvation Army leadership in this country) as Salvationists in the United States struggled to define and clarify their relationship to both the English parent organization and their American members.[87]

Booth selected George Scott Railton as his officially authorized representative to take over the Philadelphia movement in 1880. This rather eccentric, orphaned son of Wesleyan missionaries was a veteran of many revival campaigns. At the age of nineteen, Railton left his clerking job in London, sailed for Morocco, and, penniless, tried to conduct a one-man campaign to "win Morocco for Christ." Upon hearing that Railton had come to Morocco because "God had sent him there," the British consul "concluded that [the young man] was daft." With the aid of his elder brother, Railton was sent home to England where he became first an itinerant and then a local preacher.[88]

In 1873, inspired by William Booth's pamphlet *How to Reach the Masses with the Gospel*, the wildly energetic Railton joined the Christian Mission, moving quickly up the ranks to become second-in-command.[89] Unfortunately, by 1880, Railton's authority had eroded considerably, and the general's oldest son, Bramwell, now chief-of-staff, had replaced him as the elder Booth's closest associate. Railton's assignment to the United States gave him the opportunity to win America for Christ and the Salvation Army, escape an increasingly frustrating administrative situation, and perhaps recover his influence within the organization.[90]

Captain Emma Westbrook, a ten-year veteran of the Christian Mission / Salvation Army, and six other female Salvation Army officers, joined "Commissioner" Railton.[91] There are a number of reasons why Railton may have selected only female officers to accompany him to the United States. Given the Army's chronic shortage of personnel, Booth may have been more willing to sacrifice seven female than male officers. On the other hand, Railton, who was very close to Catherine Booth, may have deliberately chosen female officers in order to "show what women, inspired by the power of the Holy Ghost, could do." Furthermore, Railton apparently expected each of the women to marry an American, thus insuring, through intermarriage, "that the Army in America would be American."[92]

Even as he sent his representatives to bring the American branch officially under the Army flag, William Booth made his intention to maintain complete authority over his organization crystal clear. Before Railton's departure from England, Booth insisted that he sign a document in which he agreed to a number of conditions. The commissioner would comply with any and all commands or orders issued by William Booth. Moreover, Booth would retain an absolute veto over any orders given or persons joining the American branch of the movement. Finally, all real and personal property would "at all times be held for and on behalf of and at the disposal of the said William Booth." Having decided to embrace the American effort, Booth had no intention of losing personal control over his organization.[93]

Commissioner Railton, Captain Westbrook, and the six female Salvationists arrived at Castle Garden on March 10, 1880. The women, according to the *New York Times*, wore blue uniforms "edged with bright yellow binding," and hats with "broad bands of scarlet ribbon, inscribed with the words 'The Salvation Army' in large gilt letters." The captain carried a "flag of blue and red stuff with a large yellow sun in the centre." The reporter also noted that "their hymns were set to American tunes, such as 'Way down on the Swanee River' and 'Old Kentucky Home.' " Railton made himself immediately available for interviews in which he discussed the origins of the organization, and he handed out a "circular" with data

Six of the original seven female Salvationists who came with
George Scott Railton to the United States in 1880.
(Courtesy of the Salvation Army National Archives)

about the numbers of officers, services (indoor and outdoor), people in
attendance, and souls saved.[94]

Five days later, the *Times* caught up with the Army once again. Railton
had by then secured the support of the Christian Undenominational
Society, which made its Hudson River Hall available to the Salvationists.
The Army, according to the report, had spent the previous day visiting
various missions, including the Fulton Street Prayer Meeting, the Baxter
Street Mission, and the " 'Noonday Prayer-meeting for Business Men' "

(where they "received warm endorsement"), and then went back to Hudson River Hall in the evening. A few days later, the Salvationists connected with the venerable Jerry McAuley, who joined them in "start[ing] the hymn" at the Siloam Mission on Water Street.[95]

Although the nondenominational missionary community in New York seemed to welcome the Salvation Army with open arms, there is some indication that they were not fully informed about the group's methods. In an interview, a member of the Christian Undenominational Society (CUS) suggested that the Army's techniques resembled those of Moody and Sankey. The Army was not, he explained, "going to visit saloons and strive to pray the owners out of their business" but rather would hold daytime services at the Baxter Street Mission and evening services in the Hudson River Hall.[96] The CUS clearly did not appreciate the importance of street preaching to the Salvation Army.

While the nondenominational missions apparently embraced the Salvation Army, Presbyterians appeared a bit more class conscious and patronizing. The seven female Salvationists, wrote the New York Evangelist, were "in no way noticeable or attractive as distinguished from the many emigrants of their class." At the same time, however, the paper wished that more of "the vast foreign population" of the great American cities were "altogether such as they, by the renewing of the Spirit."[97] Presbyterians also expressed concern that the Salvation Army not compete with mainline churches but rather perform a service that was "supplementary in character." They would tolerate the Army's work only as long as it focused on those who resisted the "Gospel invitation" and then sent them on to the churches. The New York Evangelist also insisted, somewhat defensively, that there was nothing "wholly new or novel" about the work the Army was doing. "Our churches, chapels, associations and missions of various sorts," they wrote, had carried out similar work all over the city for many years.[98]

Although Railton, Westbrook, and the six officers hoped to make New York City headquarters for the Salvation Army in United States, they ran into problems with local authorities almost immediately. Political machines and trade unions or " 'rings,' " according to Railton, "prevent any party from getting any place of meeting." The commissioner did not indicate whether the machines demanded the payment of graft, but the Salvationists would not have had the resources to do so. More important, city authorities kept the group from holding outdoor meetings, a key element of their work. In New York City an ordinance restricted street preaching to ordained "clergymen or ministers of a denomination."[99] As a result, city officials, complained Railton, restricted "the main feature of our work," limited marchers to barely passable sidewalks, and threatened to "take us away before we could have got a crowd."[100]

Railton did not account for the authorities' strict control of public assembly, but it was probably a response to the New York draft riots of 1863, the Tompkins Square riots of 1874, and the nationwide railroad strike of 1877.[101] Thwarted in his efforts to establish the Army in New York City, in late April 1880 Railton moved his headquarters to Philadelphia, where the work had already been established by the Shirleys.[102]

Commissioner Railton approached his work in the United States with the determination and energy of a man who had something to prove. As the pioneer effort in Philadelphia continued to grow steadily, Railton inaugurated a program that he apparently hoped would enable the American branch to quickly eclipse the British parent. Publication of an American version of the group's newspaper, *The War Cry*, would be of particular importance in achieving his goal. The newspaper would allow him to raise money by promoting the activities of the Army in the United States. As he wrote in a letter to William Booth, "I have got no rich people to go to yet, and never shall till I can afford to send the *War Cry* out freely to such people after I have got them."[103]

In addition to publishing *The War Cry*, Railton proposed to market the Army by building on what he regarded as the special strengths of the United States: its women, its diversity, and the limitless opportunities for growth offered by the physical vastness of the nation. Soon after he arrived in the United States, Railton became convinced that American women were best equipped to help him create and lead a U.S. Salvation Army that would outshine Britain. "Those English may stick to their men as hard as they like," he wrote to Catherine Booth, "but I am certain it is the women who are going to burst up the world generally, especially American women." One American female officer under his command was, he said, "only a seamstress" and yet had the "intelligence and grasp to take in and carry out my ideas." Furthermore, Railton felt certain that he was the only one who could effectively exploit American women's strengths. "Women helpers and money I must have; I want no more from England. . . . American ladies are rapidly getting the first front places in the world. Yet no person has the wit or the diligence to make more of them."[104]

Along with the leadership potential of American women, Railton regarded the nation's diversity as an important key to growth. In the midst of a racially segregated society where even trade unions maintained a

28

MISSIONARIES TO AMERICA

"whites only" policy, Railton argued that "the Lord was no respecter of race, colour or condition," and so the Salvation Army welcomed all people.[105] Indeed, Railton envisioned an American Army that would benefit from the diversity of the nation. He naively imagined fostering a friendly marketing competition that would stimulate the growth of the organization. "If I can get the Americans, Germans, and Africans all fairly started," he said, "I hope by stirring such up to hearty rivalry to keep them at a full gallop."[106]

Finally, a 4,200-mile "scouting mission," which Railton undertook alone in the summer of 1880, convinced him of the absolutely limitless opportunities for growth in North America. The Army needed only to position itself in the right place, St. Louis, Missouri, gateway to the West. Like many Americans who regarded the West as a symbol of endless opportunity, Railton believed that the key to conquering the States for Christ lay in winning the West for the Salvation Army. "It is the chance of a generation," he wrote to William Booth; "the West, and by it the States, will be in our power in 1881." By the winter of 1880, Railton, in an escapade reminiscent of his Morocco adventure, attempted, single-handedly (the nearest Salvationists being 959 miles away) to "open fire" on St. Louis.[107]

In spite of congregations of the "most hardened scoffers" and the widely held feeling that "[t]he dollar is the God here," Railton, during his brief tenure, clearly demonstrated that a market for Salvationism existed in the United States. Philadelphia in particular showed enthusiasm for the Army; by 1880 there were six corps in that city and a seventh in Franklin, Pennsylvania.[108] Soldiers there proved very eager to help open new corps. "On Saturday afternoon at West Philadelphia," he wrote, "I called for volunteers to go out as officers, and had already got 22 ranging from 16 to 64, and including two Germans and a colored man (who particularly desires to mission England)."[109] Indeed, he finally had to take measures in an attempt to restrain the volunteers for fear of destabilizing their home corps. "Their readiness to walk miles to assist in pushing on our advance would have left the older batteries to the exclusive possession of their officers again and again had not a printed permit been required in every case."[110]

Unfortunately, Railton's fervor stirred his enthusiasm for opening Army corps (he increased the number of corps from two to twelve) but not the patience to stabilize them. Not unlike his soldiers, he was inclined to move on to the next site before existing corps could be secured. As a consequence, nearly all of the commissioner's strategies to promote the swift growth of Salvationism in the United States ended in failure. He tried (but failed) to establish any significant Salvation Army work among German Americans and African Americans and opened but ultimately abandoned his fledgling effort in the West. There was a market for Salvationism in the United States, but Railton neither properly identified nor exploited it. In January of 1881 General Booth summoned a reluctant Railton home.

William Booth selected a man with extensive business experience in North America to replace Railton. Thomas E. Moore was born in Britain in 1840 but lived in the United States a total of eleven years, during which time he reportedly made his fortune, found holiness, and "spent six months preaching in American villages and towns."[111] He joined the Salvation Army in 1879 while living in London managing a West End firm, and soon found himself appointed divisional commander for that city. Two years later William Booth sent Major Moore back to the United States to lead the Salvation Army in this country.[112]

Moore's approach to marketing the Salvation Army reflected both his business skills and his extensive knowledge of this country. Upon his arrival, Moore found many of the existing corps in precarious condition, if not already defunct. The major's first step was to consolidate the twelve corps into five (three of which were in Philadelphia) and impose some discipline and bureaucratic order on the officers. Demonstrating the inclination of evangelicals to quantify success, Moore required officers to send him a Weekly Return Form on which they accounted for their work and the numbers of souls they saved as a result.[113]

When officers resisted his efforts to track their efficiency, Moore tried to get their cooperation through the group's newspaper, *The War Cry*. The major's messages drew a connection between organizational discipline and faith by suggesting that faithfulness in carrying out mundane orders pleased God and insured the success of the Salvation Army. "You know what will become of faith," he said; "if we are faithful in little we shall be made rulers over much."[114]

Under Moore's leadership the movement grew, much as it had in England, when Salvationists took the mission with them into new cities and towns and marketed it to working-class men and women like themselves. The major apparently did not share Railton's vision of rapid growth by marketing the Army to America's diverse population. During his tenure the Army targeted British immigrants and American-born men and women and neither attracted nor specifically sought out German Americans or African Americans. Perhaps his many years in the United States had made him less optimistic about successfully breaching the formida-

Major Thomas Moore, who led the Salvation Army in the
United States until he broke away in 1884.
(Courtesy of the Salvation Army National Archives)

ble racial and ethnic divisions that separated the population. He may also
have understood that immigrants and African Americans frequently attended their own churches and were, therefore, less likely to be attracted
to the Army and its message.

As he consolidated the corps, tried to impose discipline over officers,
and presided over the steady expansion of the organization, Moore used

The War Cry to build a cohesive organization by connecting Salvationists to one another, to him, and to the marketing of the Salvation Army. Each week the newspaper published descriptions of meetings, testimonies, reports of new corps openings, and special events (weddings and funerals) which poured in from corps throughout the country. By 1883 reports were coming in from as far away as California.[115]

From the pages of *The War Cry* Moore announced promotions, explained Salvationism, and protected the group from impostors. He also sought to persuade the officers that corps reports were vital marketing tools and that they should "use the talents God has given them in ADVERTISING salvation as well as preaching it." An interesting report published in *The War Cry*, he believed, "would fire the soldiers up, make them stronger, and in fact, throw a bright aspect upon the Army work, and also ENLARGE the Cry." Moore was apparently successful. By 1884 his 230 officers were selling 20,000 copies of *The War Cry* each week.[116]

For both practical and symbolic reasons Thomas Moore became an American citizen. In doing so he made a gesture of national solidarity with American Salvationists while at the same time enabling himself to hold title to Salvation Army property in his name.[117] Waging the war for salvation in the United States, he argued, required officers who could "endure hardships" and make sacrifices, and who, most important, were citizens of the United States. "We have qualified ourselves by becoming American citizens," said Moore, "and we trust that all our officers will do likewise who are not so already." By becoming citizens, "we shall harmonize ourselves and our system of government with the laws of our adopted country."

William Booth, however, saw no reason to "harmonize" with Americans. Historically, his concept of cultural adaptation expressed itself through gestures of solidarity with class or caste rather than with emblems of national identity. In support for the lowest members of India's caste system, for example, Salvationists "adopted native dress . . . moved into the native quarters . . . lived on a native diet, walked barefoot from village to village."[118] Similarly, female Salvationists who were assigned to American or British slums "live, to all outward appearances, in strict accord with the customs of their neighbors": wearing dresses "of the cheapest material . . . rough . . . shawls or old-fashioned cloaks . . . [and] a heavy black straw hat."[119]

Because William Booth made little effort to nurture bonds between himself and the Salvation Army in America, no member of the large Booth family had visited the United States since the organization first opened fire.[120] Indeed, General Booth disappointed many American Salvationists by failing to attend the fourth anniversary celebration in Brooklyn.[121] The only contact that most American Salvationists had with William Booth was an occasional reprint of his writings in *The War Cry*.

Although Booth failed to establish personal connections with Americans, he adamantly maintained that all property in this country "given or deeded to The Salvation Army was owned by General Booth." In Britain William Booth held all property in his name for the benefit of the Salvation Army. In the United States, however, each state had different rules governing the ownership of property by foreigners making it difficult for Booth to legally hold property as the organization expanded across the country. One solution was to incorporate the organization, allowing it to hold all property. Booth rejected this approach, however, since incorporating in New York at that time would have meant that a board of directors or trustees, rather than Booth himself, would control the group's assets.[122] By way of compromise, Major Moore (as an American citizen) held title to all Salvation Army assets in the United States in his own name.

Under George Scott Railton's leadership, the contentious issue of property ownership did not arise. The commissioner's effort had been largely financed by England, and none of the corps were secure enough or had the resources to invest in purchasing buildings. Under Moore's more efficient leadership, however, the Army in America became self-supporting. Indeed, some corps exhibited new confidence in the stability of the organization by raising funds to buy or build permanent halls. As a result, a crisis developed in 1883–84. Facing public accusations that money collected in New Jersey to build a new hall was going into the pocket of Thomas Moore or William Booth in England, the local corps decided to incorporate under that state's laws. Once they incorporated, the corps demanded the return of all money collected in their state and held for them by the major. When Moore refused, he became subject to arrest in New Jersey. In December of 1883, as he held an open-air service in Rahway, New Jersey, authorities arrested him. In an article in *The War Cry* explaining his actions, he said the Army had only two ways to resolve the problem, "by conforming to the laws of the Country with regard to the property of the Army . . . or . . . [by] relinquish[ing] the work altogether."[123]

Out of desperation and in spite of Booth's explicit orders to the contrary, Moore went ahead with incorporation in 1884. A board of trustees took control of the real property as well as the insignia, crest, and *The War*

Cry.[124] With the act of incorporation, Moore severed his connection to the British organization and transformed his soldiers, officers, and all identifiable symbols of the movement from the Salvation Army *in* America into the Salvation Army *of* America. Furious at Moore's "treachery," the general sent Commissioner Frank Smith to take command of what would now be called the *Worldwide* Salvation Army.[125] It is telling that by the time Smith arrived, Booth's Salvation Army in the United States numbered only fifty officers (many of whom Smith brought with him) and seventeen "loyal" corps. Clearly, in the early 1880s, William Booth exercised even less authority over the hearts and minds of rank-and-file Salvationists than he did over the assets of the organization. As Eliza Shirley (of the pioneering Shirley family) later pointed out, most American Salvationists supported Thomas Moore because they knew little of Booth and Booth knew little of them.[126]

Born in 1854, the new leader of the Worldwide Salvation Army in the United States, Frank Smith, had been converted by William Booth's son Bramwell in 1879. After one year as a corps officer, he took over Thomas E. Moore's position as divisional commander for London; in 1884 Booth sent him to the United States to replace Moore again. Throughout his tenure as he attempted to reintroduce *William Booth's* Salvation Army into the United States, Frank Smith faced the formidable issue of national identity. In accounting for Americans' resistance to the Worldwide Army he argued that continuous waves of immigration brought a constant flood of "foreign ideas." As a result, "American citizens are continually being driven into an attitude of resistance to retain their own individuality." He suggested that as a result the Army had to undergo a period of "testing" before they could expect American acceptance.[127]

Thomas Moore, now general of the American Salvation Army, took every opportunity to stress and reinforce national differences as he publicized his version of the schism in various venues. Moore used *The War Cry* to respond to Booth's charges that his "books were in disorder, and that hundreds if not thousands of dollars . . . were unaccounted for." In the article "Incorporation," he referred to the man Booth sent to examine his books as "Herr Schaff" (as opposed to using his rank staff-captain), calling attention to the fact that the general's representative was not an *American*. In addition, Moore placed notices in *The War Cry* that clearly announced that the " 'THE SALVATION ARMY OF AMERICA' is an American institution . . . [and is] in *no way* connected with *The English Salvation Army*, under the Rev. W. Booth, of London, England."[128]

Few Americans realized that a schism had taken place. Indeed, there

Major Frank Smith, who was sent to take over the Worldwide Salvation Army after Thomas Moore's "defection." Smith led this branch of the organization until replaced by Maud and Ballington Booth in 1886. (Courtesy of the Salvation Army National Archives)

was no mention of it in the *New York Times* until March 1885, when Moore and Smith held competing special meetings in Brooklyn and New York City respectively.[129] On March 20, Moore held a "Congress" celebrating the Salvation Army's fifth-year anniversary in the United States; on the same date Smith held an elaborate "War Congress" at the Academy of Music. Smith's celebration ended up with the lion's share of the newspaper's coverage. The Brooklyn event received only eleven lines of print compared to the nearly full-page column devoted to New York's. Moreover, although the press emphasized the class nature and oddness of Smith's Congress, they also provided him with the opportunity to accuse Moore of "transact[ing] army business in his own name . . . acquir[ing] property which really belonged" to the Salvation Army.[130]

Fighting fire with fire, Moore also told his story to the secular press. A lengthy account of the schism in the *New York World* allowed Moore once again to emphasize the issue of national identity. The article variously referred to Booth as "General Booth of England," "the Foreign Commander-in-Chief," "an alien" (while Moore was a "naturalized citizen"), "the English General," "the foreign general," and "an autocratic alien." While the reporter used a cockney dialect when he quoted Moore, it was balanced by a flattering description of him as "a man of fine military bearing . . . [wearing a] uniform, his dark-blue coat being profusely trimmed with broad black braid. His hair is of the color of the raven's back, and his whiskers, which are quite white, are worn a la Burnside."[131]

In addition to *The War Cry* and secular newspapers, Moore published a pamphlet, *All about the Salvation Army of America and the Holy Revolution of 1884*, in which he emphasized Booth's cultural imperialism by accusing him of "wishing to control both the spiritual and temporal interests not only of America, but of the whole world." Moreover, by calling the schism a "Holy Revolution," he drew a parallel between the Salvation Army's rebellion against the British and the American Revolution. The pamphlet even included a letter by George Scott Railton apparently written during his American service in which he advised against "raising an American Army" using English officers since "all Americans feel . . . that they are a nation, just as the English do . . . if there were a thousand American officers in England trying to establish a concern which was to be mainly officered by Americans, they might whistle for the sympathy and support to any considerable extent."[132]

Finally, Moore even created a new version of the Salvation Army's story of origin, which he published in a book entitled *Positive Facts Regarding the Salvation Army of America*. Organized in a FAQ style (Frequently Asked

Questions), Moore responded to the questions "When, where, and by whom was the Salvation Army originated?" Without ever referring to William Booth or his first official representative, George Scott Railton, Moore connected his Army directly to the earliest work of the Holy Spirit. The Army originated, he said, "In the City of Jerusalem, nearly 1900 years ago, when the day of Pentecost came round, and the followers of Jesus were all baptized with the Holy Ghost. Incorporated in the United States October 24, 1884."[133]

As Smith and his cadre of English officers attempted to regain lost territory in the United States, he acknowledged that the group faced considerable "national and political prejudice." Even William Booth expressed concern at the "desperate efforts to discredit the Army in the States as being altogether English."[134] In the face of this opposition, Smith and his "reinforcements" orchestrated a two-and-a-half-year campaign to rebuild the organization and forge bonds of loyalty between the British and U.S. branches.[135] First, Smith moved swiftly to market the Worldwide Army in regions where he would not be competing directly with Moore and the American Army. As soon as he was appointed to "replace" Moore, International Headquarters in Britain informed the Pacific Coast Division that Smith would be their new leader.[136] Then he sent William Evans, his wife, and Captain Gay (whose concertina would later be stolen) to open up Chicago and the Midwest. Finally, he sent A. D. C. Pugmire on a "Colored Expedition" to finish the work that the Civil War and the Thirteenth, Fourteenth, and Fifteenth Amendments had begun because "a whole race remained to be not only liberated, but civilized and saved." Pugmire, according to Smith, "cut himself off to a certain extent from the white community" and lived among the African Americans, who "affectionately" referred to the young man as the "curly headed white man."[137] Smith hoped that Pugmire's work would help the Worldwide Salvation Army make its mark by being the first to break down the color line.[138] Smith proved to be an excellent "organizer and publicist" and within his two and a half years in the United States increased the Worldwide Salvation Army's corps from 17 to 143.[139]

Moore changed the national identity of the Salvation Army in legal fact by becoming a citizen and incorporating the organization under American law. Smith took a more symbolic approach that integrated American patriotic symbols into Salvation Army culture at every opportunity. The new Salvation Army emblem, for example, now sported "a gallant eagle" (looking suspiciously like an American eagle) above the "Blood and Fire" crest replacing the crown which adorned the English version.

American flags now appeared in all Salvation Army halls alongside of the Army banner.[140] Salvation Army weddings and funerals also featured American flags. On one occasion forty Salvation Army women stopped traffic when they appeared in a wedding parade wearing "white dresses, Stars and Stripes sashes and red liberty caps." Furthermore, at a funeral a newspaper reported, "On each side of the casket stood the color bearers, holding two beautiful silk flags bearing the stars and stripes."[141] According to Stuart McConnell, the "cult of the flag" that surfaced in this period "show[ed] native born whites groping toward a new definition of what American meant."[142] Perhaps Smith and the leaders who would follow him embraced patriotic symbols in an effort to include the Salvation Army in the emerging redefinition of "American."

Smith also used the pages of *his* version of *The War Cry* to define the relationship between his and Booth's Armies and to attack Moore. Identifying himself variously as commissioner of the "USA Forces" or "of the U.S. Section of the Salvation Army," he established that his Army was the *American* part of a larger international Salvation Army. At the same time he denied accusations that England controlled the American Army. He wrote, "statements made, that the American section cannot be governed from England[,] we answer by saying, it never has been nor is it intended [that] it should be." He went on to ascribe the problems which led to the schism not to the relationship between the British headquarters and the American outpost but rather to internal difficulties in "the financial department of the American section" which "got into the unfortunate state of confusion . . . giving rise to well founded suspicion and mistrust."[143]

To facilitate bonds of loyalty between the "American Section" and British Headquarters, Smith took steps to ensure that Americans understood the nature of their connection to the general. In what would become a weekly feature in *The War Cry*, the general wrote a column in which he made explicit the paternal relationship he envisioned between himself and his soldiers and officers around the world. "The father writes his weekly letter to the boys and girls who have left the old homestead, and gone up and down the country, or wandered to distant lands; and with the dutiful ones the post is regularly looked for, and the letters are eagerly read. Perchance it may be so with mine . . . I shall write at least with the pleasing assurance . . . that our people scattered abroad everywhere will read its facts with interest, consider its councils, and carry out, at least to some extent, the actions I recommend."[144] Booth's articles reveal that he regarded himself as the father, and the loyal soldiers of the Salvation Army the "dutiful" sons and daughters who followed his councils. However, his letters also demonstrate a failure to grasp that a growing number of Salvation Army officers in the United States were born in this country and were not "boys and girls who have left the old homestead" in Britain.

In addition to his weekly letters in *The War Cry*, Booth built closer ties to American Salvationists through his 1886 visit to North America.[145] In Chicago alone, thousands came out to see the general's Army march through the streets and to hear him preach. The *Chicago Tribune* reported that more than 4,000 people jammed the Army's hall hoping to see the general; a religious newspaper indicated that he spoke to a "vast congregation."[146] At the same time, however, the general encountered evidence of national feeling on his visit. According to a newspaper report, at a large meeting in Scranton, Pennsylvania, "When . . . Gen. Booth said: 'God bless England!' there was a feeble 'Amen'[;] when he exclaimed 'God bless America!' . . . this called forth an enthusiastic and hearty 'Amen!' from all parts of the house." Said the General, " 'The vote seems to be in favor of America.' "[147]

The year following his tour, William Booth sent his son and daughter-in-law, "Marshal" Ballington and Maud Booth, to replace the ailing Commissioner Frank Smith.[148] From 1887 until 1934, there would be literal blood ties between the leadership of the Salvation Army in the United States and Britain.[149] Although the number of corps and officers declined during the period of transition from Smith to the Ballington Booths, the pace of corps openings and the growth of officership soon steadied. Under Maud and Ballington's leadership, efforts to promote American national identity continued unabated. The couple soon became citizens of the United States; American flags began to wave alongside Salvation Army colors in all street parades; and a small American flag began to appear regularly in the upper left-hand corner of the Salvation Army banner. Each of Booth's representatives in America learned that successfully marketing the Salvation Army in the United States meant developing and promoting an American identity for the organization.

Although Thomas Moore's efforts had resulted in a serious schism, for nearly a decade during Ballington Booth's tenure as national commander, the British and American branches established an uneasy truce. Ballington protected American assets by holding the property of the unincorporated organization in his own name on behalf of his father. At the same time, he asserted the American identity of this British-born organization through his zealous use of American national symbols. William Booth returned to his policy of sullen neglect. Back at International Headquarters, however, the general never reconciled himself to an American national identity for the U.S. branch of the Salvation Army. He believed that the small-group loyalties created by membership in the Salvation Army connected his followers across categories of class, caste, race, gender, and nationality. The worldwide nature of the organization, he argued, transcended any single national identity. Furthermore, Booth probably regarded Americanization as a potential threat to his authority over the organization and its ever-increasing resources.[150]

Ballington Booth was the second child of William and Catherine Booth. The *Detroit Free Press* described him as "over six feet tall and very slender ... narrow-chested ... [with] long arms and a long black beard."[151] Born in 1857, by the age of 23 he had joined the family business and taken charge of the Salvation Army Training Home for male officers in Clapton. After a year in Australia as co–territorial commander, he returned to Britain where he married Maud Charlesworth in 1886.[152] Maud was the daughter of Anglican minister Samuel Charlesworth. By 1885 she was thoroughly estranged from her father as a result of her connection with the Salvation Army, and she was living with her future in-laws, William and Catherine Booth.[153] According to the *New York Times*, Maud had "a petite figure, bright and attractive face, and an agreeable and modest manner."[154] Soon after their marriage, the couple took command of the Salvation Army in the United States.

Until Maud and Ballington's administration, Salvation Army leaders in the United States focused their energies on typical missionary goals, "the proclamation of the gospel and the planting of churches."[155] Early in their administration, however, the new American leaders expanded these goals to include rescue work in city slums. They were well aware that in Britain the Army's participation in the 1885 campaign to raise the age of consent "brought rescue work to the forefront of the Salvation Army's mission," as well as public recognition and inclusion in national committees "such as the National Vigilance Association."[156] In October 1886 *The War Cry* proudly announced the opening of Morris Cottage, the Army's first " 'rescue home for fallen or falling women,' " in New York City.[157] Morris Cottage shared many characteristics with rescue homes opened by Protestant missionaries throughout the nineteenth century. Like the first home opened in 1834 by the New York Female Moral Reform Society, Morris Cottage initially focused on the prostitute. The Booths also believed that the cottage should re-create "the ideal Christian home of Victorian rhetoric." "Our first desire as regards the home itself," claimed the announcement, "is that it may be in every sense what the term im-

Maud Booth, who with her husband, Ballington, led the Salvation Army in
the United States from 1886 until 1896, when they resigned.
(Courtesy of the Salvation Army National Archives)

plies ... as a place were the comforts, the sympathies, and all the genial
surroundings of that far off place where father and mother still mourns
[*sic*] the absence of the lost one shall be found." Three years later the
Army organized a slum "crèche" that provided childcare to working or
incarcerated mothers.[158]

In 1889 the Salvation Army also began to institutionalize a working-
class style of mutual aid when it organized its "Slum Brigade." Unlike

Unidentified slum officers in "uniforms" worn by the
women in this branch of Salvation Army service.
(Courtesy of the Salvation Army National Archives)

settlement houses and urban home missions, Salvation Army slum work
did not establish a physical space for religious meetings or secular cultural events. Instead, female officers known as Slum Sisters moved into
small, dingy, sparsely furnished tenement rooms. Living little better than
their neighbors, these women went out each morning to pray, distribute
bits of scripture, tend the sick and dying, assist working mothers with
meals for children, and perform other "neighborly" duties.[159]

The more traditional missionary goals of Railton, Moore, and Smith
encouraged them to market the Salvation Army by advertising salvation
to either the racially and ethnically diverse American laboring population or working-class, native-born Americans and British immigrants.
With the addition of the rescue programs, however, Maud and Ballington
began a vigorous campaign of marketing the Salvation Army to respect-

able, moneyed Americans. Backed by Mrs. John Wanamaker, wife of the Philadelphia department store mogul, Maud spoke at small "drawing-room" gatherings as well as huge meetings before "hundreds of the most influential and wealthy members of society." In these sentimental talks she emphasized "uplift" as she described the work of the Army and the sacrifice of the Lasses among "the babies and young children of the very poorest and the most depraved classes."[160] Audiences were reportedly "so affected by her accounts of the Army's 'great work . . . that they wept, opened their purses and . . . donated their rings and jewelry on the spot." Marshal Ballington Booth held a series of "special noon gathering[s] of . . . businessmen."[161]

Maud Booth so "charmed" New York society that newspaper reports suggested the Army was "evidently aiming to work an entirely new field." Indeed, she soon began to organize "a new series of meetings among the higher classes."[162] The Booths' approach to this audience paid tribute to its elevated social standing in a number of ways. At services attended by both the fashionable and the "slum element," the democratic seating arrangements of most Army meetings gave way to segregation by class. At a "consecration service," for example, the "ladies and gentlemen from aristocratic circles," who made up two-thirds of the audience, "occupied all of the seats" while the slum element "crowded against the four sides of the room."[163]

Beyond seating arrangements Maud Booth stated explicitly that some meetings were designed for an affluent audience. While no one would be turned away, she said, "we desire that the attendance at these meetings shall be confined as much as possible to the class of society that we are seeking to interest in our work." Moreover, Maud's fashionable support-ers insured the exclusiveness of the meetings by arranging that admission be "by invitation only" as determined by the "patronesses of the affair."[164]

American Salvation Army leaders were wildly enthusiastic about their work among "high society." An 1889 article in The War Cry reported that "[n]ever before was the United States branch of The Salvation Army so much recognized as a power for good as now. Mrs. Booth, through her drawing-room meetings, has done wonders, and the press are lavish in their praise." Seizing the moment, Maud and Ballington resuscitated the Salvation Army Auxiliary League.[165] First established under Thomas Moore, the league was intended to raise money and cultivate allies for the organization but languished until given new life by Maud and Ballington. They used it to identify and maintain the support of upper- and middle-class supporters around the country.[166] Auxiliary meetings differed radically from regular Army meetings in style and content. The league, composed of middle- and upper-class auxiliary members, supported the social rescue evangelical work without committing themselves to the Army's religious principles and methods.[167] As a consequence, the boisterous religious rituals, raucous singing, hell-fire preaching, and calls to the penitent form generally associated with the Salvation Army played no role in auxiliary meetings.[168]

Although popular with the Booths, there is some indication that many full-fledged Salvation Army members did not approve of the auxiliaries. In an interview some years after his retirement, Commissioner Edward J. Parker indicated that auxiliaries ultimately proved ineffective as a "money making scheme." Moreover, many rank-and-file members resented that auxiliaries seemed to regard themselves as full-fledged Salvation Army members. Said Parker, many auxiliary members "got the wrong idea. Thought if they paid their $5 they were members [of the Salvation Army]." From the perspective of many Salvationists, financial contributions could never replace religious commitment.[169]

Maud and Ballington's increasing enthusiasm for auxiliary work may have disturbed William Booth in a number of ways. First, their work among the upper classes appeared to outstrip that done among the masses; by 1896 there were eight times more auxiliaries than local corps.[170] Furthermore, by continuing to concentrate almost exclusively on rescue work, Maud and Ballington appeared to reject William Booth's new social Christian approach to poverty inaugurated in 1890 with the publication of his book *In Darkest England*.[171] The "Social Scheme" became a critical part of the Salvation Army's program to advertise salvation to the poor but did not really get under way in the United States until after Maud and Ballington resigned.

The tenuous truce that had been reached in 1886 when Maud and Ballington took command of the United States began to unravel in 1894 during the elder Booth's second visit to North America. In the years since his last visit, the general had come no closer to accepting expressions of American national identity or what he began to call "Yankee Doodleism." Upon arrival he found American flags greeting him at every turn. They were featured prominently at the head of parades, and Ballington issued a medallion of the general "surmounted by TWO American flags." An indignant William Booth even found his son's home "decorated with national flags."[172]

The culminating demonstration of national identity came at the 1896 International Congress in London. Salvationists from other countries

MISSIONARIES TO AMERICA

Commander Ballington Booth and the United States party on the steps of
the Congress Hall, Clapton at the Jubilee International Congress, 1894.
Seated in front are Richard Holz (left) and Ballington Booth (right).
(Courtesy of the Salvation Army National Archives)

honored their home culture by marching in some form of their "native"
costume. Americans, in contrast, defined themselves with their flag, a
symbol of national identity; the men in the American contingent sported
Stars and Stripes tunics while the women wore sashes of the same design
draped across their chests. In 1904, when the Americans appeared at the
Congress under the leadership of Evangeline Booth, symbols of American culture (cowboy outfits) replaced symbols of nationalism (flag-
uniforms).

William Booth clearly regarded these displays of nationalism as a serious threat. He began to consider combining Canada and the United
States "into three divisions, [to] break down this National feeling."[173] For
his part, although Ballington publicly called his display of the Stars and
Stripes "innocent," he may have envisioned a time when the American
branch of the Salvation Army would surpass Britain in membership and
resources and, having developed a clear national identity, would be able
to declare independence.

As in 1904, the American contingent of the Salvation Army
at the International Congress in 1914 wore cowboy-style western
costumes as opposed to symbols of nationalism — flags.
(Courtesy of the Salvation Army National Archives)

Eleven months after William Booth returned from his visit to North
America in 1896, Chief-of-Staff Bramwell Booth issued "farewell" or
transfer orders to Ballington and Maud.[174] It is not entirely clear why the
general decided that Ballington and Maud had to be removed. It is likely,
however, that the elder Booth believed that the emphasis on national
identity combined with his son's cultivation of wealthy Americans might
allow the Army in the United States, as Railton had predicted, to surpass
the parent organization. Booth may even have feared that his son would
be able to seize the International Salvation Army and remove the organization from his control. American newspapers regarded the elder
Booth's actions as an example of British aggression. Wrote one newspaper, "[F]inding his own name under an eclipse, the General of the
army, a typical John Bull in aggressiveness, discipline, and personal authority, sought to reinstate himself in the United States and set up a
personal salvation machine of which he would be the boss."[175]

In contrast to the earlier Moore schism, the New York press gave the
removal of Ballington and Maud a considerable amount of attention. As
indicated above, a recurrent theme in the newspaper coverage was the
British challenge to American national identity. General Booth, claimed
the *New York Times*, "was not favorably impressed with American institutions" and recalled Maud and Ballington as part of an effort to "re-

MISSIONARIES TO AMERICA

Anglicize the movement."[176] The paper also emphasized the wide support the couple received from their friends in fashionable New York. Within two weeks of the recall, luminaries like Chauncey M. Depew, Josiah Strong, Lyman Abbott, and Grace H. Dodge organized a mass meeting in Carnegie Music Hall. The meeting was designed to "express public opinion on the subject" and to persuade the general to reconsider his position.[177]

Rather than accept reassignment, Ballington and Maud decided to retire from the Army.[178] Religious and secular newspaper opinion on their decision varied. While a few papers argued that the Ballington Booths ought to accept their orders and so set an example of unquestioning obedience "for the class which most [needs] wholesome discipline," most argued that their defection demonstrated that the Salvation Army in the United States ought to operate independently of Britain.[179] One newspaper, however, argued that Ballington Booth loved the easy life he found in this country. "The truth seems to be," wrote the *Chicago Daily News*, "that Commander Booth has a soft thing in the United States and will not give it up."[180]

In contrast to the 1884 schism, response among the Salvation Army rank and file was muted; after an initial period of confusion, few officers and corps broke with the organization to join their former leaders. Some Salvationists may have resented the Booths' efforts among the upper classes. According to one newspaper, the rank and file did not approve of his focus on the elite. "He has abandoned the old 'back alley' campaigning and taken the army into 'Swell Parlors,' " they wrote, "[i]n fact, the army has always been proud of its influence with the typical tough and its ability to make him religious, whereas under Ballington Booth it has, to quote an officer, 'given the tough the marble heart.' "[181] At the same time, Ballington and Maud chose not to retain control of the property, name, or insignia with which Americans identified the Salvation Army. After years of commitment to the flag, uniform, and crest of the organization, many soldiers and officers may have been reluctant to leave those symbols behind.[182] Furthermore, Frank Smith's earlier efforts to connect William Booth more closely to American Salvationists may have succeeded in finally garnering the loyalty of most members.

Once again General Booth responded to the crisis swiftly by sending other family members, his daughter and son-in-law Consul Emma Moss Booth-Tucker and Commander Frederick St. George de Lautour Booth-Tucker, to take command of the United States.[183] From this point forward, changes in American leadership would proceed more peacefully.

The Booth-Tuckers led the United States until the consul was killed in a train accident in 1904. Evangeline Booth replaced her brother-in-law and served as national commander from 1904 until 1934, when the international leadership elected her to the generalship.

In the meantime, although William Booth and his successor, General Bramwell Booth, never became reconciled to Americanization, the eagle remained atop the crest and American flags and other national symbols continued to play a prominent role in Salvation Army culture in the United States. Experienced officers advised that "three things were needed for a successful open-air meeting: a chair, a light, and an American flag." A torch provides the light, the chair provides the pulpit, and the outstretched flag would receive the collection.[184] Indeed, in the midst of the 1896 schism when the general sent Evangeline Booth to try to gain control of the American forces, it was only by playing the "Star Spangled Banner" and waving an American flag that she was able to calm an unruly meeting of officers.[185] As late as 1926, General Bramwell Booth complained that in some parts of the United States the eagle on the Salvation Army crest had grown "larger and more imposing" and threatened to overwhelm the Salvation Army part. "I hope," he wrote, "this matter will be watched."[186] William Booth may not have approved of "Yankee Doodleism," but no American leader had found a more effective way to market the Salvation Army in the United States.

CHAPTER TWO

"RED HOT MEN AND WOMEN" IN THE SALVATION ARMY, 1879–1896

The prospects are tremendous but what we need, what we want, what we cannot do without are thoroughly consecrated men and women, red hot men and women, soldiers and officers that will stop at nothing.

— D. O. EVANS, "Volunteers for Life"

By the time Arthur D. Jackson turned fourteen in 1893, he was living in Higginsville, Missouri, wheeling coal in the mines.[1] He recalled that as a young man he spent all of his leisure time and money drinking with his friends. On more than one occasion he found himself in the middle of a brawl. "In many instances," he said, "fights terminated in the death of one or the other of the men who fought." Indeed, as Jackson noted sadly, his elder brother died at the hands of a man who "got drinking and challenged my brother to a fight . . . stabbed my brother in the heart and killed him." When he was nineteen, the Salvation Army came to town and began to hold revival meetings. After a year as a soldier Jackson left the mines to become an officer in the Salvation Army, rising through the ranks for the next four decades.[2]

Nellie Upham grew up in the late 1840s in Lawrence, Massachusetts, where she worked as an operative in a textile mill. By the age of fifteen she had surrendered "to the cursed allurements of drink" and came "very near the gates of hell." After drifting around New England living "the gay life" at one moment and confined in Tewksbury Almshouse in another, Nellie eventually "made the acquaintance of . . . this most extravagant band of frights, in timbrels and coal-scuttle bonnets," the Salvation Army. Five months after the Captain persuaded her to join the ranks, Nellie applied and was accepted as an officer in the Salvation Army.[3]

Elizabeth and Susan Swift were the college-educated daughters of a middle-class businessman and his wife. Finding their children too restless and unhappy to remain at home, the Swifts packed the young women off to Europe hoping to restore their spirits. In Glasgow, Scotland, in May 1884 the Swift sisters attended their first Salvation Army Holiness Meeting. In short order, both Susan and Elizabeth joined the organization. Taking advantage of the women's education, Salvation Army leaders put Elizabeth to work teaching cadets basic writing and arithmetic, while Susan became editor of the Army's newest magazine.[4]

In the 1880s Samuel Brengle attended Indiana Asbury University and then Boston Theological Seminary studying for the ministry. In 1885, while serving as a student pastor, Brengle got his first glimpse of William Booth. Brengle admired the general's "virile address" and soon, inspired by Booth, dropped out of seminary to begin work as an itinerant preacher. Two years later, through his courtship of Elizabeth Swift, Brengle became an officer in the Salvation Army, quickly rising to administrative staff positions at the district, provincial, and divisional levels.[5]

Although the Salvation Army recruited most of its officers from among the young native-born, white working class, the institution also attracted much smaller numbers from middle-class backgrounds, many of them, like the Swift sisters and Samuel Brengle, college graduates.[6] For all of these men and women Salvationism offered, first and foremost, an intense religious experience which provided both discipline for a sanctified life and opportunities for Christian service that bought meaning and purpose to their lives. The egalitarian nature of the group's theology, moreover, established the spiritual authority of all members regardless of class, gender, or race. By institutionalizing equality, the Salvation Army offered all men and women opportunities to hold positions of leadership unheard of in religious organizations of that period and well beyond.

The men and women who joined the organization also found themselves attracted to the sacred community created within the Salvation Army. As a man or woman made a moral commitment to the organization, each took on a new identity as an officer in God's vanguard of the Millennium. At the same time, the Army became its members' exclusive social world in which they found supportive homosocial relationships and appropriate partners for divinely sanctioned marriages. They also created new definitions of manhood and womanhood that included sacrifice, service, and vigor. Between 1872 and 1896 Salvationists created a working-class-dominated, cross-class organization devoted to advertising salvation and waging a spirited battle for souls.

"RED HOT MEN AND WOMEN"

Salvation Army records indicate that during the late nineteenth and early twentieth centuries single men and women consistently made up more than 80 percent of the Salvation Army's shock troops, the field officers. (See Appendix, Table 1.) Data for rank-and-file soldiers is very difficult to find; of the few Soldiers' Roll Books that survive, most date from the early twentieth century and reveal that nearly equal numbers of married and single people became Salvation Army soldiers. Of these, 55 percent were men and 44 percent were women.[7] Among the officers who began their careers between 1880 and 1899, more than 65 percent were single and more than half were young (fourteen to twenty-two), white, native-born Americans.[8] Unlike pre–Civil War churches in which women made up 60 percent to 70 percent of the ranks, until 1900 men entered training as Salvation Army officers in greater numbers than women.[9] (See Appendix, Tables 2–5.)

The available occupational data suggests that between 1880 and 1924 well over half of all Salvation Army officers worked before entering training.[10] More than half held jobs in factories, domestic service, agriculture, and transportation. Salvation Army female officers had a much higher rate of participation in the labor force than most American women. While wage earning among all women in the United States reached approximately 23 percent by 1920, nearly 60 percent of female Salvation Army officers between 1880 and 1924 had spent time in the paid labor force prior to becoming officers.[11] The high rate of female Salvationists' participation in the work force may be a factor of their age and marital status. Over three-quarters of those employed were between the ages of fourteen and twenty-four, and 60 percent were single when they joined the organization.[12] These women would be among those most likely to have been employed prior to becoming field officers.[13] (See Appendix, Table 6.)

Among men who became officers in the Salvation Army between 1880 and 1924, nearly half had worked in manufacturing, agriculture, and transportation, and only 16 percent had held clerical, sales, and/or domestic service jobs. Moreover, while a little more than 20 percent of Americans were self-employed by 1920, not one of the men in my sample claimed this status.[14] Furthermore, in the organization's first two decades in this country, none of the men in my sample had been clerks, and only four had worked in sales. Twenty-four men reported working in offices between 1900 and 1924, in a period when 59 Salvation Army women also worked in this sector of the economy as stenographers, typists, and bookkeepers. The larger number of male Salvationist clerks in the post-1900 period suggests these men gained greater access to education. However, the much larger number of women in these jobs reflects the fact that clerking had by this time become increasingly routinized, feminized, and less likely to provide a springboard to promotion to higher positions.[15] (See Appendix, Tables 6–8.)

Although the Salvation Army recruited most of its officers from among young working men and women, the institution also attracted smaller numbers from middle-class backgrounds, many of them, like the Swift sisters and Samuel Brengle, being college graduates.[16] Although their numbers were small, many middle-class Salvationists rose quickly to positions of power within the organization. Unfortunately, Salvation Army records hold little data about officers from middle-class backgrounds in the late nineteenth century; among those for whom I do have information, all had been born during the Civil War and all came from religious households.[17]

Not only were most Salvationists working class, they were also primarily English-speaking, white, native-born Americans or English immigrants. (See Appendix, Table 4.) Explaining the Atlantic Coast Province's inability to convert more of the area's population of 12 million souls, Lieutenant-Colonel Alexander Damon wrote, "The mixed population of our cities frequently makes a successful work impossible, and the predominance of foreigners, who do not acquire the English language, has forced us many times to close corps."[18] These non-English speakers and their children, according to Damon, were "un-get-at-able." Only Scandinavian immigrants showed much interest in the Salvation Army.[19] By 1908, the Army counted separate Scandinavian corps in eight states. In the same year, the group boasted only one Italian and two Chinese corps.[20]

Official Army policy on race was quite unusual for a predominately white organization in the nineteenth and early twentieth centuries. Indeed, as early as the mid-1880s, Commissioner Frank Smith denounced the color line in the United States. The Army, he said, must be "among the first Christian communities of America who will faithfully and wholly break down the wall of partition, separating the white from the colored, whom the Lord has bought from a common captivity and bondage."[21] Indeed, in 1889 *The War Cry* published a report from Frederick, Maryland, that described a meeting advertised "for colored people." The event, at which whites outnumbered blacks five to one, was "led by the sergeant-major of [corps] No. 2 (colored)" and featured "white and black, rich and poor, [who] testified, sang, jumped and praised God."[22]

However, although the Army made several attempts to attract African Americans "ready to die or . . . ready to live and fight for Jesus" by undertaking "expedition[s] to the South in order to work with black people," few actually joined the organization.[23] In 1961 one long-time African American officer suggested that the Salvation Army in the United States "has been principally a white man's Army—not by design, but because of racial attitudes here."[24] Nevertheless, a sufficient number of African Americans joined the organization so that the Army opened a "Colored Corps" in Frederick (1889), one in Cleveland (1891), and three in New York City in the 1920s.[25]

The lack of self-employment among native-born, white, working-class male Salvationists in my sample clearly reflects the declining opportunities for independence and upward mobility available to Americans in this period. Fewer men owned their own farms, and machines relentlessly replaced the work of many skilled laborers.[26] By 1920 most men in this country found themselves working for wages in an unending series of low-skilled, dead-end jobs. The numbers of native-born, male Salvation Army officers who performed low-skill manual labor and the dearth of self-employment among them suggest that many male Salvationists felt disappointed with both their jobs and their prospects. According to Stephen Thernstrom's study of Boston, first- and second-generation immigrants in the economy usually "served as platforms that boosted the position of Yankees." In white-collar work, for example, native-born Americans tended to be concentrated in the highest ranks, while "second generation youths tended to cluster in the less attractive and less well-paid white-collar jobs" as store and office clerks.[27] Considering these trends, native-born, American male Salvationists probably felt keenly disappointed in their own lack of progress.[28]

By 1880, twenty-eight-year-old future Salvationist John Milsaps had failed as both a small proprietor and a gold miner. Forced to earn wages, the young man traveled around the West picking up work as a herder, a railroad dining-car waiter, a road grader, a store clerk, and a paint factory operative.[29] Frustrated by his inability to achieve independence, he wrote, "Am knocked about the world from pillar to post, enduring hardships, wearing poor clothes, eating poor grub, sleeping in cheap lodging houses, and am looked down upon and treated as one of the mudsills of society. Why this is so is a mystery to me. I am ambitious and both wish and try to better my condition and yet do not succeed."[30]

For men like John Milsaps, the new industrial economy created two separate roads, sending some into dead-end jobs and others, like Samuel

Brengle, into a prolonged period of preparation for potentially open-ended careers.[31] These new opportunities for advancement appeared primarily in the white-collar sector of the economy, where access to good jobs increasingly required a formal education. Families able to manage without their children's wages might provide sons with the necessary schooling to get jobs as bookkeepers, accountants, engineers, lawyers, and business managers. Access to education often determined whether or not a young man would reap the benefits of the expanding industrial economy or find himself a "mudsill of society," permanently confined to the bottom levels of the social and economic structure. As Joseph Kett has pointed out, "the boy who dropped out [of school] at 12 or 14 was in serious trouble."[32]

Few Salvationists boasted more than a meager education. The economic demands of his family, according to Arthur Jackson, meant that "I got to go so little, and the breaks in my schooling were so long and so frequent, that I only got into the fourth reader by the time I was fourteen years old." John Milsaps had even less formal education: "two years covered the entire period of my school days," he wrote.[33] Indeed, many painfully written letters from young officers testified to the deficiencies in most Salvationists' education. "[D]ear Mother and father . . . they thot I am the smartest and best Capt that has ever been here. . . . [A]n infidel who hates the Army . . . changed his mind and when I began to talk he was attention and before he went out it cost 175 he gave 25 cents to the door and bout a song of susie and gave her 25[.]"[34]

Industrialization also affected women in the late nineteenth century by drastically reducing the need for their household labor while at the same time expanding opportunities in semi/unskilled labor for those willing to leave home to live in cities and towns. One long-time Salvation Army member recalled that in turn-of-the-century Burlington, New Jersey, there was not much work for the daughters of workingmen. "[T]he girls? Not too much for them. Dressmaking, millinary, — perhaps clerking in a dry goods store."[35] Eva Thompson from South Manchester, Connecticut, said that she felt bored and lonely at home just helping her mother care for the other children. She longed to "go out West where many of my friends have gone."[36] Other women who became Salvationists expressed a desire for independence, or, as one woman put it, to "be the Captain of my own ship." May Harris of Frederick, Maryland, recalled feeling restless during her last two years of normal school, especially when she saw her friends going off to work. Although her father wanted her to become

"RED HOT MEN AND WOMEN"

a teacher, she begged to leave school so that she could get a job, even threatening, "when I got of age I should do as I chose."[37]

Ironically, the very opportunities that promised young women autonomy also created problems that actually circumscribed their ability to be independent. All female workers contended with both low wages and occupational segregation. Employers paid women a family wage on the assumption that they lived with kin who assisted with their support. At the same time, the sex-segregated occupational structure prevented women from getting better-paying jobs.[38] Compounding the problem, young women confronted a housing market where rents, also based on a family economy, exceeded their means.[39]

While working-class men and women grappled with low-wage dead-end jobs, middle-class men and women faced their own set of frustrations in the new industrial economy. Although their education opened up opportunities for advancement, middle-class men discovered that success had become difficult to measure in the late nineteenth century. Still believing in a tradition of individual responsibility for achievement, they faced a reality in which highly organized corporations made individual action and control impossible.[40] Increasingly success no longer implied independence but rather meant slowly ascending the ranks of a bureaucracy, spending years as an " 'apprentice — as an assistant to someone' " in the "bureaucratic web of a large business corporation."[41] These men "tried to live by the Victorian values of their parents at a time when those values seemed to become outmoded and unworkable."[42]

Samuel Brengle, like so many other middle-class men, hoped to "succeed grandly at some important work" but confronted a lengthy career path as well as the ambiguous meaning of success in the late nineteenth century. Within the complex bureaucracy of the Methodist Episcopal Church, the young man faced years of "poor appointments and small memberships." Yet when Clement Studebaker offered Brengle the pastorate of "a large and wealthy congregation" in Indiana, giving him the opportunity to "leap over [hurdles confronted] by the average preacher," the young man rejected the post.[43] Perhaps he recognized that as an employee of Studebaker's church, he could not hope to achieve the independence he associated with success. Instead, his career would depend on his ability to please the church's sponsor and diplomatically "handle" wealthy church members.[44] Reflecting his yearning for independence, Brengle said he preferred the life of an evangelist who "move[s] about largely care-free. If people do not like him, he does not feel the responsibility of adjusting himself to them, for he soon passes on and hears of them no more." Brengle believed that his success as an itinerant evangelist would be associated with the numbers of people "converted and sanctified under his preaching" and not his ability to negotiate social relations within a church bureaucracy.[45]

Middle-class women in the late nineteenth century faced their own dilemma as they sought on the one hand to uphold Victorian domestic ideals while at the same time longing for a productive career. Throughout the nineteenth century women exercised significant moral influence and authority based on their domestic roles as wives and mothers.[46] According to the domestic ideal women created homes that served as sanctuaries from entrepreneurial grasping while at the same time preparing men for the individualism of the marketplace by teaching them self-restraint and industry.[47] As changes in the economy and workplace weakened individual autonomy, however, and as success increasingly depended on slow and steady progress up a bureaucratic ladder, the role of the modern home and hence the moral authority of women became less clear.[48]

At the same time, women faced new competition for moral authority as middle-class children spent long periods of time under the influence and authority of unmarried female schoolteachers. Moreover, fraternal organizations explicitly challenged women's monopoly on moral authority in the late nineteenth century. The Masons, for example, portrayed themselves as "morally self-sufficient," arguing that "men could attain morality through participation in an all-male brotherhood." The notion that the Masons could "inculcate morality without feminine intervention . . . challenged [women] in the central area reserved for them by the canons of domesticity."[49] As a consequence, although many middle-class women may have longed to fulfill the older domestic ideal, they discovered the basis for their moral authority in the family undermined.

Expansion of the domestic sphere into various reform activities in the nineteenth century also challenged the Victorian domestic ideal, creating new expectations for usefulness and drawing many young women into higher education by the late nineteenth century. Unfortunately, the lack of opportunities for work outside the home meant that these women faced nearly insurmountable barriers when they attempted to apply their education to meaningful occupations. One college-educated Salvationist woman wrote that she grew restless with the countless hours she spent on "wool-work" (needlepoint) and "wondered why women need do such things when so many useful better deeds were undone."[50] With few late-nineteenth-century professions opening their doors to women, many, like the Swift sisters, found themselves sinking into a debilitating lethargy after returning from college to keep house for their families. Like so many others of their class, these future Salvationists found themselves in limbo, unmarried and without career options after graduation. The Swifts, like Jane Addams who recovered by throwing herself into reform work, would not be restored until they found some way to combine traditional female responsibilities with their college education to carry on meaningful work.[51]

Although it is not possible to say with any absolute precision why men and women joined the Salvation Army, the conversion narratives and memoirs of working-class Salvationists emphasize "the practical aspects of sin and salvation" by expressing a desire to escape some of the riskier aspects of their world.[52] Some male Salvationists, for example, expressed concern that their "continual association with the wicked" exposed them to sins of the flesh. At a boardinghouse in Sherman, Wyoming, for example, John Milsaps found himself sorely tempted by a number of prostitutes plying their trade. "There were three or four fat girls here," he said, "one good looking. Their actions and talk were such with some of the boarders, that my passions were inflamed." On another occasion Milsaps recalled attending the Belle Union Theatre in San Francisco where he was treated to a "liberal show of female limbs."[53]

Most commonly, however, men described the destructive impact of drink and the violence it promoted either through fights, accidents, or criminal behavior.[54] As noted above, Arthur Jackson lost his brother when drink led to a deadly fight.[55] Another young man recalled driving recklessly home in an express wagon with his employer, "so drunk that we did not know what we were about." The older man was killed when he "fell out of the wagon . . . breaking his neck," while the younger man broke his arm and was unable to work for six weeks.[56] After another young man took a job as a waiter in a saloon, he not only began to drink but soon found himself working for a ring of thieves by slipping into buildings through small spaces and "opening . . . the dwellings to be plundered." Before long he had "spent altogether, some seventeen years behind the prison bars."[57]

Working-class women expressed concerns about dangers associated with the world of "cheap amusements." Among women's testimonies published in the organization's newspaper during 1890, 65 percent cited the risks of "worldly pleasures," including parties, fancy dress, dancing, and theater, all of which were associated with drink. Indeed, working-class Salvationist women used "worldliness" as code for risky sexual behavior. Over half of the Army women concerned about "worldly pleasures" specifically mentioned dancing. Their fears could easily reflect the overtly sexual conduct frequently found in the heterosociality of the dance hall; there, couples who barely knew each other danced in sexually charged embraces and fondled one another in balconies or remote corners of the dance hall. Moreover, drinking was closely associated with dancing. With dance halls often located next door to saloons, owners increased their profits by selling drinks during dances.[58] The vivid personal testimony of Salvationists like Nellie Upham warned that the sexual intimacy of dances combined with consumption of alcohol could make any woman a sinner.[59]

In contrast to working-class men and women, middle-class Salvationists fretted that a life of ease had made them soft and "anemic."[60] Sedentary office work, they lamented, kept young men working in offices day after day rather than performing strenuous physical labor in the open air.[61] Middle-class Americans also worried that commercial culture persuaded them to overindulge in items of "comfort and convenience."[62] Indeed, when middle-class female Salvationists complained of "worldliness," they did not mean the sexual dangers lurking in commercialized "cheap amusements." Instead, they referred to the comfortable, self-indulgent, middle-class life which, they felt, sapped their spiritual (as well as physical) strength and placed them at odds with the notion of true Christian self-sacrifice.[63] Like many women in early-nineteenth-century revivals, middle-class Salvationists "conclude[d] that they had been hypocrites: moral behavior had masked indifference to religion."[64] For many middle-class male Salvationists, the stark contrast when measuring themselves against the heroic sacrifices of the Civil War generation exacerbated concern for their own "softness" and "overcivilization." The war, many believed, having toughened and ennobled those who fought in it, "the warrior's life personified wholeness of purpose and intensity of experience."[65]

Neither middle- nor working-class Salvationists found relief in mainstream Protestant churches. While most working-class Salvationists claimed that their parents had been "Christians," few reported more than passing association with any denomination.[66] By the late nineteenth century, most middle-class Anglo-American Protestants believed that their churches "had to a large extent lost touch with . . . discontented groups." Indeed, the religious community in both the United States and Britain worried that the " 'neglected and poor' threatened to become a dangerous vagabond class if left isolated from the social and religious influence of the church."[67] Recent research on the working class and religion suggests, however, that although working-class men and women felt uncomfortable attending middle-class Protestant churches, "the basic message of evangelical Christianity was a familiar and welcome one to most workers, when presented within a culture and language with which they could identify."[68]

Middle-class Salvationists also came from "Christian" backgrounds, and although they often reported extensive experimentation with religion, they claimed to have found little spiritual solace in a liberal Protestantism that sought to "accommodate modernist thought," including evolution, comparative religion, and higher criticism of the Scriptures.[69] Men found little comfort in churches that had, according to Josiah Strong, become "too soft." "There is not enough of effort, of struggle, in the typical church life of today to win young men to the church. A flowery bed of ease does not appeal to a fellow who has any manhood in him. The prevailing religion is too utterly comfortable to attract young men who love the heroic."[70] Similarly, although the Swift sisters had "attended the Methodist, Presbyterian and Episcopal churches by turns," they claimed their spiritual needs went unfulfilled. These women mistrusted their outward behavior and religious observance and longed for some concrete sign of saving grace. They came to the Salvation Army searching for tangible evidence of their utter submission to God. By obediently carrying out the divine work of the Salvation Army, a middle-class Salvationist received assurance that she conformed to God's will.

The Salvation Army's doctrine of individual holiness attracted these restless men and women by promising to provide a discipline for a sanctified life that established a clear set of behavioral norms. In a body of prescriptive literature, the organization articulated standards of behavior that characterized submission to a holy life. As early as 1878, the Salvation Army in London codified these norms in several books of *Orders and Regulations* for members of the Army.[71] In addition to the basics of Salvation Army religious doctrine, these books taught members that their outward behavior served as a witness to their own salvation and the divinity of the Salvation Army. "The eyes of the world are upon him," warned the general, and are judging him and "the whole Army." A Salvationist ought to "avoid all giggling, foolish conversation, silly joking, childish games, or flirtation. He should cultivate a steady dignity of manner. His very walk and carriage should say, 'I am a soldier of the King of Kings.' "[72]

Along with decorous deportment, *Orders and Regulations* described appropriate physical appearance, personal hygiene, family relationships, and worldly ambitions. The Army took a particular interest in courtship since it affected both the individual and the organization. Marriage, said *Orders and Regulations*, is a "step which, closely bears upon [Salvationists'] . . . future happiness and usefulness, and which is also intimately connected with the welfare of The Army and the Salvation of souls." Regulations also established the rule of endogamous marriage, reflecting the concern that a union to someone outside the Army could undermine a member's commitment and willingness to submit to the authority of the organization. Regulations also advised Salvationists to mute their worldly aspirations; all ambition, the organization suggested, should be directed toward usefulness within the Army.[73]

Conversion stories also served a prescriptive role. For working-class men and women, the often vivid personal testimony of Salvationists like Nellie Upham and Arthur Jackson cautioned that drink and "cheap amusements" could expose men to uncontrollable violence or give a woman her "full diploma as a sinner."[74] These testimonies did more than simply warn, however; they also served as a marketing tool by arguing that a moral commitment to the Salvation Army provided the power to resist this fate and, more important, could *redeem* the man or woman who had fallen. After his conversion experience, one man called the organization "the bridge that carried me over."[75]

People often make moral commitments to a community as part of a personal search for direction or purpose. In exchange for accepting the authority and values of the community, they receive "identity, personal meaning, and the opportunity to grow." This kind of commitment, according to sociologist Rosabeth Moss Kanter, takes place in two ways. First, the process of "mortification" allows one to separate from one's previous life, "to undo those parts of himself he wishes to change." Second, "transcendence" allows the individual to find within the group a greater power and higher meaning within which one can forge a new identity. "Mortification causes the person to 'lose himself'; transcendence permits him to find himself anew in something larger and greater."[76]

For working-class Salvationists, holiness served as a process of mortification to help them forsake sins of the body and sever themselves from their previous lives. For working-class women, sins of the body included drinking and the sexuality that pervaded the world of commercial amusements. For working-class men, these included all manner of "manly" entertainment, including drink, gambling, pugilism, and saloon going.[77]

For middle-class men and women, mortification meant relinquishing their lives of ease to take up a strenuous life for Christ.

Salvationists often testified that their "comrades" played a critical role in helping each other relinquish old behaviors. Using the language of communal bonds so common to evangelicals, William Booth told Salvationists that in the Army, "you will find some brothers and sisters who will . . . appreciate your trials, lend you a hand in the strait places in to which you must of necessity come, weep with you when you weep . . . cheer you in the dark valley of death, and sing you right up to the very threshold of the golden city."[78] Indeed, men like William Day and Charles Malloy frequently testified to the ease with which they slipped from salvation to sin without the "watchful care" of the Salvation Army.[79]

Mortification severed Salvationists not only from old behaviors but also from familiar places and people. Field officers, for example, seldom remained in one village or city for very long. In their testimonies officers described their Army lives as a peripatetic existence that nearly defies the imagination. As soon as she became an officer in 1885, the Army assigned May Harris of Brewster Station, New York, to Meridian, Connecticut. By the time she took over the leadership of Boston 1 corps the following year, she had served in Bristol, Wallingford, Torrington, West Winsted, and Norwalk, Connecticut, as well as Taunton, Cambridge, Worcester, and Fall River, Massachusetts.[80] Middle-class officers also found themselves leaving friends and family behind. Fannie Lawson, for example, left her friends and family in Nevada City to begin her Salvation Army service at a corps in Chico, California, Alice Lewis was sent to serve in the United States from her native Britain in 1896, and Charles McAbee left his family in Columbus, Ohio, in 1884 and by 1887 had served in Michigan, Indiana, and California.[81]

While becoming a Salvation Army officer meant severing oneself from friends and family, the Army compensated by providing the opportunity to become part of a community. A number of special rituals of membership helped Salvationists achieve transcendence by integrating them into the body of this sacred community. This sense of solidarity was particularly important for Salvation Army officers assigned to lonely corps in small towns around the nation. After nineteen-year-old Phillip Gerringer was assigned to a corps in Valley City, North Dakota, loneliness became a recurring theme in his diary. "Glad that the Capt had come home it had been so lonesome without him for a week," he wrote. "All alone during day. No meeting at night. No one came"; "I was left all alone"; "All alone all day"; "Still alone and tired."[82] Similarly, after he had spent three unhappy months assisting in the city of Bath, James Price was given command of an even less promising corps in Brunswick, Maine. Although he had been feeling discouraged by his situation, after spending ten days at a "Congress" with other members of the division, Price seemed transported by "the true brotherly comradeship of officers and soldiers . . . the glowing testimonies of the uniformed hosts, so different from what I had been experiencing in Brunswick and Bath." For these officers, colorful "Congresses" and camp meetings where officers gathered to recall "war memories" proved indispensable to both prevent personal "backsliding" and maintain a strong sense of community.[83]

In addition to camp meetings and "Congresses," rituals of membership included wearing uniforms that set Salvationists apart from "worldlings" and openly professing their faith. To Salvationists, the uniform symbolized the power of individual holiness they found in the Salvation Army; divesting themselves of "worldly dress" became an important physical manifestation of the power of sanctification to change their behavior.[84] For working- and middle-class Salvationists, wearing the Salvation Army uniform publicly announced their rejection of either sins of the body or a life of luxury and ease. In addition to uniforms, other rituals included religious performance, that is, ingenious methods and individual exhibitionism designed to bring about conversions, contributions, and public attention; and a special military language to describe corps religious activities, organizational structure, and phases of each soldier's life cycle.[85] Through these rituals each member gained a new identity and a new mission, "as a Salvation Army officer, baptized and anointed of God, to carry the Gospel to perishing souls."[86] Rituals also served as the language of Salvationists' Christian witness that they not only shared with other soldiers and officers but also used to advertise salvation and bring outsiders into their fellowship.

Once incorporated into the sacred community, Hallelujah Lads and Lasses in many cities found themselves immersed in a constant round of activities and a large social network made up of Salvationists and adherents. A continuous round of religious meetings, selling of *The War Cry*, and assisting or leading corps filled the days of most Salvation Army officers. Moreover, he or she socialized almost exclusively with Salvation Army members. Some Salvationists even resided in lodging houses that catered solely to Salvation Army soldiers.[87] Within this community some officers not only established lifelong friendships but also "ran together in double harness," serving as a unit throughout their careers in the Army. Although Army leaders generally discouraged such teams due to the chronic shortage of officers, Captains Shaw and Williams were separated only twice in six years from the moment they left the Training Home in Malton, Yorkshire, through a variety of appointments in the United States. Similarly, Captains Libbie McAbee and Clara Long apparently "served for many years together as a team of officers." And Charlie McAbee "was permitted to take his faithful companion, Lieut. Murphy" with him to his assignment in Jackson, Michigan.[88]

I have uncovered no evidence that would provide insight into the texture of these relationships. However, a "brief" or report issued by Mrs. Colonel Higgins in 1903 hinted that these friendships often replaced family ties and played a critical role in keeping officers connected to the Army. "Captain O—— and Adjutant A—— are very much attached to each other," she wrote. "They fit in beautifully together and one is a good deal dependent upon the other. Captain O—— is also of a rather frail makeup, and apart from being with A—— would I think be quickly discouraged and return to her home, where they would be very glad to have her."[89]

Tensions and contradictions permeated the meaning of family and family ties within the Army. On the one hand the group's publications sentimentalized family relations emphasizing the power of mothers especially to save the lost.[90] On the other hand, the organization confronted the reality that many parents resisted when their sons and daughters joined the Salvation Army. Indeed, Army critics warned that the organization divided families, especially by "entic[ing] girls from their homes and set[ting] them in opposition to their parents."[91] In coping with this conundrum, Salvationists embraced the family-like quality of Christian fellowship and promoted the organization as "a sort of family bound together." The corps, wrote the general, was not only "a regiment of soldiers," it was "also a family—a brotherhood, having all the family responsibilities for caring for, watching over, and promoting the interests of every member."[92]

Nevertheless, Salvationists frequently found themselves caught between their duty to family and to the Army. Family illness or financial need frequently exerted pressure on young officers. Some left the organization to return home, while others, like Captain James Taylor, sought transfers because his family kept "bothering him for money and assistance, of various kinds." When a Salvationist asked, "My Mother or My God?" Army leaders typically hedged by suggesting that "God and His wish in all things is your first consideration." Although God commanded us to honor our parents, "the greatest dishonor you could bring on your mother and father would be to live in disobedience to God's call." If the voice of God called a Salvationist to save souls, then commitment to the Salvation Army took priority over all other obligations.[93]

In addition to providing a family-like social network solidly planted within the Salvation Army, membership also frequently led to marriage between Salvationists. As with birth families, however, married Army members faced tensions caused by competing demands. Wrote one observer, "[E]arly officers . . . work[ed] very hard and family matters had a lower priority."[94] The Army's rules on marriage and courtship may, in part, have been an attempt to minimize the pressure. *Orders and Regulations*, for example, established that "[n]o Soldier should commence courting with anyone who is not already a Soldier, or unwilling to become one immediately." Moreover, the Army insisted that a superior officer be consulted before any soldier or officer "commence[ed] courting, or enter[ed] into an engagement, or arrange[d] to be married." These rules clearly attempted to establish and preserve the supremacy of Army authority by trying to ensure that Salvationists married only other members fully committed to the mission of the organization.[95]

Tensions aside, endogamous marriage assured working-class female Salvationists of marriages to men who willingly subjected themselves to the discipline of a holy life. Testimonies by working-class married couples suggest that holiness and membership in the Salvation Army often ended a husband's abusive behavior toward his wife and encouraged a more equitable sharing of household resources.[96] For middle-class men and women finding spouses in the Salvation Army ensured support for both a man's rejection of worldly success and a woman's active service for Christ. Indeed, Army literature characterized marriage as a partnership; selfish men, it said, "ought to be without wives." A Salvation Army husband should help with household chores and caring for children. He should especially encourage his wife to develop any talents that would assist in the Army's mission and "always consult her on questions affecting the interests of the family, both as it regards their temporal and spiritual interests."[97] Single Salvation Army officers could easily feel reassured that the men and women they met in the organization would make good mates and that fellow Salvationists would not tolerate selfish or abusive behavior.[98]

In addition to encouraging companionate marriage, Army doctrine also taught that men and women enjoyed equality before God. Salvationists learned that they had a responsibility to ensure the "effectual carrying out of the Savior's law of brotherhood, and the Apostles great theme

"RED HOT MEN AND WOMEN"

of Oneness." Indeed, the Army boasted that it welcomed all the classes of the world, since "there will be but two classes at the Judgment Day those on the right hand, those on the left, those who have accepted Christ, those who have rejected Him."[99] In contrast to most nineteenth-century Protestant evangelical denominations, the Salvation Army officially declared the right of women to preach the Gospel as a "critical and vital doctrine" of its theology.[100] *The Doctrines and Disciplines of the Salvation Army* asserted that people with pure hearts who serve a divine organization must, *regardless of gender*, have equal opportunity to carry out the work of Christ.[101] In 1878 the Salvation Army made itself one of the few mixed-sex organizations that institutionalized egalitarianism by allowing a woman to "hold any position of authority or power in the Army, from that of a local officer to that of the General."[102] Speaking at the World's Congress of Representative Women, Maud Booth said, "We make no difference in our work between the man and the woman. We do not give her a separate sphere of the work, or organize her efforts as though she were in any way disqualified for standing shoulder to shoulder with man at the battle's front. Every position that can be held by man — every office and duty that can be performed by him — we throw open to her."[103]

Service in the Salvation Army opened a world of opportunities to officers regardless of class or gender. By training both men and women in Army methods, the group gave them all the chance to develop and exercise spiritual and organizational authority.[104] Until the first training garrisons opened in the 1880s, men and women received training in the field as they assisted at various Army locations. Training consisted of carrying out the daily responsibilities of corps operation such as visitations, selling *The War Cry*, and holding morning, afternoon, and evening indoor and open-air services. At meetings the cadets learned to sing, preach, take collections, and, especially, keep order.

Coping with disorder gave female officers, particularly, the chance to exercise their leadership skills and demonstrate their capacity to take risks, make sacrifices, and innovate for the cause. At Bristol, Pennsylvania, for example, Salvation Army meetings had been plagued by men wearing white sheets "trying to impersonify [*sic*] ghosts." In retaliation for the men's arrest, someone set the Army hall on fire. With the savvy of an experienced propagandist, Cadet May Harris turned the disaster to advantage by holding an open-air meeting, "upon the smoking ruins," which drew many people appalled by the destruction. "They gave us a good collection," wrote Harris, "we made many more friends, and the press came boldly out on our side."[105] The willingness of women like

Harris to place themselves on the front lines of a holy battle helped to establish the authority of all female Salvation Army officers as spiritual leaders who could be relied upon for their experience, courage, and thorough knowledge of the work.

While the Army was unique in the authority it offered female officers, women were actually underrepresented in the upper ranks of the organization. Women, who often equaled or outnumbered men as officers of local corps, lagged behind them in staff officer positions. Furthermore, very few women (other than William Booth's own daughters) rose to the highest leadership positions. It was not until March of 1890 that *The War Cry* announced the appointment of England's first female divisional commander.[106] Part of the problem was the way in which the Army dealt with the careers of married couples. Beginning in the nineteenth century, when Salvation Army officers married they took on a single administrative identity; the organization merged their professional lives into a single career sheet. From that point forward they received joint appointments and promotions. If Captain Lucy Smith married Adjutant Mark Jones, they became Adjutant and Mrs. Mark Jones. (Women seldom married men with lesser rank; they either waited until the men received a promotion or lost rank themselves.) The Army did not treat married officers as separate people with separate careers. It did not assign married officers to different posts, nor did it pay the family the equivalent of two single officers' salaries.[107]

While this arrangement obviously penalized female officers, I think that the Army's purpose, in part, was to find some way to forestall the loss of the female officer's spiritual and administrative labor after marriage. As indicated, the group encouraged Salvationists to marry others within the group for fear of losing authority over the couple altogether. At the same time, Salvation Army leaders fretted that when Salvationists married, the organization frequently lost its most capable officers to domestic duties.[108] In response, the Army came up with a unique solution. By creating the status of "Officer-wife," the Salvation Army institutionalized the role of the minister's wife in which she held joint rank and assisted her husband in his staff position. In February of 1888, for example, the *Disposition of Forces* listed Brigadier and Mrs. Evans as heads of the divisional headquarters in Chicago.[109] In creating this special status, the group recognized that which has gone unacknowledged (even today) in most religious, business, and political organizations, the critical role played by the "professional" wife.[110]

Single, educated, male and female middle-class Salvationists found themselves promoted quickly into staff or administrative positions. Like the Swift sisters, other well-educated women performed important administrative work for the Army. Alice Lewis assisted Consul Emma Booth-Tucker when the latter commanded the Army in the United States.[111] Officers like Brigadier Elizabeth M. Clark, a Bryn Mawr graduate, wrote for the Army's magazines and newspapers, in addition to publishing biographies of important Salvationists. Likewise, middle-class men like Samuel Brengle and Charles McAbee quickly moved from field to staff positions.

Although the education and business skills of middle-class officers meant they moved quickly into administrative positions, it would be a mistake to suggest that the Army limited positions of authority to middle-class officers. The number of middle-class Salvationists was small, and the Army's need for leadership was great. As a consequence, working-class men and women also moved up the ranks to hold significant positions of power. Emma Westbrook, one of seven single, working-class Hallelujah Lasses sent to the United States in 1880 rose to the rank of major.[112] Similarly, over his fifty-year career John Milsaps, who joined the group in 1885, moved up the ranks of the organization from corps captain to editor of the national edition of *The War Cry*, eventually achieving the rank of major.

When working-class men and women relinquished or resisted sins of the flesh, the Salvation Army provided them with tangible rewards, which included not only promotions in rank and responsibility but also a vigorous defense of their personal virtue. The Army regularly argued that it targeted the men and women who wallowed in the very depths of sin and shame. "Trophies of Grace," degraded men and women redeemed by the work of the Salvation Army, not only demonstrated the effectiveness of the Army's methods but were themselves a *cause* of the organization's success. As a consequence of their own experience with wickedness, the organization argued, these Salvationists were particularly suited to work among the heathen masses. This position was particularly important for working-class women; when the Army publicly promoted the uprightness of Hallelujah Lasses, it established the principle that even a "fallen" woman could be redeemed, invested with moral authority, and become an asset in the redemption of others.[113]

Furthermore, when working-class Salvationists advertised the blessings of salvation to others like themselves, they invented a popular theology that gave them a profound sense of purpose. Saving souls and promoting the Army's sacred community expressed an ethic of mutuality common to working-class families and neighborhoods. In contrast to the market values that ruled most social relations of the era, the Salvation Army revival meeting could be regarded as a place of *spiritual* "mutual aid." Instead of sharing resources (rainwater, sinks, cutlery, bedding, or cooking pots), the working-class Salvation Army officer shared the keys to the Kingdom, salvation.[114] Moreover, well before the institutionalization of social work in the Salvation Army, it was not unusual for officers to provide temporal mutual aid on an ad hoc basis by permitting a down-and-out man or woman to sleep in corps buildings.[115]

While saving souls brought meaning to the lives of working-class Salvationists, teaching holiness satisfied middle-class men and women who, much like those drawn to settlement houses, felt "strong emotions and sense of purpose . . . helping others."[116] In contrast to the working-class notion of mutual aid, however, these officers found meaning in helping others quite *unlike* themselves. True holiness, they believed, released in them a desire to undertake active salvation work among the lost; in the Army submission to God entailed arduous Christian service. Of course the Salvation Army was not the first religious movement to make a connection between sanctification and Christian service. Since the early nineteenth century, one of the "fruits" of salvation had been energetic effort to convert others. Indeed, many historians have noted the close connection between evangelical Christian revivalism and social reform during the antebellum period. The Salvation Army's brand of Christian service, however, was *unusually* demanding.[117]

As a result, most middle-class sympathizers avoided the strenuous demands of the Salvation Army by joining the Auxiliary League. One league member, Mr. R. Lodge, wrote his enamorata (a Salvation Army officer) that he found Salvation Army Christian service too arduous. He preferred the sort of "practical holiness" advocated by Hannah Whitall Smith, whose early work preached a more passive "gospel of submissiveness." According to Smith, conforming utterly to God's will often meant accepting one's limitations rather than taking up active work in "the Lord's harvest field."[118] In contrast, Lodge found in the Army's teachings on holiness "just a *little bit* of harshness, in the sense of a painful service to God." Auxiliary member Lodge admired the Salvationists but did not feel he had the "fortitude" to perform such a rigorous service, even for God.[119]

The active nature of submissiveness apparently influenced other areas of Salvationists' lives. Mr. Lodge seemed somewhat amused (and perhaps discomfited) by the brand of female submissiveness exhibited by the object of his affections, Captain Mary Hartelius. In a letter he wrote, "[W]hile you delegate to me all your authority, and allow me to say whether or not you shall do certain things, yet you very contentedly assume, that when you decide these questions yourself, it is I that do so; and when you do just as you like, I am to feel happy at having complete jurisdiction over you. Well — I have taken a long breath — Amen."[120] Holiness and the arduous Christian service it inspired apparently encouraged Salvation Army officers to view submission as a kind of call to action.

Like this interpretation of submissiveness, Salvationists constructed a maleness and femaleness that combined the contradictory elements of nurture and self-sacrifice with vigor and boldness.[121] In explaining what attracted him to the organization, Samuel Brengle said, "Two or three things appealed to me when I first met the Army. One was their *sacrificial* spirit. The other was their *virility*. I shall never forget going down to Boston #1 and seeing the officer in charge . . . coming in — blowing his trumpet — marching *erect* and with *vigor*—and preaching sermons with *fire and bite* in them."[122] Salvationists seemed "virile" and "vigorous" to Brengle, particularly in contrast to the "soft," "easy," and "anemic" students who surrounded him at Boston Theological Seminary. And yet Salvationists also had a "sacrificial" or self-sacrificing spirit, a quality most often associated with the female experience.

To men like Samuel Brengle and Charlie McAbee, William Booth, the cofounder of the Salvation Army, personified a virile Christian manhood that included physical vigor and strength of personality.[123] In his mid-fifties when he visited the United States in 1885, the general cut a striking figure. His "iron-gray beard" streamed over his chest. Under his military tunic he wore a "flaming red guernsey" on which there was a "blazing crest with the words 'Blood and Fire' fairly shouting at the observer." The general walked with "great strides" to the platform and "carried his . . . audience by storm." Brengle's reaction to Booth's presence was very emotionally demonstrative; the sight of "God's greatest servant" caused him to "burst in to tears."[124]

Like men, the personal vigor and power of women leaders attracted many female Salvationists to the Army. Catherine Booth and her daughters, for example, served as models of strenuous motherhood successfully combining the domesticity and self-sacrifice of mothers with the bold leadership of "women warriors." Elizabeth Swift reported that when she was given an audience with Catherine Booth, "the greatest woman preacher of the age [was] patching her husband's shirt!" Another daughter, Catherine (Katie) Booth, the "Marechale," opened Army work in

Paris in 1881 and in Switzerland in 1882. She was expelled from the latter in 1883 and imprisoned when she reentered Switzerland to try again.[125] The marechale captured the imagination of Maud Charlesworth, the sixteen-year-old daughter of an Anglican minister, who defied her father's wishes by becoming actively involved in Salvation Army campaigns. Perhaps the most charismatic and powerful of the Booth daughters was Evangeline Cory Booth, who held the post of national commander in the United States for thirty years (1904–34) and then served as general of the International Army for a five-year term.

The public did not always respond warmly to the Army's definition of manhood and womanhood or to its defense of its members' moral character. Newspaper articles in this period often portrayed the group as encouraging civil and sexual disorder. Particularly horrified by the sight of men and women marching in the streets, "the army," they reported, "was a public nuisance and attracted bad crowds." Furthermore, they warned, there was danger of "immorality among the women and men engaged in the fantastic crusade."[126] Arguing that the group "violat[ed] . . . all instincts of propriety," another newspaper wrote, "Religion is nothing if it does not regulate conduct, and in regulating conduct it may properly be expected to avoid that extravagant and bizarre deportment which invite[s] ridicule."[127]

To combat their critics and reassure officers, particularly women, of the righteousness of their "blood-and-fire, dare-devil spirit," the organization again invoked its concept of *corporate* holiness and suggested that God would not sanctify the Army if He found its principles offensive. As a consequence, leaders argued that the devil was behind any effort to discourage officers from boldly wielding their influence in the name of Christ and the Salvation Army. "One of his most effectual plans," the group argued, "is in raising the question in the heart . . . 'Isn't it unwomanly?' " Women must not mistake "the devil's voice for God's," cautioned the Army. For "[a] lass who is led of the Spirit will not be wrong, even if it is beyond the bounds of what the world considers propriety." Refusal to carry out the Army's work meant that "they choose to obey man and certain rules and conventionalities laid down by man, rather than God."[128]

As Ballington and Maud Booth gathered support for the social rescue work in the mid-1880s they also promoted a positive public image of the group's young officers. In meetings they described the work of the Army and the sacrifice of the officers among "the very poorest and the most depraved classes."[129] The holy boldness of male and female officers, argued Maud Booth, was critical to reaching the "masses." While not entirely successful in shaping public opinion, some press reports began to appear articulating the Army's standard defense of its principles and its methods. Wrote the Chicago *Citizen*, "When we listen to [Maud Booth's] powerful words . . . we learn to have patience with the cymbals and the drums, and to understand that the inhabitants of the slums can never be reached by the usual priest and minister, or by fine rhetorical phrases and logical statements."[130] In spite of some signs of support, however, public opinion about the work of the Salvation Army and its officers would not change significantly until the turn of the century, when the organization began to advertise salvation to the heathen through its own style of social Christianity.[131]

When the Salvation Army appeared on the American religious landscape in the late nineteenth century, although it attracted small numbers of the middle class, it found its true market niche among young, native-born, white, working-class Americans. Salvationism provided these men and women with a religious experience that not only helped them reject sins of the flesh but also demanded that they undertake an arduous Christian service. The Salvation Army offered more than religion, however; it also created a family-like sacred community in which members, regardless of class or gender, found enduring friendships, suitable marriage partners, moral and administrative authority, and meaningful careers. In this unique working-class-dominated religious organization, Salvationists redefined the meaning of manhood and womanhood and advertised salvation by placing men and women together on the front lines in the battle for souls.

CHAPTER THREE

THE WORLD SALVATIONISTS MADE

Democracy and Autonomy in the
Salvation Army, 1879–1896

As my soul in darkness wandered to and fro,
I was roused by the beat of the drum,
And the flaming torch showed the way to go,
While the drum and the light said, "Come!"
— Joe the Turk's Experience, in
The Salvation Army Special Songs and Solos

Forty-eight hours after they landed in New York City in 1880, a small contingent of the Salvation Army held its first public meeting at the infamous Harry Hill's Variety Theater. The enterprising Hill, alerted by newspaper reports of the group's arrival from Britain, contacted their leader, Commissioner George Scott Railton, and offered to pay the group to "do a turn" for "an hour or two on . . . Sunday evening."[1] In nineteenth-century New York City, Harry Hill's was one of the best-known concert saloons, and reformers considered him "among the disreputable classes" of that city. His saloon, they said, was "nothing more than one of the many gates to hell."[2]

The advertising for Sunday's performance announced: "the Salvation Army will attract [attack?] the Kingdom of the Devil in Harry Hill's Variety Theater on Sunday, March 14, 1880 commencing at 6:30 p.m. sharp, after which the panorama of 'Uncle Tom's Cabin.' Admission 25c."[3] Commissioner Railton was somewhat troubled by the fact that his little group would be "tak[ing] part in a Sunday entertainment for the people for which admission money was charged," and local friends had warned him that respectable people would reject the Army if they went "to such a den to begin with." He confessed, however, to feeling "a savage satisfaction in having this notorious sinner open his door to us before any church did so."[4] That Sunday, Railton and the seven Salvation Army Lasses who made up the group climbed onto Harry Hill's stage and formed a semicircle around the commissioner in minstrel show–style. "Mr. Railton's opening prayer," reported the New York Times, "was very much such a prayer as may be heard at any camp-meeting." Then, according to the New York World, with Railton kneeling and the Lasses surrounding him in " 'various and curious positions' " reminiscent of a tableau vivant, the Salvationists proceeded to sing hymns (including one to the tune of "Rosalie, the Prairie Flower"), exhort the audience, recite "obviously memorized" testimonies, and pray.[5] While unanimously rejecting the invitation to repent, the audience reportedly applauded the effort, perhaps entertained by the Salvationists' use of the minstrel-show idiom and music-hall venue for religious ends.[6]

As the Salvation Army entered the crowded American religious marketplace, its largely working-class membership invented an autonomous and surprisingly democratic religious culture. In an urban analogue to the frontier camp meeting, Salvationists established new ways for working-class people to experience and express religious feeling. When the eight Salvation Army officers ascended the music-hall stage to sing, pray, and strike curious poses before an audience of sinners, they put working-class forms of popular culture in service to an experiential evangelical religion.[7] Throughout the late nineteenth century the Salvation Army in the United States held raucous indoor and open-air meetings at which both men and women worshipped God with their bodies as well as their souls. To the alarm of mainstream Christian society, Salvationists combined the culture of the saloon and music hall with a frontier camp-meeting style and took it onto city streets. There, the Army successfully marketed itself and its religion to working-class men and women in America.

In addition to its religious culture, the institution created by Salvationists demonstrated unexpected levels of autonomy and democracy. In spite of continuing efforts by General Booth and American leaders to represent the organization as a military-style autocracy, these high-ranking officers faced critical realities that undermined their efforts. Throughout the late nineteenth century, distance and weak lines of communication undermined centralized authority and encouraged local autonomy. Moreover, since British and American headquarters relied heavily on local corps and scores of voluntary members for financial support and legitimization, rank-and-file Salvationists wielded considerable power to resist all levels of authority. In spite of claims to the contrary, the Army's national leadership never fully controlled the periphery of the organization. Indeed, the Salvation Army's administration demonstrated a persistent tension between autocracy and democracy.

One of the impulses that encouraged Salvationists to create an autonomous religious culture fit into a "long tradition of democratic religious authority" in the United States. Beginning in the late eighteenth and early nineteenth centuries, according to Nathan Hatch, ordinary people reshaped Christianity and "molded it in their own image." The common folk not only favored local control but also preferred "unpretentious" leaders who made religion accessible by using everyday language as a means to communicate simple and practical religious beliefs.[8] These movements also legitimated the "spiritual impulses" of ordinary people by allowing them to create a religious culture in which they could express their spirituality physically as "enthusiasm" or "religious ecstasy." Salvationists not only looked to each other to provide moral, spiritual, and administrative authority, but the organization also accepted its members' "deepest spiritual impulses at face value" and allowed them to "defin[e] the nature of faith for themselves."[9]

Along with religious tradition, democratic aspects of working-class popular culture also influenced Salvationism. "The saloon," for example, "was actually a 'democracy' of sorts . . . where all who could safely enter received equal treatment and respect." Saloon culture, argued Roy Rosenzweig, rejected the mentality of market exchange and celebrated instead an ethic of mutuality and reciprocity among equals. Not only had group drinking become an important symbol of equality, since "all men were equal before the bottle," but treating, that is, the custom of paying for one's friends' drinks, served as a way in which working-class men could declare their solidarity with their mates.[10] As we will see, however, the democratic impulse based in male working-class saloon culture broadened in the hands of the Salvation Army to include women as well as men.

The religious world Salvationists made brought the early-nineteenth-century frontier camp meeting into the city and gave it the vernacular expression not of southern "plain folk" but of the northern urban working class. The plain folk who created the frontier camp meeting shared many characteristics with Salvationists. Both populations were economically, politically, and socially marginalized, the plain folk as subsistence farmers in a southern plantation economy and the northern working class as low-paid unskilled workers in an expanding industrial economy. "Neither rich nor starving," Salvationists, like the plain folk, believed in self-reliance and upward mobility. They seldom, however, controlled their own destiny and almost always (like John Milsaps) ended up as "mudsills" of society, moving restlessly around the country in search of elusive opportunities. For some plain folk and working people, "drinking and violent 'sports' " provided release from the contradictions in their lives. For others, religious sects offered an "alternative way of life" that spelled out "proper relationships between individuals," clearly defined the rules they needed to follow, and "provided an alternative sphere of action where people could assert themselves in ways other than those denied them by secular . . . society."[11]

The goals and structure of frontier camp meetings and Salvation Army religious services also shared important characteristics. For both groups, conversion was the major point of religious exercises, and "every aspect of the meeting contributed to that end."[12] Each group also sanctioned intense physical manifestations of religious experience. In a recent article Ann Taves called this condition a "dissociative state," in which "something that is 'not me' can be present in place of or along side what I experience as or believe to be 'me.' " In these states people disengage from both sensory input and voluntary motor control, experiencing visions and voices or physical spasms and jerking. In a Christian context these dissociative experiences have been called " 'ecstasy,' 'enthusiasm,' and 'inspiration.' "[13]

Reports of the camp meeting at Cane Ridge, Kentucky, in 1801 describe "bodily agitations or exercises" that including "falling down . . . jerks . . . dancing . . . barking . . . laughing . . . running [and] . . . singing." For many Salvationists, worship was similarly "a physical sensation" or "a tactile experience" and fostered a loss of control over bodies and voices.[14] In his memoirs Salvationist James Price recalled that on one Saturday night during a " 'hallelujah wind-up,' " he nearly passed out. "I seemed to be lifted out of myself," he said, "and I think that for a time my spirit left my body." While he did not faint, "mentally, for a time I was not at home." When he regained awareness, he found himself "on the platform among many others singing and praising God." "[S]uddenly finding myself in the midst of a brotherhood with whom I was in complete accord; without the shadow of a doubt regarding its divine mission, and then the great meetings climaxing in scores being converted, all this affected me like wine going to my head."[15]

According to Taves, dissociative phenomena reached a high point "in the interracial and interdenominational frontier camp meetings in Kentucky and Tennessee," after which it began to die out among European American Methodists. For Salvationists in the late nineteenth century, however, physical manifestations of spiritual feeling were an integral part of worship. "Many of the soldiers," wrote the *National Baptist*, "rock[ed] themselves backwards and forwards waving and clapping their hands, sometimes bowing far forward and again lifting their . . . faces, heavenward. The singing was thickly interlarded with ejaculations, shouts [and] sobs."[16] Salvationists had created an urban working-class version of the frontier camp-meeting style of religious expression.

The Salvation Army also institutionalized "enthusiasm" or the physical expression of a "continuous revival of feeling."[17] Beginning with conversion, Salvationists experienced their religion with striking physical intensity. When an iron miner came "under conviction" and approached the altar to pray for forgiveness, according to Salvationist Arthur Jackson, "[h]e prayed on his knees at the altar for a while, then he sat down on the floor in front of the altar and prayed, and then he lay down on his back on the floor and prayed, and then he seemed to get into a sort of convulsion or an agony. He turned over and lay on his stomach and prayed." Jackson also recalled an elderly woman who, when saved, "jumped from her seat like a jack out of a box and began to shout. . . . She pounded the back of the bench in front of her with her hands and screamed for joy."[18]

Although one might expect that the initial conversion experience would be intensely felt and expressed, in the Salvation Army even daily prayer was a loud and physical experience. While dining with a captain at a Salvation Army training garrison, a startled visitor reported hearing "a roar, as of thunder, and a noise as if fifty sledge-hammered men were pounding on the floor over our heads."[19] Creeping upstairs, the guest discovered "fifteen stalwart, hearty, powerful-lunged fellows upon their knees at prayer. They prayed with their voices, their feet, and both hands, and as each one possessed of a pair of hands and feet, which were going for all they were worth."[20] Leading prayer was also a physical experience. One young captain reportedly "would lean away over to one side, then lean the other way and wave his arms, throw back his head, putting his whole body into the exercise."[21]

In addition to physical expressions of spiritual feeling, the structure of both camp meetings and Salvation Army services provided a total experience for those attending by holding meetings all day long. Both religious movements followed a typical sequence of services. Camp meetings began with the gathering of the congregation. Each day opened with family prayer followed by morning prayers for the whole camp. After breakfast there would be a morning service with testimonies and perhaps a sermon; small tent meetings followed afternoon services and the day ended with a lengthy evening service. Similarly, Salvation Army meetings were held all day everyday and frequently began with a street parade through the neighborhood that gathered a congregation or audience. Each day's exercises began with a knee drill (morning prayers). Local corps also held morning, noon, afternoon, and night meetings, some of which were held in the "open air." Every Friday there would be one meeting devoted exclusively to holiness.[22] Furthermore, the camp meetings and Salvation Army services had similar effects on participants by undermining the structure of their old lives, and replacing it with a new order and a new identity that provided assurance.[23]

Salvationists were not the only ones to adapt the camp meeting in the late nineteenth century. After the Civil War the holiness movement in the North transformed the nature of camp meetings, making them very different from those of the antebellum period. In contrast to southern plain folk and Salvationists, however, sponsors and participants in northeastern camp meetings came from the urban middle and upper classes. Unless they lived nearby, the costs of transportation made it impossible for ordinary working people to attend. These rural or coastal camp-meeting grounds soon became quite elaborate, as camp-meeting associations built permanent buildings and "shareholders" built family cottages on surrounding land. As several historians have demonstrated, late-nineteenth-century camp meetings provided the urban middle and upper classes with a place of retreat from urban life. Trips to camp meetings soon became vacations where Christian families found nature and nurture. Wrote one critic, "People flock to summer camp meetings . . . half in search of health and half in quest of religion. . . . [They] mix Christianity and sea-bathing a little too confusedly."[24]

While Salvationists shared much with the plain folk, each used a very different vernacular to express their spirituality. The plain folk reached into their southern rural experience, while the Salvation Army looked to the world of the urban working class for ways to demonstrate religious feeling. Salvationists occasionally used forms that recalled the traditional work-centered culture of the artisan. The roots of the Salvation Army's "trade union nights" can be found in eighteenth-century street parades, where "craftsmen . . . presented themselves as members of a corporate body, as contributors to the social good through their practice of a useful, productive skill." They acted out this identity by performing their crafts before audiences gathered along the streets. While these traditional parades excluded representations of casual labor, however, Salvation Army trade union nights counted all manner of work and workers, skilled and unskilled, male and female among the "honorable trades."[25]

According to the *Chicago Blade*, meetings on Salvation Army "trade union nights" began with a street procession in which female Salvationists formed a "broom brigade" and the men, dressed in "overalls and jumpers carrying the tools of their trade," drew a large and enthusiastic crowd to the hall. When the people entered the hall, they found that the stage was filled with men and women busy at their trades. A barber gave shaves and haircuts. A violin maker made repairs on a fiddle, a lather put up lath after which a plasterer put on the "rough coat" of plaster and a paper hanger made preparations to paper the wall when the plaster dried. These meetings represented female Salvationists' work as domestic servants with "a little sitting room . . . partitioned off from the rest of the platform, [where] two girls showed how they swept floors and cleaned houses during the day."[26]

While a few Salvation Army religious rituals adapted the sedate and respectable aspects of artisan culture, more often the group embraced urban working-class forms of popular culture that promoted sociability. The group instinctively understood what labor organizations discovered by the late nineteenth century, that is, the critical role of sociability in working-class subculture. This world, according to one labor historian, "demanded both individual commitment and group solidarity." Working-class leisure activities helped to "maintain the commitment of members through sociability rather than wait to test solidarity in the crucible of a strike." Similarly, sociability allowed the Salvation Army "to compete for the allegiance of workers" and maintain group solidarity. However, in stark contrast to the male world of labor unions and working-class leisure culture that circumscribed "participation from women and children," sociability Army-style was heterosocial.[27] Like the women who participated in trade union nights or mounted the stage at Harry Hill's Variety Theater, female Salvationists participated along with their men in the Army's use of lively and often rowdy working-class leisure forms for religious ends.

The Army's use of songs and music illustrated the wedding of religion and working-class saloon and music-hall culture in their services. When Salvation Army captain Daniel E. Smith stopped going to saloons, where he used to "sit at the piano . . . and play and sing . . . until the morning," he sacrificed alcohol but not the rousing music.[28] Highly participatory

HELLO! WHAT NOW?

DON'T YOU KNOW? NO! WHAT?

Why the Salvation Army is going to have a Big United Meeting
in the Tent, cor. of Ontario and St. Clair Sts.,

Wednesday, Sept. 28, 8 P. M.

A REGULAR

Trades Union Meeting!

(Under Major Stillwell's Management,)

When the Blacksmiths, Carpenters, Printers, Machinists, Plaster-
ers, Draughtsmen, Stenographers, Type-Setters, Dressmakers,
House-Maids, and others, will perform some part of their voca-
tion in Meeting. COME AND SEE.

GOOD MUSIC, GOOD SINGING

AND SPEAKING

Will make this one of the most novel and interesting meetings
ever held in Cleveland. Be sure and secure a ticket at once.
Proceeds to go towards clearing debt on tent.

Ordinary Tickets 10c. Reserved Seats 20c.

Salvation Army poster advertising a "Trades Union Meeting."
(Courtesy of the Salvation Army National Archives)

saloon-style sing-alongs played a critical role in Salvation Army services. "The meeting began with singing," reported the *National Baptist* in 1880. "The lung-power and unction that these people throw into their singing is immense.... [T]here is a clapping of hands, keeping time to music.... [R]efrains . . . are repeated an indefinite number of times. No particular person starts the tunes; each of the officers, man or woman, takes a hand at it as the spirit moves; often before a new verse of the hymn can be commenced, a voice strikes in with the chorus once more."[29]

The Army put considerable effort into accumulating songs suitable for its lively services. Rejecting slow and stately hymns, the Army encouraged budding songwriters to co-opt secular tunes. Said an announcement in *The War Cry*, "[A]ll you who undertake to write songs for the War Cry just let us have some jolly good songs to rattling tunes."[30] Adjutant Smith contributed the following hymn, entitled "The Experience of Ash-Barrel Jimmy: The First Salvation Army Convert in America," set to the tune of "I'm Captain Jinks of the Horse Marines."[31]

> Once I was a Water street bum,
> Full all the time with five-cent rum,
> The devil had me under his thumb.
> When I was in his Army,
> Oh! yes he had me in his grip.
> I cared for nothing but a nip,
> I down the road to hell did slip,
> In the damnation Army.
>
> *Chorus:*
> But now my sins are washed away,
> Are washed away, are washed away,
> I'm fighting for Jesus night and day,
> In the Salvation Army.[32]

Where "talent" and the availability of instruments permitted, musical accompaniment also played an important part in Army services. In the early years the Salvation Army relied heavily on easily mastered percussion instruments like bass drums, cymbals, and tambourines, and did not demand much in the way of melody from brass horns. The *Chicago Inter-Ocean*,[33] reporting on the "musical" consequences, noted, "The blare of the trumpet, the 'umtra-umtra' of the trombone, and the 'biff biff boom' of a particularly corpulent bass drum filled the auditorium . . . shook the rafters, and set the windows rattling like a grip car off the track. Melody got twisted into weird noises resembling the blended symphony that the lonely donkey sings at the moon, the Wagnerian strains evoked from a battered tin-pan by a small boy and the soul-stirring agony of a violin student's first attempt."[34]

One of the most important elements of any Salvation Army meeting was gathering the congregation. Since local corps could not afford high rents, they frequently found rooms or halls located in alleys and back courts where attracting an audience could prove to be quite a challenge. To address this problem, the Salvation Army regularly used street parades to promote meetings and literally lure people to its indoor and outdoor religious performances. In 1879, for example, a Philadelphia newspaper described a small parade led by Salvationists Eliza and Anne Shirley, who "walk[ed] backward . . . down German Town road, singing a rousing hymn, and keeping step to the air." The march reportedly attracted a great deal of attention as "windows and doorways . . . filled with spectators[, and the group was] . . . followed by almost everything that had legs." The crowd then piled into the Salvation Factory, wrote the reporter, filling the small building to capacity. On another occasion a newspaper drew an explicit parallel between a Salvation Army parade and the circus. Wrote the Paterson *Daily Guardian*, "The women of the procession, and the Army attracted almost as much attention as Barnum's street parade."[35] Salvationists promoted their meetings with lively campaigns that exploited the power of street spectacle to attract public attention.

A report in *The War Cry* from Schenectady, New York, clearly acknowledged the theatricality of its street performances (which were often followed with arrests) by describing the events as if they had been part of a dramatic presentation with numerous "scenes." "Scene 1 — Street — Nearly 8 o'clock p.m. — Saloon close by — people going to hell — saloon keeper disturbed on account of losing trade — police sent for — two girls arrested." "Scene two," at the court house where the judge "Pronounced [the Lasses] guilty — Exit to the common jail." "Scene Three" upon the women's release a "[t]riumphant procession hallelujah welcome — General rejoicing . . . enthusiastic crowds."[36]

The group also seized every opportunity to emphasize its similarity to popular entertainment, at times even referring to itself as the "Hallelujah Circus." The Salvation Army in San Jose, for example, attached itself to the coattails of a genuine circus by having handbills distributed in town falsely announcing twice as many performances as were actually scheduled. After the real performers departed, the Salvationists set up their

THE WORLD SALVATIONISTS MADE

own tent, and held "a monster open air on circus grounds," not only "netting souls" but also reportedly accumulating "[t]he largest offerings received in any one day since we opened fire here." That the audience or congregation not only failed to object to the Army's bait-and-switch technique but expressed its satisfaction with larger-than-usual donations suggests that the people found the Army nearly as entertaining as the circus.[37]

A War Congress in New York City revealed the minstrel-show elements often found in Salvation Army meetings. Like minstrelsy, these performances were divided roughly into three parts and included several specialty roles; unlike minstrelsy, however, women also participated in the various acts.[38] Part 1 included the entire company. Three hundred Salvationists waving flags, jingling tambourines, jumping and waving their arms filled the stage of the music hall, reported the *New York Times*. Major Smith, acting as a kind of interlocutor or master of ceremonies, leaped onto the center stage, fell to his knees, and prayed. After hymns as well as some heckling from the audience, Part 1 of the performance closed with a group song and dance, including the full company praying on their knees, stretched out full length on the floor, standing, rocking, crying, and shouting.

Next came the variety section or olio. Here Major Smith invited "Ash-barrel Jimmy" to the center of the stage for the following exchange:

Smith: "Who would have thought once that 'Ash-barrel Jimmy' would have performed on the stage of the Academy?"
Jimmy: (scratches his right ear thoughtfully)
Smith: (claps Jimmy on the back) Jump in, but not into the ash barrel.
Jimmy: I 'ardly know which end to begin at.
Smith: Start at the middle and work to both ends.

After Jimmy came Captain Wallace singing a hymn to the tune of "Captain Jinks" and "danc[ing] a jig at the close of each verse . . . [while swinging] his banjo around his head in true minstrel style." He was replaced by Captain Dean whose husband, Billie, stood next to her "look[ing] uncomfortably while his wife . . . told of his shortcomings." Billie then sang a hymn he composed. The War Congress's concluding act included a skit reenacting "how the Salvation Army rescued sinners." Here "21 women marched around the stage . . . [while] the leader played a bass drum [and] the rest banged tambourines [and] the remainder of the Army danced and shouted."[39]

While not all corps services were this elaborate, personal testimonies often injected melodrama or comic relief into a service. At a corps meeting in Higginsville, the man who had killed Salvationist Arthur Jackson's brother spoke movingly about his experience. Reported Jackson, "This man . . . said no matter where he went, whether he was going to sleep or waking up, or whether he was working or resting — no matter what he did, everywhere he went and everything he did reminded him of my brother, and the fact that he had in a temper taken his life." The man went on to testify that the Salvation Army showed him God's willingness "to forgive even so base a sin as he had committed."[40]

Some testimonies were not quite as dramatic. Indeed, some "experiences" sounded more like bad burlesque routines. One "comrade" claimed, "[I] once went into a public house and saw some pickles so I asked the landlady to give me some, but she refused after I had spent all my money . . . so I went to the Salvation Army instead. Here I soon got into a pickle, for God shook me on account of my sins; these I at once forsook. Now thank God, I am saved and a soldier, and mean to fight for God, and I buy my own pickles."[41] On another occasion a convert's comic testimony played on public criticism of the Army as a "money making business." This was true, he said, "because when I first joined them I only had $1.95 a day and since I have joined them my boss said he would give me an advance in my wages but at that moment another man came up and asked me to work for him for $2.25 a day. Glory to God! Salvation pays because it rescues a man from a drunkards [sic] grave and sets him on his royal road to heaven."[42]

Apparently, not all Salvationists successfully delivered entertaining testimonies. In an article called "Hints for Testimony Meetings," the Army established guidelines for making testimony and prayer interesting and effective. Those giving testimony and prayers should be on time, sit together, and speak loudly, distinctly, and briefly. Remember, the article pointed out, "Peter's prayer was short and was answered as was the Publican's." Most important, do not bore your listeners, "[d]on't go back into the dim, uncertain past of sixty five years; don't tell too frequently about your experience of the last twenty years."[43]

In addition to snappy testimonies, sermons or "lectures" also borrowed from working-class culture in order to deliver religion and entertainment. At a particularly spectacular meeting, "the devil and his works were burned in effigy."[44] After a parade through the streets and some hell-fire preaching by Mrs. Staff-Captain Winchell, her husband proceeded to dramatize his wife's major points. As the audience watched,

Winchell held up one after another of the devil's works, pointing out the dangers of each in turn. "1st: The devil of pride — a large over-trimmed women's bonnet, such as can be seen in any church or theatre; 2nd: The devil of unbelief, infidelity, higher criticism, Bob Ingersoll, book and papers; 3d: The theatrical devil — a huge bill-board poster; 4th: The political devil; 5th: The tobacco devil — cigarettes, pipes, etc.; 6th: The whiskey devil, which included politics, gambling, the sin of scarlet." At the end of the "lecture," the Winchells dimmed the lights, placed the devil's works in a pile, and topped it with an effigy of Satan himself. Before a spellbound audience they set the pile aflame, and within a few seconds not a trace of the devil remained.[45]

The Army also kept a pool of "specials," officers not assigned to a particular corps or staff position, who traveled around the nation holding "special meetings."[46] The dime-museum or circus-sideshow style of some of these officers' acts made them excellent drawing cards. One particularly colorful and successful "special" was "Joe the Turk." Joseph Garabedian, a six-foot-two, Turkish-born Armenian shoemaker living in San Francisco, joined the Salvation Army in the 1880s.[47] After serving two years as "doorkeeper . . . a combination of head usher and bouncer" at San Francisco No. 1, Joe the Turk went on the road.[48] Joe sported a "fierce looking mustache" and dressed in "shimmering crimson pantaloons," a heavily braided and decorated Army tunic, and a fez. He led marches and services playing a trumpet with doubtful skill but "loud enough to wake up the devil." He also carried his famous and ever-popular umbrella made in stripes of yellow, red, and blue, with the following slogans painted on it: "Jesus is the drunkard's friend," "Prodigal come home," "Sinner, stop and think!," "Where will you spend eternity?," "No cross, no crown," "Jesus wants to save," and "God is love."[49] Indeed, at a time when public interest in scientific wonders heightened, the umbrella began to get its own billing in program announcements as "the only illuminated umbrella in the world . . . of great size and illuminated by nine electric lights of different hues."[50]

In addition to Joe the Turk, the pool of special acts included the likes of: "Tom-Ma-He-Kum," a converted Delaware Indian "who always dressed in buckskin clothing trimmed with feathers and beads . . . and adopted the name of Logan and the title of Doctor for use in civilization"; Lena Behrandt, "the Hallelujah Midget" who "wore the conventional dark blue dress of the Salvation Army, with little poke-bonnet trimmed in red ribbon"; and Staff-Captain Walsh, "the Converted Minstrel" who

Joe the Turk in one of his colorful costumes.
(Courtesy of the Salvation Army National Archives)

THE WORLD SALVATIONISTS MADE

played the banjo and "always spoke in the idiom of the Blacface [*sic*] Comedian," all of whom who toured the country raising money as well as the profile of the Salvation Army.[51]

Even Salvation Army weddings captured the flavor of working-class entertainment culture. In contrast to the private style of middle-class weddings which brought together family and friends, the Army often used weddings between officers as another form of special act and invited the public (for a modest admission price) to join in the celebration.[52] The Hallelujah Weddings themselves often opened with colorful parades. "There were large numbers of flaring torches, banners and bannerettes and hundreds of smiling soldiers . . . but the great[est] attraction of all was the forty bridesmaids all dressed alike with white dresses, Stars and Stripes sashes and red liberty caps, with the Salvation Army red band around them. These lasses caused such an attraction that traffic was completely stopped."[53]

Not only did Salvationists adapt the form of their religious performances from working-class popular culture, but the halls in which they held their services often struck outsiders as having the look and feel of working-class entertainment spaces. Wrote the *Chicago Tribune* in 1886, "[T]he Princess Rink was well filled yesterday afternoon. . . . The sawdust-covered floor, the chinese [*sic*] lanterns, and noisy band suggested the circus as much as anything else, and the exercises were somewhat on that order."[54] Indeed, the Salvation Army so successfully reproduced the environment of various working-class amusements that audiences frequently treated meeting halls much as they would treat a saloon or music hall. After a meeting that had been held in a rented church, a distressed church official pulled the Salvation Army officer aside and took him over to a spot where some of the "usual crowd" had been chewing tobacco and spitting on the floor. "I could almost cry to see this," said the church warden. "Never has such a thing occurred in this church before." Wrote the officer, "Of course I felt sorry for the man, and sorry for the carpet, and equally sorry for the man who had given the cause for complaint, but I could not help making a note of the inference, that the Salvation Army is the place where tobacco chewers do come, and are welcomed too."[55]

Of course officers did not always appreciate the extent to which their audience felt at ease in Salvation Army surroundings. To the discomfort of one young officer, some men and women who came to his meetings treated the hall as if it were the infamous theatrical "third tier." He recalled later that prostitutes sometimes used his Decatur, Illinois, corps as a place to meet with potential customers. "There were about a dozen

Poster promoting a late-nineteenth-century Salvation Army "Hallelujah Wedding." (Courtesy of the Salvation Army National Archives)

prostitutes and street walkers . . . and there were possibly twenty-five or thirty men who were interested in such folks, and they seemed to make the Salvation Army hall a rendezvous for an opportunity to make dates and meet up with each other."[56]

The religious use of popular culture was not limited to the Salvation Army in the late nineteenth century. Master revivalist Dwight Moody frequently performed in secular amusement spaces, used secular-style songs in his services, erected "circus-like tents . . . for Sunday services," and used "Gospel Wagons" equipped with "lanterns, a small organ, and two horses" to promote his services. His elaborately staged and costly performances adapted aspects of modern popular culture in an effort to attract people and to provide an evangelical substitute for an urban middle-class culture of commerce and consumption. According to James Gilbert, Moody not only failed to replace or change that culture, but his revivals served instead to "broaden the appeal of popular culture" to his middle-class, largely female, and "already churched" audience.[57]

In contrast to Moody's adaptation of urban middle-class commercial culture, the Salvation Army in the late nineteenth century employed male working-class forms of popular culture as a language and style through which members could express religious feeling. By making it available and accessible to women, however, Salvation Army performances anticipated the emerging *heterosocial* world of modern commercial leisure culture. In this way Salvation Army meetings may have ultimately expanded the appeal of modern popular culture to working-class men and women accustomed to a sexual division of leisure activities.[58]

The Salvation Army's sanction of working-class popular culture created tensions with middle-class Americans. In spite of well-to-do New Yorkers' enthusiasm for Maud and Ballington Booth and their rescue work, published criticisms of the Army frequently emphasized the group's "otherness." Pointing out its working- or lower-class nature, newspapers expressed alarm at the boisterousness and physicality of its religious performances. Reports stressed Salvationists' use of minstrelsy or variety-show styles, their dialects, and their similarity to volunteer firemen, and likened their services to "[N]egro camp-meeting[s] in the South."[59] Furthermore, although the Army insisted that it was "impossible to make a drawing room saint out of a saloon sinner," middle-class religious folk believed that the Salvation Army methods bred "blasphemy and irreverence" toward Christ. Was it possible, they asked, for "blackguards . . . to cease to be sinners without ceasing to be roughs"? Said a letter to the editor in the *Chicago Daily News*, " '[R]eal belief in a Divine Savior must inspire reverence and dignity of character.' "[60]

According to a Chicago judge in 1885, the Army's activities amounted to blasphemy. He described the Army as "a monkey show" and complained that the organization "gather[ed] together all the worst types of people." He was particularly appalled by the Army's "[r]idiculous street parades, blatant discourses before gatherings of hoodlums, and [their] . . . imitation of religious rites." These sacrilegious "parodi[es of] religious ceremonies," he said, "made the organization more than just a nuisance" because they fostered among "the ignorant and unthinking, a contempt for the religion these street performers profess."[61]

Middle-class Christians also believed that the Salvation Army's "motley groups of 'Captains,' 'Lieutenants,' and 'Sergeants' " encouraged public disorder. Calling their services "hysterical," newspapers most commonly reported complaints about the noise Salvationists made while marching in the street or holding open-air meetings. In New Haven, for example, the Army was accused of "making night hideous with amateur performances on drums . . . cymbals, tambourines, banjos and trumpets." Said one Chicago police officer in 1888, "They disturb the peace with their drums and tom-toms. They cause teams to break loose on the streets. . . . They drive simple-minded people crazy with their singing and praying and shouting. They are a public nuisance." Prompted by these criticisms, city officials regularly dispatched police to arrest the Salvationists for disturbing the peace and obstructing the streets as they held open-air services and marched to their hall.[62]

Concerns for order were not entirely lacking in merit. When the Army attempted to "open fire" in some neighborhoods, the response could include beatings, theft of members' belongings, threats to tar and feather the Army officers, and arson. Irish Catholic residents were often especially hostile to the Salvation Army, not only because it was a Protestant organization but also because of its British roots.[63] In other cases the Army's emphasis on temperance provoked angry and violent responses from saloon owners and their working-class customers. On one occasion locals invaded a corps hall and proceeded to wreak havoc by "taking up the chairs and breaking them over the heads of the soldiers, and then turning over the stove with the fire in it. The mob barricaded the doors and refused to let anybody go in or out." In 1892, according to the *New York Times*, seventeen-year-old Frederick Pratt and his pals "interrupt[ed the Salvation Army's] services with ribald songs and obscene remarks." They then "blew out all the gas jets in the room," attacked a Salvationist as he tried to shut off the gas main, and set off "a big bunch of fire-crackers right in the midst of the panic-stricken men, women and children in the place." On another occasion, reported *The War Cry*, "the devil's agents got on the top of the hall . . . threw a keg full of ashes and herrings through the skylight on the platform then followed this up with a can full of kerosene, no doubt hoping to set the hall on fire."[64]

Open-air marches were particularly dangerous, and Salvationists could not always count on police protection. Since municipal governments often had close political ties to saloons, the police generally made little effort to protect the soldiers and officers as they waged their campaigns against the sin of intemperance.[65] At one march, reported *The War Cry*, "under the glaring lights of electric lamps and police all along the line of march," a "cowardly tough" punched an officer, knocking her to the ground, and "a volley of stones cut the brigadier's lip open . . . bruis[ed] his head. . . . Stones, blows, pushing and profanity was heaped upon us. Ash boxes were opened and the contents thrown upon our soldiers."[66]

In addition to concerns about blasphemy and civil disorder, a considerable amount of press attention focused on the sexuality of Salvation Army men and women. At one extreme, a newspaper accused General Booth's daughter of excessive prudishness. "Miss Booth," said the article sardonically, "announces that she is about to produce a 'sacred drama with a decorous ballet.' " Playing with ballet's reputation as "leg business," the paper suggested that "the mere suggestion that legs exist would of course strike Miss Booth as indecorous." Moreover, it said that in her decorous dance the "ballet girls' " legs would be "hermetically sealed" in "skirts made after the pattern of meal bags," after which the young women would be "mounted on small movable platforms . . . and . . . wheeled about the stage by elderly supernumeraries."[67]

More frequent, press reports implied that female Salvation Army officers' sex appeal played an important role in recruiting and keeping men in the organization. An 1883 article, for example, noted the work of a "very pretty young female lieutenant" who had a voice that could make a man believe he "might do worse than to be a private in the Salvation Army under her." Another article described a free-and-easy social exchange between male and female officers that might easily have taken place at a dance hall. At an Army "feast," a male officer "pick[ed] out the prettiest" female officer, walked up to her and said, "Hello, dear." To which she replied, "Hello, dear . . . What yer got ter chew?" "[G]allently harpoon[ing] a sandwich with his thumb," the couple dined together and then marched with the rest of the company to the evening service.[68]

Finally, press reports warned more ominously that Salvationists could turn out to be sexual predators, women as bigamists and men as seducers. In 1885, the *New York Times* reported the arrest of Mrs. Jennie A. Moore, a.k.a. Captain Jennie A. Wilson of the Salvation Army, on the charge of bigamy. The article described Mrs. Henry Moore (whose other married name was Frey) as "a prepossessing blonde, with pleasant manners" who had been "a roller skater, book agent, [and] domestic" before joining the Salvation Army. The report suggested that Mrs. Moore-Frey was not the least bit embarrassed by her arrest and quoted her as brazenly saying, "You can bet your life that Henry Moore will be sorry for this. . . . I am only too glad to get rid of him."[69]

The *Times* also published reports about young women being seduced by male Salvation Army officers. In 1884, the paper noted, a "young and handsome daughter of poor but highly respectable parents" joined the Army only to be "ruined" by a young male officer. In 1885 the newspaper reported that a male "Captain of the Salvation Army" took a seventeen-year-old girl to "a sailors' dance house" where men and women "sat at tables drinking beer." After she began to cry, however, the proprietor called the police, who arrested the young man for "abduction."[70]

In addition to the sexuality of Salvation Army officers, a subtext in some public criticism implied that the excitement of the group's services risked heightening sexual desire. Reports like the one for the *Chicago Herald* employed sexually charged language to describe Army religious performance and the passions it provoked. Sounding more like a seduction than a religious service, the writer described "caressing" voices, exhorters who "woo[ed]" sinners, and base drums that "throbbed, like [a] pulse." Passions built up as Salvationists marched "[a]round and around . . . faster and faster, wilder and wilder," igniting "a vast enthusiasm" as the audience became "over-wrought." In climactic moments, according to the report, drums exploded like "minute gun[s] at sea," while "words crashed forth like a shot of musketry," and "shouts of hallelujahs . . . rent the air like skyrockets."[71]

Alarmed critics wrote that if "the Salvationists [are] allowed to continue . . . their singular performances," citizens could expect to hear of even greater "violations of all instincts of propriety." "Elsewhere," they hinted, "there have been disclosures of vice so gross that the authorities have been compelled to interfere in the interests of all decency."[72] Fears that this "motley" group would either provoke or be unable to prevent civil and possibly sexual disorder were no doubt heightened by the fact that both male *and* female Salvationists exercised spiritual and administrative leadership within the organization.

Salvationists' invention of a rowdy and physically expressive religious culture also troubled some high-ranking middle-class Salvationists. As noted earlier, middle-class officers were more educated, and although their numbers were small they tended to rise quickly to positions of power within the organization.[73] These men and women feared that the Army's boisterous religious performances obscured the "shallowness [and] spiritual ignorance" of many Salvationists.[74] Indeed, when one of the Army's few college-educated captains discovered that very few of the soldiers at his corps actually "professed to be sanctified," he decided to get them sanctified or have them dismissed from the Army. For their part, the soldiers refused to accept his contention that they did not measure up to Salvation Army standards of belief, and the young officer found himself plagued by a host of "internal difficulties" during his tenure at the corps.[75]

This young middle-class officer questioned the authority of the common people to define the nature of their own faith and invent their own religious culture. He unwisely tried to convince his working-class soldiers that "[t]he shout of hallelujahs and the noise of tambourines won't feed the soul, nor will stirring appeals to sinners six nights out of the week, and scathing anathemas against tobacco and bustles the seventh night, build up soldiers and make them robust men in Christ."[76] What this young Captain failed to understand was that it was *precisely* the hallelujahs and tambourines and stirring appeals which "built up" many Salvation soldiers and made them feel emotionally committed to the Salvation Army and its religion. Like the sociability of the saloon, the camaraderie of a boisterous meeting was the Army's most potent tool in winning converts and building solidarity among the soldiers in the late nineteenth century.

The Salvation Army attempted to mitigate tensions created by ecstatic experiential religious performance through its special application of the doctrine of holiness. In addition to legitimizing the movement and its principles, corporate holiness sacralized its members' expressions of individual religious feeling through rowdy working-class leisure culture. As a creation of God carrying out His work on earth, all Salvation Army expressions of faith were clearly sanctioned by the Lord. He would not, after all, allow the Holy Spirit to fill an organization whose religious practices offended Him. At the same time, corporate holiness enabled Army leaders to argue that although their actions may horrify more refined Christians, the Army's "methods" had been successful among the masses and this very success was proof that "the blessing of the Master has been with them." As a consequence, wrote an outside supporter, "when a 'boxing man who is now boxing the devil' sings a song or the 'one-legged prophet' gives a talk or 'Glory Sam' or 'Hallelujah Maggie' breaks out recklessly, though it may shock us let us charitably and with all humility call to mind the fact that these are laboring where we would not, and drawing souls to Christ whom we persistently neglected and left to die in their sins — and let us hinder them not, but rather, bid them God speed."[77]

Although the Army defended the religious culture its members created by invoking the doctrine of corporate holiness, it also took pains to reassure critics that the organization's leadership actually exerted significant control over its boisterous members. William Booth, for example, repeatedly asserted the importance of the military model and his autocratic control over the entire Salvation Army.[78] Only a single, all-powerful leader, he said, could achieve "Oneness of Direction"; any resistance to his authority was treason. "Those who are disobedient must be degraded, punished, expelled."[79] Authoritarianism, he argued, allowed him to discipline and organize the "disorganized and hopeless" poor; permitted efficient operation of an expanding movement; was effective, that is, "it worked"; and created a unified Army which served as a model of the coming kingdom of God on earth.[80]

American Salvation Army leaders also stressed the importance of hierarchical authority. Commissioner Frank Smith wrote in 1886 that being a salvation soldier required a "willingness to lose our own identity," that is, one must be willing to sacrifice individual goals and follow the orders of commanding officers.[81] Even some rank-and-file Salvationists argued that the Army exercised considerable control over its membership. In contrast to churches, which wielded authority by committees, one officer noted, "The Salvation Army . . . demanded strict obedience to the rules and discipline of the movement, and the officer in charge saw to it that they were enforced."[82] Even today, while historians of the movement disagree on the virtue of Booth's authority, none question that he actually wielded such power.[83]

The promise of effective social control probably comforted an urban middle class gripped by the fear of working-class violence. The great railroad strikes of 1877 and other late-nineteenth-century examples of working-class militancy inspired middle-class leaders to restrict street parades in cities like New York and build huge, ominous armories in many urban areas. Moreover, the popularity of Edward Bellamy's *Looking Back-ward* indicates the broad appeal of the military model and discipline as a solution to the problem of an unruly working class. In his description of a worker's military parade, Bellamy's Julian West captured the promise many Americans saw in Booth's autocratic control of his Army. "Here at last were order and reason, an exhibition of what intelligent cooperation can accomplish. . . . [I]t was their perfect concert of action, their organization under one control, which made these men the tremendous engine they were, able to vanquish a mob ten times as numerous."[84] Rationally organized workers, according to Bellamy, could be controlled and turned into a great machine capable of defeating irrational, threatening mobs of working men and women.

Clearly many Americans supported the Army's principle of hierarchical authority. An article in *Living Church*, for example, admired the group's "strictly military organization, with its inculcation of implicit, unquestioning obedience to orders," and called it "[t]he most meritorious feature of the Salvation Army."[85] Less sanguine Americans regarded absolutism as dangerous. Wrote the *Advance*, "If every Salvationist in this country must be absolutely obedient to orders from headquarters, then we have another papacy in this country."[86] As late as 1916, John D. Rockefeller expressed concern about "the principle of military absolutism, which lies at the basis of the Army organization."[87]

Although the Salvation Army successfully popularized the notion that it exerted complete control over its membership, in reality the organization's bureaucratic, like its religious, culture permitted surprising levels of democracy. Thwarted by inadequate lines of communication, the bureaucracy's financial dependence on the rank and file, and the voluntary nature of membership, the Salvation Army failed to exercise absolute authority over its members throughout the late nineteenth century. A number of factors contributed to communication problems between Army leaders and the rank and file. First, just as distance made it difficult for the center in London to control events and decisions at its American periphery, so headquarters in the United States frequently faced problems when it tried to assert its authority over local corps affairs. As we have seen, the efforts of London to assert its power triggered two schisms that nearly destroyed the American branch of the organization. Similarly, Major Thomas Moore's inability to control events at the New Brunswick, New Jersey, corps in 1883 enabled them to incorporate locally in direct defiance of international policy.[88]

The lack of lateral coordination (from one corps leader to his/her

successor) and the inability of headquarters to provide accurate information to incoming officers about the financial and spiritual state of their
new corps also reveal the inability of the Salvation Army to assert its
authority. In a letter to headquarters, one officer complained at the end
of his first week that he was unable to fill out the report forms adequately.
Not only had the previous officer failed to "leave any figures or information re the attendance open-airs etc. etc.," but he or she also left no
information about the corps' total indebtedness. What seemed most ag-
gravating to this officer, however, was that headquarters had told him that
this corps was already well organized. Said the captain, the "12 or 14
soldiers that you represented we should find here on our arrival have
failed to materialize but instead we found three or four young girls and
two young men who seem to expect to occupy the platform, but do not
act as though they had salvation and will not testify that they have any
[except] when they are called out and plead with till we get ashamed to
urge them any longer."[89]

Frequent shifts in the location of national headquarters, numerous
changes of national leadership, the nonstop opening and closing of
corps, and constant turnovers in corps personnel exacerbated the already feeble lines of communication, coordination, and enforcement between headquarters, local corps, and officers. Between 1880 and 1885,
the location of national headquarters changed five times, and through
1904 there were six shifts in national leadership.[90] Furthermore, since
the Salvation Army seldom owned property in its early days, a local corps
might change locations many times within a single year or close down
entirely if a town proved to be a "hard shop."[91] Even if a corps did not
move or close down, the young officers in charge moved repeatedly from
one assignment to another, either on their own impulse or reassigned by
their leaders.

Communications problems apparently made efforts to implement policy a frustrating exercise for high-ranking Salvation Army officers. In
1881, an announcement appeared in *The War Cry* in which field officers
were asked, *yet again*, "to send, properly filled out the weekly return
forms." These reports, which required (among other things) an accounting of how officers spent their time, needed much more careful attention, complained the announcement. "Please answer the questions
plainly," wrote an exasperated Major Thomas Moore, and "in answer to
questions as to time spent in visiting, state exactly—don't say about. That
sort of thing don't look well on my field state book." Failure to comply

would not go unpunished, the notice threatened; "the names of the delinquent officers" would be advertised on the front page of *The War Cry*.[92]

In addition to communications problems, the impulse for autocracy contended with the Salvation Army's dependency on the rank and file for financial support. Like most nondenominational evangelical missionary organizations, the Army expected each corps to be self-supporting. Officers sold *The War Cry* in the streets and saloons and took up collections at open-airs and meeting halls in an effort to meet expenses and pay salaries. At the same time, without independent sources of revenue, headquarters relied entirely on the local corps for its own financial support. When Army leaders made concerted efforts to regularize its system of financing, they faced complaints from the field.

One method of fund-raising required that a percentage of sales of *The War Cry* be returned to headquarters. Leaders assigned each corps a set number of issues to sell and worked out the amount due H.Q. each month, based on that number whether or not all of the papers actually sold. In 1887 one officer complained that her corps quota was too high. She wrote, "200 Warcries [*sic*] is to [*sic*] many for us to take here. I sent to headquarters for them to send 130 but they still send 200 and we don't sell them all."[93] In addition, the Army insisted that each corps forward to headquarters 10 percent of all money collected by the local group from other fund-raising activities. Moreover, wrote one officer, "four times a year the total collections for the week-end, Saturday night, and all day on Sunday had also to be turned over to headquarters." If any of the money was withheld, he said, "the ammount [*sic*] was carried on the books at headquarters as a debt against the corps, and monthly statements were received appraising us of that fact."[94]

Attempts to regularize the financing of headquarters inspired the implementation of more elaborate bureaucratic methods. In order to keep track of collections, headquarters required each corps to appoint a secretary, "whose duties will be to keep account of all the monies received and expended by the Corps." Headquarters even devised a printed balance sheet for the secretary to fill out and "return quarterly to their divisional officer."[95] For its part, to encourage an increase in fund-raising at the local level, the Army periodically implemented special projects. In the mid-1880s, for example, leaders asked Salvationists in the United States to join a self-denial effort in which each soldier and officer would "put aside money from some pleasure for the sake of the cause."[96]

While leaders hoped to stabilize funding for headquarters, the evidence suggests that the soldiers' and officers' limited resources undermined those efforts. Frequently, corps officers simply found themselves unable to collect enough money to both take care of their own needs *and* send some on to headquarters. As one officer explained, "[I] cant send any this week but will do my best to sent it along next week. you see I had to borrow $3.00 for my care fare and have to pay $1.00 to day and had to get coal and wood so it make me short." On another occasion the same officer not only failed to forward any money to headquarters but also sought financial assistance from his colonel. "I am Verry sorry to hear that your have done any with the Relief Fund because I was going to asked you to give me $3.00 fore a pair [of] shoes has my is all gone and my feet is on the ground. . . . I just tell you that I hardly can get Enouth to Eat but have to used the Collectionto live on."[97] Still another officer wrote, "It seems very hard the past three weeks to get money but I am going to keep believing for better times."[98]

Grand efforts by headquarters to help corps raise money easily backfired and inspired resentment. James Price recalled that in the wake of a performance by the Staff Band designed to help the Fall River corps "raise money for a local need," the corps actually found itself $5.00 deeper in debt. Wrote a disgruntled Price, although "[w]e took in over $100 . . . the expenses—so-called, of the visitors were $105.00 and we were left holding the sack with our debt unpaid, the people drained of ther [*sic*] money, and we deeper in debt than ever." Living so close to the edge themselves, many Salvationists resented and resisted having to pay "expenses" for visiting staff officers. Indeed, when one corps realized that 10 percent of the money collected by local officers corps went to headquarters, the soldiers "naturally were in rebellion."[99]

There may also have been some resentment over policies that did not allow local officers to take their wages out of collections until "all operating expenses, assessments and debts have been deducted." Indeed, according to Salvation Army rules, although poor Captain Seely apparently struggled desperately to survive on the collection from week to week, he violated Army policy by using the collection to pay his personal expenses.[100] Salaries for staff officers, on the other hand, were guaranteed. Even when the Army sent Staff Captain John Milsaps to the Philippines during the Spanish-American War as an unofficial chaplain to Salvationists serving in the armed forces, headquarters agreed to provide his "regular salary."[101]

Soldiers and officers apparently found small ways to withhold money, including not putting sufficient postage on all mail addressed to headquarters. Complaining that over the course of a year headquarters laid out nearly $100, a notice in *The War Cry* said, "The paying of extra postage upon insufficiently stamped letters and packages is becoming a very severe charge upon our funds and as it arises wholly from inattention on the part of the senders, it appears to be an unlawful outlay of the Lord's money, especially at a time when there are so many legitimate channels for every cent entrusted to us."[102]

In addition to wrestling with leadership over financial support, local corps and officers actually exercised significant levels of autonomy. Indeed, it was not uncommon for local corps to make independent decisions that supported an officer's freedom of movement, the corps' right to decide where meetings would be held, and their use of "specials" as field officers. Announcements in *The War Cry* suggest that administrative officers repeatedly tried to assert the authority of headquarters over these questions which corps apparently regarded as local decisions. Leaders instructed that field officers "under no circumstances" were to leave their corps assignments or "hold meetings in any place but their barracks without having consulted with and received sanction from their divisional officers." Furthermore, high-ranking officers warned corps to refrain from using "specials" as corps officers unless "sanctioned and commissioned by Headquarters."[103] Nine years later, headquarters had still not successfully established its control over many of these decisions, as NHQ once again issued instructions for field officers to cease using non–Salvation Army facilities for meetings or special services without permission from the divisional officer.[104]

Army leaders could not even claim to exercise complete authority over religious doctrine at the local level. In its newspapers and other publications, the Salvation Army made efforts to explain and teach the doctrine of individual holiness. As we have seen, however, some Salvation Army soldiers failed to comprehend the full meaning of the second blessing, a fact that created tensions with officers more committed to asserting official Army theology. Many salvation soldiers apparently preferred their own popular theology that encouraged the physical expression of religious feeling and saving the souls of sinners. One long-time field officer even called holiness an "impossible theory" and inaccurately suggested that by the 1890s few leaders actually preached the doctrine.[105]

Officers and soldiers in the late nineteenth century also exercised considerable autonomy in designing one of the key symbols of membership, the Salvation Army uniform. During its early years in the United States, the Army had not yet developed an official uniform. In the first contingent George Scott Railton sported a " 'dark blue suit, cutaway coat and a high peaked hat,' " while the Lasses wore "short blue dresses, blue coats trimmed in yellow, and 'Derby hats' " decorated with a red ribbon on which "Salvation Army" had been stitched in gold letters. Generally, soldiers and officers invented their own uniforms by applying trim to "an exotic collection of makeshift and multi-colored apparel." Women officers often wore the black straw bonnet advocated by Catherine Booth; men's headwear, on the other hand, expressed considerable individuality and included: "pith helmets, toppers, cowboy hats, sailor hats, and discarded military band helmets."[106] Regulations about men's hat styles appeared in 1891. According to the chief secretary, "[t]he Commander has decided that in future all male Field Officers are to wear the Regulation Cap as supplied by HQ. They are also to discontinue wearing caps that are not uniform style. Cloth vizors [*sic*] on caps must not be worn."[107]

The enormous effort expended by the Army to promote the importance of wearing the uniform suggests that soldiers and officers frequently decided for themselves when and whether they would comply. Articles like "Why should I wear [the] uniform" and "When should a salvation soldier take off the uniform" regularly appeared in *The War Cry*. Uniforms, these reports argued, should be worn every single day, not just "on the way to and from the barracks and perhaps all day on Sunday." Uniforms were important because they served as a witness of one's faith, could serve as a defense against worldly temptations, and advertised salvation to others.[108] As late as 1898, headquarters suggested that "the wearing of the uniform is not keeping pace with our onward march, and, indeed, . . . in some parts of the country there has been declension." They expressed particular concern that the "sister comrades" had taken "license . . . to discard the habitual use of the regulation bonnet," electing instead to wear summer or bicycling hats."[109]

Tensions between autocracy and democracy not only plagued relations between corps and headquarters but also stirred unrest within local corps. Although the captain of a corps was "in command," in reality soldiers could exercise considerable power by making the captain's job a misery. James Price reported that soldiers in his West Sommerville, Massachusetts, corps registered their dissatisfaction with his leadership by remaining outside of the tent and refusing to assist with services. The soldiers claimed to have "lost faith in [him]." They accused him of "neglecting to call on the members; of spending too much time on matters not connected with the corps . . . and . . . going off to [a] camp [meeting] without taking it up with the soldiers first." These soldiers felt they had a right to expect a certain level of service from their captain, and they demanded that he consult them before he made plans to absent himself from the corps. Price was ultimately able to soothe his soldiers' wounded feelings; but had he not succeeded he would have been forced to seek a transfer.[110]

In addition to withholding their cooperation, soldiers exercised their democratic power in other ways. In 1890, upon his return from a meeting of the Salvation Army's National Congress in New York, Lieutenant Morher found himself facing angry soldiers at his Buffalo corps.[111] He nervously wrote to Major Holz that upon his return from New York, he found "some of the Soldiers terribly out of sorts because I took the Banquet money and went to the Congress." Hoping to defuse potential trouble, Morher wrote to warn Holz that the soldiers "threatened to write to you and to do lots of things." By threatening to report him to his superior officer Morher's soldiers used the hierarchical structure of the Army to rebuke the officer and express their dissatisfaction with his personal use of local funds. They may also have withheld financial support as a means of punishment. In his letter Morher also reported, "We have had very good meetings but small collections."[112]

Finally, like soldiers, officers also exerted power in relation to their "superiors." Since the Salvation Army suffered from a chronic shortage of officers, the organization rarely acted arbitrarily on matters of concern to field forces.[113] As a consequence, these men and women managed to resist the authority of their superiors at both district and national headquarters in a number of ways. One common form of resistance used by field officers was to refuse an assignment. After a brief and violent stay at the Astoria corps on Long Island, New York, where he and his lieutenant were surrounded by "roughs" who hooted and jeered at them and "pelt[ed them] with mud and whatever else they could lay their hands on," James Price advised his superiors that he could not take his family into that environment and "they would have to find some other place for us." His leaders responded by shifting his assignment to Passaic, New Jersey.[114]

While officers and soldiers exercised significant levels of democratic power within this supposedly authoritarian organization, the Army did make efforts to promote discipline and obedience. In the late 1880s, for example, Army leaders began a "Training Garrison" system of preparing officers for the field; until that time nearly all officers had learned on the job.[115] Centralizing training in a separate facility not only ensured uniform training in Army administrative methods but also allowed leaders to indoctrinate cadets with Army discipline.[116] When Arthur Jackson balked at following Army rules at the training college, for example, his adjutant reminded him that "it would be necessary for me to conform to all the rules in order to get along properly with the program of training."[117] Army leaders also used the training schools to build national and international allegiances capable of competing with officers' local loyalties.[118]

In the late nineteenth century the Salvation Army insisted that its authoritarian military style made it uniquely suited to bringing salvation to the intractable "heathen masses." The evidence suggests, however, that Salvation Army leaders failed to impose absolutism because they were locked in continuous tension with the democracy and autonomy actually exercised by the group's voluntary membership. First, working-class Salvationists invented ways to express their religious feelings that drew heavily on democratic forms like the frontier camp meeting and working-class leisure culture. Moreover, instinctively understanding the Army's need for the democratic legitimization of its rank-and-file members, they found many ways to resist and exercise their individuality (as soldiers or officers) and their democratic power (as local corps) against demands of the Salvation Army hierarchy. As we will see, by the turn of the century, the balance between autocracy and democracy would be threatened when the Salvation Army decided to institutionalize a new approach to advertising salvation—social service.

CHAPTER FOUR

A NEW MESSAGE OF TEMPORAL SALVATION

Reinventing the Army at the Turn of the Century

Amid all your joys don't forget the sons and daughters of misery.... Brought it on themselves do you say? Perhaps so but that does not excuse our assisting them. You don't demand a certificate of virtue before you drag a drowning creature out of the water nor the assurance that the man has paid his rent before you deliver him from the burning building. But what shall we do? Content ourselves by singing a hymn, offering a prayer or giving a little good advice? No, ten thousand times no! We will pity them, feed them, reclaim them, employ them. Perhaps we shall fail with many, quite likely. But our business is to help them all the same and that in the most practical, economical and Christlike manner. — WILLIAM BOOTH, "Messages by the Founder," 1905

To celebrate their founder William Booth's first visit to the United States in 1886, the Salvation Army held a grand march through the streets of Chicago. Four drummers thumping "with fists as well as drum-sticks" and a "squad of sisters" jingling tambourines led the parade. Next came General Booth in his carriage, followed by men "wav[ing] torches," the Army band, and a troop of "Blood and Fire" soldiers. "The General," reported the *Chicago Tribune*, "stood up in his carriage[,] waved his canary-colored gloves, shouted 'Hurrah for Jesus!' and sat down again. The band played on and the army, about 200 in all, sang."[1] Twelve years later in October 1898, Salvationists at Army Headquarters in New York City worked furiously to prepare for a demonstration and street parade set to begin in front of Carnegie Hall. The centerpiece of the march was a windmill with four large hand-operated paddles. On the night of the demonstration, "derelicts of all description enter[ed] the mill at one side as the paddles turned, and on the other side . . . emerge[d] a procession of well-fed, well-dressed men and women . . . illustrat[ing] the Social rehabilitation work of the Army."[2]

Street theater was a very popular means of nonliterate communication in nineteenth-century American cities; one historian called them the "cultural equivalent of descriptive representation." Americans paraded to express or create identity as well as to signify democratic legitimization of popular politics. Parades, wrote Susan Davis, were "public dramas of social relations" with concrete goals and results. The participants defined who were and were not "social actors" and determined "what subjects and ideas are available for communication and consideration."[3] During its first two decades in the United States, the Salvation Army took to the streets and made a joyful (and ear-splitting) noise unto the Lord praising the redemptive power of Christ. The goals of these marches were to "capture" souls for Jesus, attract an audience to corps meetings, and collect enough money both to finance their religious work and provide a livelihood for the officers.

The 1886 march also represented the Army's identity as the sum of its different parts. The focus of the parade was the general in his carriage surrounded by the individual instruments of Christ. The individual soldiers and officers (male and female) constituted the Salvation Army and ranked second only to the general as social actors. Indeed, by giving the "squad of sisters" such a prominent position in the parade, not as auxiliaries or symbols but, rather, representing themselves as Blood and Fire soldiers and officers, the Salvation Army publicly acknowledged the importance of women in the organization.[4] The parade also communicated the hierarchical nature of the group. Riding in a carriage high above the marching, uniformed ranks, the general established his position as leader of an organization characterized by military order and discipline. At the same time, however, the hundreds of enthusiastic marching participants demonstrated the visible endorsement or democratic legitimization of the general's authority by the rank-and-file members.[5]

Finally, Salvation Army street theater in 1886 transmitted its most important concept, the transforming and redeeming power of the Army. As the sanctified instrument of Christ, the group had turned each of these men and women from a sinner into a militant soldier of the Cross. Salvation Army parades climaxed with a service either at the local hall or in the "open-air." Here the most important performers were individual salvation soldiers like "Shouting Annie," "Charlie, the Salvation Wonder," and "Glory Milt," whose conversion stories told of a life steeped in sin and their rescue by the Salvation Army.[6] These examples of personal transformation communicated a message about the power of Christ, acting through the Salvation Army and each salvation soldier, to redeem the worst of sinners.[7]

By 1898 Salvation Army street performances had taken on new meaning as political acts and described a different set of goals and social relations. The social-work windmill in the 1898 parade advertised the redeeming power of the Army's social service, enlisted the public's support for the work, and, most important, inspired the crowd to help fund the social institutions. In its effort to represent and promote the social work, however, the Army unintentionally redefined, at least in the public mind, the group's "social actors" and its identity. Instead of featuring the spiritual power of individual soldiers working through the Army, the parade suggested that the Army's many social programs were the *true* instruments of redemption and that Jesus, working through these institutions, gave the Army the power to transform derelicts into respectable citizens.

The 1898 parade advertised the Army's new approach to the salvation of the poor introduced in William Booth's 1890 book, *In Darkest England*. Until then, Salvationists, like most evangelical Christians, argued that sinful human nature not environment caused destitution; hence only spiritual salvation offered any enduring solution to poverty. In 1883, for example, *The Bitter Cry of Outcast London* asserted that before the poor could be reached by Christian missionaries they must get "the right to live as something better than the uncleanest brute beasts." At that time William Booth responded, "[T]he way to help the prodigal son was not to build him a comfortable hut . . . but to get him to see and acknowledge his sin, and . . . be put morally right."[8]

By the late 1880s, however, Anglo-American notions about the root causes of poverty began to change. A growing number of studies and revelations of urban misery undermined the authority of traditional evangelical solutions to poverty.[9] William Booth, like many in Britain and the United States, began to reconsider how best to save the perishing masses. The result was his book *In Darkest England*. His plan consisted of three interconnected phases. In the first stage the Salvation Army would establish a "city colony" which included "various REFUGES, WORKSHOPS, and other Establishments for Industrial Labor." From the City Colony, men and women would be sent "to the FARM COLONY . . . with its Villages, Co-operative Farms, Mills and Factories." Lastly, the Farm Colony could prepare people for "emigration to . . . a colony overseas."[10]

Most researchers agree that Salvationist Frank Smith and William T.

Stead, editor of the *Pall Mall Gazette*, each played a critical role in influencing the general's conversion to social Christianity. Smith developed an interest in social reform in the early 1880s while he commanded the Worldwide Salvation Army in the United States. At that time he read and had been deeply affected by Henry George's book *Progress and Poverty*. After returning to Britain as the general's private secretary, Smith began vigorously lobbying the leader to embrace social reform. By 1890 he took over direction of the Army's social work in England and moved swiftly to implement the Army's program of social Christianity. He opened an employment bureau, a factory, and "Salvage Brigades," which picked up waste materials for sale as scrap or for resale to the poor while providing temporary employment for the "out-of-works." Smith, however, was more committed to social justice than was the general, and he left the Army in 1890 because William Booth reportedly was displeased with his overtly political activities.[11] General Booth, according to Victor Bailey, regarded the Army's social work as a means to achieve individual salvation by removing the barrier of privation. In contrast, the new Social Wing leader described poverty "not simply as a bulwark against individual salvation . . . but as a social injustice in itself."[12]

Bailey also argues that W. T. Stead influenced William Booth by helping the Salvation Army leader turn his new impulse for social reform into the elaborate program outlined in his 1890 book. Furthermore, Stead reportedly exposed the general to the ideas of social imperialists who advocated emigration and the use of colonization to solve Britain's labor problems. Booth's embrace of rural panaceas also reveals the influence of the emerging social gospel movement. Editorially, Stead assisted the general in turning his chaotic notes "into a manageable manuscript, to which Booth then added his own evocative vernacular and some of the singular proposals."[13]

William Booth invested his version of social Christianity with his own understanding of the character of the poor, the causes of their poverty, laissez-faire political economy, and traditional solutions to the problems of the impoverished. I would argue that these ideas ultimately proved much more significant and enduring than any specifics of his plan. Booth argued that as a rule, poor men and women wished to work. Backing his assertions with interviews of tramps and homeless men, he demonstrated that loss of work at home and the search for employment in other towns drove these men to the road. Moreover, he argued that inadequate wages drew many women into prostitution. Said Booth, "[T]he number of young women who have received £500 in One year for the sale of their person is larger than the number of women of all ages who make a similar sum by honest industry." Many years later Booth told a reporter that "[t]he men who won't work are very few. . . . *They are very good fellows; only they need leading—directing.*"[14]

In his analysis of the causes of poverty, Booth inverted the Charity Organizing Society's basic assumption: lack of work caused drunkenness, disease, and immorality, he argued, not the reverse.[15] Indeed, although he believed that individuals must take responsibility for their own predicament, he also argued that society often created conditions that encouraged men and women to degenerate. Society's "habits, its customs, and its laws" said Booth, have "greased the slope down which these poor creatures slide to perdition."[16] The general also rejected laissez-faire political economy. He called its advocates "anti-Christian economists" because they "hold that it is an offense against the doctrine of the survival of the fittest to try to save the weakest from going to the wall, and . . . believe that when once a man is down the supreme duty of a self-regarding Society is to jump upon him." Booth also denounced the notion, so fundamental to the scientific charity movement, that some people are simply beyond help and that only the "deserving poor" ought to receive assistance. Calling the thrifty and industrious the "aristocracy of the miserable," he condemned any solution that singled out "an elect few who are to be saved while the mass of their fellows are predestined to a temporal damnation." Instead, he pressed for "a Temporal Salvation as full, free, and universal, and with no other limitations than the 'Whosoever will,' of the Gospel."[17]

He also warned that remedies ought to offer at least the minimum standard of life enjoyed by a London Cab Horse. His "Cab Horse Charter" entitled men and women to be lifted up when they are down and to have at least food, shelter, and work. "That," he said, "although a humble standard, is at present absolutely unattainable by millions . . . of our fellow-men and women in this country." It should be noted, however, that although Booth argued that lack of employment caused social problems, that laissez-faire economics was un-Christian, and that a minimum level of help ought to be open to all, he did not address the root causes of unemployment or offer systemic social solutions.[18]

William Booth never fully implemented his *In Darkest England* scheme. Of its three-part program, every one of the Farm Colonies failed, and the Over Seas Colony found little support. It was the City Colony with its various programs for meeting the temporal needs of the urban poor that left the greatest imprint.[19] Significantly, however, Booth's ideas about the character of the poor endured in Salvation Army social work. As one study of homeless transients during the Great Depression revealed, occupants at the Army's Gold Dust Lodge felt that, in contrast to other shelters, "Army personnel made every effort to . . . treat the men with dignity."[20]

While few American social Christians in the 1890s embraced the plan's recommendations uncritically, most acknowledged that the book awakened public interest in social reform by dramatizing efforts to eradicate poverty. Said Richard T. Ely in 1891, the book "is a trumpet-blast calling men to action on behalf of the poorest and the most degraded classes of modern society." Booth's book popularized the notion that any attempt to achieve the moral and spiritual salvation of the poor must also address their physical needs.[21] Implementation of the social scheme in the United States, however, lagged well behind its progress in Britain. Indeed, it was not until after the resignations of Maud and Ballington Booth in 1896 that their successors inaugurated the program in earnest.[22]

The arrival of a new Salvation Army administration in the United States and its implementation of the social mission unleashed considerable turmoil and led to the decline of democracy and autonomy in the movement. Consul and Commander Emma and Frederick Booth-Tucker vigorously publicized the social scheme and soon made the new programs synonymous with the organization in the public's mind. At the same time, ambivalence among all ranks of Salvationists about the spiritual value of their new category of Christian social service, as well as external criticisms of the social scheme prompted the Booth-Tucker's to make changes in the group's administrative structure. They relentlessly pushed their new mission by centralizing authority while at the same time separating the organization into two specialized branches, spiritual and social, the latter advertising salvation through a variety of social services rather than experiential religious rites.[23] None of these changes took place easily. The more the Army expanded the social scheme, the more dissatisfaction surfaced among the membership about the time, effort, resources, and control expended offering temporal salvation to the poor.

Emma and Frederick St. George de Lautour Booth-Tucker arrived in the United States in the midst of the chaos created when the general ordered Maud and Ballington Booth to "farewell" from this country. Sentiments ran high among mainline church leaders and New York City's elite who organized public rallies supporting the Ballington Booths. For weeks it was unclear how the couple would respond. With all Army properties held in his name, Ballington could have easily followed Thomas E. Moore's earlier example and simply taken over the group, lock, stock, and insignia. Instead, they resigned, and within months, using their many contacts among well-placed New Yorkers, began their own organization, the Volunteers of America.[24]

Through the uncertain days of February and March 1896, National Headquarters (NHQ) fairly buzzed with intrigue and excitement. While the *New York Times* suggested that "members of the Army . . . from Staff Captains down to privates . . . were without exception on the side of the popular Commander," internal sources indicate that there was considerably less unanimity of sentiment. According to one twenty-two-year-old officer at NHQ in this period, "everyone is on the tip toe of expectation. . . . Little knots of people all over the place talking the topic of the day over and over and over again. Some on one side and some on the other[,] almost all had taken sides some way." For several days running, he described "private councils" where Ballington or his sister, Evangeline, who acted on behalf of her father, William Booth, aired their grievances to officers gathered at NHQ.[25]

In February two British officers, Colonels Nichol and Eadie, took command of the American forces in what the *New York Times* characterized as "a sort of regency, pending the appointment of a successor." Colonel Eadie, who had been assigned to the United States two years earlier, very quickly came to symbolize what the *Times* cited as the "foundation of the whole trouble" the effort to "Anglicize" the movement. As described in the newspaper, this criticism had two elements, one class-based and the other relating to centralization of authority. First, the paper suggested that the educated Ballington's "ways and methods" as well as "the personality of his refined and tactful wife" had "won the hearts of the people here." Colonel Eadie, on the other hand, represented the "clumsier, sterner and less American system of the draconic [*sic*] colonel," who, the paper pointed out condescendingly, had been "a sailor before he joined the Salvation Army."[26]

A second aspect of the newspaper's criticism cited efforts at centralization as evidence of English domination.[27] Eadie stood accused of "introduc[ing] English methods into the conduct of the affairs of the army," including invasions of privacy and challenges to individual autonomy. First, according to the newspaper's sources, Colonel Eadie insisted that he had the right to open "all telegrams and cablegrams addressed to officers and others." Moreover, wrote the paper, he tried to prevent American Salvationists from taking out loans to purchase homes, maintaining a horse and carriage for their own use, and riding bicycles. Not all Salvationists agreed with the *New York Times*'s assessment, however. John Milsaps, for example, believed that "Col. Eadie . . . was loyal . . . [and so I] went to him just before the Carnegie Hall meeting & told him he could count on me to stand by the colors."[28]

In addition to the chaos created by Ballington Booth's resignation, as one historian of the Army remarked, the Booth-Tuckers' administration "began and ended with tragedy."[29] When Consul Emma Booth-Tucker arrived in New York on March 28, 1896, she learned that her third child had died. The couple had left the six-week-old baby boy in England in the care of a nurse; sadly, the child died while they were in transit to the United States.[30] Thirty-six-year-old Consul Emma Booth-Tucker was the fourth child and second daughter of William and Catherine Booth. Before her wedding, Emma operated the Army's London Training Garrison for female officers. In 1888 she married Frederick Tucker and went with him to India to continue his Salvation Army missionary work in that country. In 1891 Emma became ill, forcing the couple to return to England, where they served International Headquarters as foreign secretaries "in charge of the entire work of the Army outside the United Kingdom." Her husband, Frederick St. George De Lautour Booth-Tucker, was born in Bengal, India, "the son of a Commissioner in the Indian Civil Service." After attending Cheltenham College in England, Tucker returned to India where he, too, entered the Indian Civil Service rising to the rank of assistant commissioner. In 1881 he left the service and the following year he and a few English Salvationists donned "native dress and moved into native quarters" in order to preach to Indians of lower castes.[31]

Ten days after their arrival in the United States, the Army held a large welcome meeting for the Booth-Tuckers at Carnegie Hall. As one young officer observed, the new commanders "received a welcome such as I never recall anyone to have before in the S.A. in U.S. They both spoke FINE GRAND."[32] The Booth-Tuckers followed up that meeting with a flurry of activity designed to solidify their control. They established their presence at NHQ by leading officers' councils in prayer. They identified "loyal" officers and, with British reinforcements, sent them out to "stay the tide of revolt." They rewarded officers who returned to the fold and quickly began touring the country introducing themselves to their American forces.[33]

Most important, the Booth-Tuckers quickly and forcefully established an action-packed agenda that demanded energy and commitment of the

Emma and Frederick Booth-Tucker and family.
(Courtesy of the Salvation Army National Archives)

Army's members. An officers' council in late June 1896 generated considerable expectation among the staff at NHQ. "Another day of mistery [*sic*] we can see the Brigs coming and going from the council chamber on the 7th floor," wrote an officer. "There shall start from this a work I believe which shall make the whole world train their eyes towards America even more than they have during our late trouble." The following day the Booth-Tuckers announced "all the schemes that they expect to carry out," which consisted of a myriad of City and Farm Colony programs.[34]

Over the next seven years, in addition to expanding the Rescue work, Children's Homes and Slum Brigades, the Booth-Tuckers opened Hotels for Workingmen, delivered "Cheap Fuel and Ice" to the urban poor, and established Salvage Brigades, Second Hand Stores, Industrial Homes for the Unemployed and employment bureaus. Indeed, a 1898 report titled "The Social Work in the United States," noted that in just one year the total number of social institutions had increased from 28 to 85.[35] In addition to expanding the City Colony, between 1898 and 1899 the Booth-Tuckers opened three farm colonies: one in the Salinas Valley of California, another in Colorado near the border with Kansas, and a third in Ohio near Cleveland.[36] The Booth-Tuckers' social scheme joined similar efforts by institutional churches and settlement houses that offered community programs in some American cities at the turn of the century.

In contrast to institutional churches, however, the Army's programs focused much more attention on finding or providing work for men. Moreover, unlike settlement houses Salvation Army efforts aimed at temporary material amelioration not long-term goals of social reform.[37]

The American social Christian community generally welcomed the Army's program. One minister supported the plan because it attempted to deal with "the awful problems of social misery and degradation and sin."[38] A number of social gospel luminaries also endorsed the expansion of the Salvation Army's social work. Josiah Strong, for example, wrote in glowing terms of the Salvation Army's "Christian philanthropy," which, he said, "fundamentally differentiate[s] the Army and its work from the churches and their efforts," and accounts for its success. Similarly, sociology professor Charles R. Henderson said that Booth's social scheme reminds us all "that they who touch the soul must minister to the body, as Jesus did."[39]

Predictably, some Americans leveled a traditional Christian evangelical critique, condemning what they regarded as the plan's emphasis on the physical rather than the spiritual life of the poor. Wrote one Baptist minister, "I think the proposed scheme goes at it in the wrong way. The soul degrades the body more than the body degrades the soul, and to suppose that the betterment of the mere physical part of man will effect his reformation is viewing the matter in the wrong light."[40] Critics also questioned the plan's core assumptions about the poor, suggesting that the program would fail because of the voluntary nature of idleness and sin; very few unemployed men "honestly want work but cannot get it," and "female outcasts" prefer that life and will not stay reformed.[41] More sanguine critics suggested that New York simply had less poverty than London did and that the United States, in contrast to Europe, had no class system. "[W]e have no such stratification," said Washington Gladden, "the poorest people do not willingly admit that they are members of a class."[42] Still other critics pointed out that although the plan might work among Londoners who were "Protestants, English born and English bred," the Salvation Army would find it much more difficult to reach the "motley multitudes" in the United States. "At least nine-tenths of our poor people," they argued, "are of foreign extraction, more than half of them are nominally Roman Catholics, and a large proportion of the other half are Hebrews."[43]

Probably the social scheme's most outspoken opponent was the organized charity movement. Edwin R. Solenberger, general manager of the Associated Charities in Minneapolis, reported in 1906 that his investiga-

A NEW MESSAGE OF TEMPORAL SALVATION

tion of the Salvation Army's social relief work revealed serious problems. First, the Salvation Army placed too much responsibility on society and not the individual for causing poverty; as a result, its work did nothing to improve character. In the lodging houses, the report complained, Salvationists failed to "exert any moral influence over the men." Furthermore, the program was neither "scientific" nor "rational." In dealing with the unemployed the Army simply offered temporary work instead of recognizing that this category of men and women actually "represent[ed] many different types" requiring "[i]ndividual treatment carefully suited to their varying needs." In addition, he argued that Salvationists duplicated the work of other organizations by refusing to coordinate relief efforts. "All of these defects," wrote Solenberger, "make the Salvation Army un-American and ill-adapted to carry out progressive and rational measures of social relief."[44]

In their campaigns for public support, Emma and Frederick Booth-Tucker remained loyal to William Booth's fundamental assumptions about the poor. At the same time, however, the Booth-Tuckers worked hard to undermine charges that the program was "un-American," that is, inappropriate for the United States, and to answer critics' charges. In a carefully crafted argument, Frederick Booth-Tucker sought to establish the group's credentials and the program's suitability. To Josephine Shaw Lowell, who suggested that the Army limit its work to "moral and spiritual care," leaving the temporal care of the poor to experts, the commander pointed out that the Army was well qualified in "practical sociology." While the group was limited in "theoretical and literary study," it had investigated the pauper problem "from a *world-wide*, a *national* and a *people's* point of view."[45] He added that although the extent of poverty in the United States was far less than in England, Americans still had the responsibility to "mitigate this almost inconceivable mass of human woe."[46]

In his discussion Booth-Tucker cannily injected arguments suited to an American audience. For example, he tapped into American fears of class warfare made real by the violent confrontations between authorities and workers during the last two decades. He suggested that punitive policies which require examinations of character, move the poor from city to city and "nail poverty to a cross of shame or treat it as a crime" are not only "contrary to the spirit of our American institutions," but could easily turn the poor into "Socialists, Anarchists, Dynamitards of the most dangerous and desperate character, the manufacture of our own cold-blooded brutality." In response to charges that the Salvation Army refused to cooperate with the organized charity movement, he enlisted the language of industrial capitalism and touched public concerns about the impact of trusts on individual opportunity and independence.[47] Arguing that "unity of purpose [not] . . . uniformity of method" should be its goal, Booth-Tucker compared social work to the "commercial field" suggesting that "competition" is more beneficial than "monopoly" because it introduces "new machinery . . . [and] novel plans." Furthermore, he said, "the multiplication of efforts . . . cultivate[s] the spirit of energy, independence, and enterprise." He even argued that each organization had the *right* to develop its own approach to the problem. Extending the notion of individual liberty to organizations Booth-Tucker also said, "to me the individual liberty of each organization to do the best it can and the most it can in its own way is very nearly as valuable as the liberty of the individual citizen to do the same."[48] Far from being unsuitable for this country, he argued, the social scheme proved more faithful to American institutions and beliefs than those of the Army's critics.

Finally, in his explanation of the cause of urban poverty and his adaptation of the social scheme to the United States, Booth-Tucker emphasized a rural romanticism that appealed to Americans. Although the "Pauper Policy" and *In Darkest England* emphasized the role played by unemployment, Booth-Tucker placed *land* at the center of his promotion of the program while William Booth stressed the centrality of the *city colony*. In the general's description of the plan the City Colony took center stage and from it flowed the rescued men and women to the Farm Colonies. In contrast, Booth-Tucker emphasized the creation of "*centrifugal* forces" aimed at luring both the poor and the criminal back to the land in order to counteract the "strong *centripetal* forces of the city" which "attract too many workers for too few jobs." Furthermore, Booth-Tucker's "Pauper Policy" opened with an American version of colonization referring to settlement in the western United States as the "Western Canaan . . . large tracts of 100,000 acres of land and upwards in the Far West." It is telling that of the four major elements of the Pauper Policy, Booth-Tucker chose to mention the settlement of western land first even though he acknowledged that it "must be necessarily the last portion of the scheme to come into actual operation."[49] Clearly the Commander recognized that many Americans still regarded the West as the country's best hope for solving urban problems.[50]

The second element in the American social scheme was the Farm Colonies which, if placed close enough to overcrowded cities, would draw population back to the land. Booth-Tucker went on, however, to add a third policy which is unique to the American program, City Garden Allotments or Potato Patches. Borrowing from a program already established in Detroit, the commander advocated urban gardens as "a stepping stone between the city and the farm, creating a love of the land and a knowledge of how to handle it."[51] Significantly, although the City Colony was the most elaborate part of the Army's program and the core element of the British social scheme, Booth-Tucker took up his discussion of the City Colony only as the final part of the "Pauper Policy." In both his defense of the plan and his articulation of its elements, Booth-Tucker altered *In Darkest England* for an American audience.

In addition to framing the scheme in peculiarly American terms, the Booth-Tuckers went on tour to vigorously promote the social scheme to the public. While Maud Booth advertised the Army's social rescue evangelism by giving sentimental talks in the parlors of the well-to-do in the 1880s and early 1890s, the consul took elaborately produced shows incorporating new technologies of mass culture to large audiences gathered in American theaters and opera houses around the nation.[52] The Booth-Tuckers and their successor, Evangeline Booth, proved so successful at popularizing its social work over the next decades that many Americans lost sight of the religious aspects of the group's mission. In the 1890s, Americans knew the Salvation Army exclusively as a working-class religious organization. By the 1920s, however, the Army and its social services became synonymous. Indeed, a 1924 study noted that the Salvation Army "is not uncommonly regarded as a distinctly social agency in which religious worship plays a subordinate part."[53] Public perceptions have not changed significantly in the past 65 years. In 1989 the *New York Times* pointed out that "many people assume . . . the organization is a social service agency . . . rather than a church with clergy and lay members."[54]

Even as the expanding social wing gained popularity with the public, Salvationists revealed considerable ambivalence about social work as a legitimate category of Christian expression. Historically in the Army, service as a sign of true faith meant advertising salvation through inventive religious rituals designed to convert sinners. Booth's scheme, however, created new goals and a new class of Christian service, temporal salvation through social work. Salvationists, from the general on down, placed greater value on directly spiritual efforts in the field than more indirectly religious work in social institutions. Many members felt unconvinced that both kinds of service were equally valuable.

In a revealing 1903 letter, William Booth articulated his own complex feelings about the direction in which he had taken the group thirteen years earlier. On one hand, Booth sanctified social service by arguing that it was the Christlike thing to do. "If a man had a brother who was hungry and homeless and naked," he said, "his first sense of duty would be to feed and house and clothe him, doing it in the spirit of love and talking to him about his soul all the time." Furthermore, he argued that the scheme had proved useful to Army public relations because it "lifted us up to a position in public esteem, the world over, which we should never have gained in all human probability for perhaps a Century without it."[55] At the same time, however, he expressed skepticism that the effort spent in social service actually provided the same benefit as that "spent in purely spiritual work." As a result, while committed to social service, when it came to the distribution of financial and human resources, Booth fervently believed that the Army should reserve its own economic assets as well as the best and the brightest officers for the spiritual effort. Said Booth, "We have a number of people . . . who can do this work [social service] and who cannot do the other [religious service]. Let us employ them and make the world pay for it. What I object to is using the time and ability of men and women for Social Work who are required for the Spiritual and using money after the same fashion."[56] Booth's attitude helped ensure that in Britain social services operated quite separately from the group's spiritual work.

Emma and Frederick Booth-Tucker brought this complex mix of sentiments with them to the United States. Thus, even as they enthusiastically pressed forward with the social scheme, the leaders argued that the spiritual effort demanded more from officers than the social work. In 1899, for example, the commander suggested that social officers needed to be honest, attentive to detail, and spiritual. "These," he said, "are qualities which are often possessed in a large measure by officers who are not particularly successful in the Field." Operating a corps, he argued, was more difficult than managing a social institution since corps leaders must also preach convincingly while social managers simply needed business skills that required only "a little training." At the same time, however, many Americans moved by the promotional efforts of the consul and commander regarded social officers as "a Samurai caste," and believed that "the officers on the spiritual side have . . . more emotion and less intelligence."[57] Under the Booth-Tuckers' leadership, the social and spiritual branches would begin to develop separate administrations and identities.

Criticism from the organized charity movement also contributed to the Army's decision to separate the administration of the social from the spiritual work. In contrast to William Booth's concern that religious resources would be invested in social work, the Associated Charities charged that the Salvation Army used funds raised for social work to support the organization's worldwide religious agenda. The group, said Rev. Henry R. Rose, was "not doing Good Samaritan work solely and purely from the love of such work but as a part of its plan to build up a powerful denomination in the United States."[58] The Associated Charities' accusations posed a serious threat to the group's fund-raising efforts in the community at large. In Cleveland, for example, the Army's ability to raise money from local businessmen required the endorsement of the Chamber of Commerce. Unfortunately, the secretary of the Associated Charities gained control of the chamber's charitable committee and refused to give the Salvation Army its stamp of approval. Ultimately, the Army won endorsement in Cleveland but not until they waged a lengthy campaign among the city's businessmen. Salvationists believed that their initial exclusion from the list of acceptable charities had long-term financial effects in Cleveland and that they needed to develop some mechanism to reassure the community that religious and social finances would be kept separated.[59]

The complex demands of an expanding Social Wing along with the need to create clear administrative boundaries between the spiritual and social work placed tremendous bureaucratic pressures on the Salvation Army in the United States at the turn of the century. In addition to supplying personnel, overseeing expansion of its religious activities, and coordinating funding for National Headquarters, the organization now sought to establish and operate an elaborate nationwide network of social institutions. To address this goal, Emma and Frederick Booth-Tucker introduced a business ethic of efficiency, rationality, centralized control, and accountability which they immediately applied to the American administration. These managerial changes looked to a corporate model and in many ways mirrored the "internal organizational changes" experienced by the Charity Organization Societies and the Settlement House movement by the 1920s.[60] Both of the Booth-Tuckers came well equipped with experience in bureaucracy and Salvation Army administration: the consul through her leadership of the London training "garrison" and the commander from his years in the Indian Civil Service.

Starting with National Headquarters, the Booth-Tuckers inaugurated changes that they believed fostered efficiency and rationalization of responsibility. They created a plethora of new "departments" whose responsibilities and oversight expanded significantly over the next years. Under Maud and Ballington, NHQ bureaucracy consisted of individual officers with special responsibilities like Notary Public, Legal Adviser, Auditor, and Slum Work, or single departments with multiple functions such as the "Statistical, Field Report, Property and Local Commissions Department." Moreover, before 1896 districts and corps exercised significantly more power than NHQ. As we have seen during Major Thomas Moore's administration, one corps, on its own initiative, incorporated itself under New Jersey law. In the hands of the Booth-Tuckers, however, NHQ expanded to fifteen distinct units including separate Financial, Legal, Statistical, Property, and Musical Departments. Most significantly, however, they established a separate Social Wing which, although as yet with little power, consisted of a separate Colonization Department, a City Colony Department, and, by 1900, a Slum and Rescue Department, each reporting directly to the consul and commander.[61]

In addition to rationalizing responsibility in new departments, the Booth-Tuckers also tried to bring efficiency to the funding of NHQ and the expansion of the City Colony. First, they implemented cost-saving mechanisms by centralizing Salvation Army printing and merchandising functions in the Reliance Trading Company that took over the ownership and publication of *The War Cry*. Reliance not only provided printing services for other departments but also sold a variety of Salvation Army merchandise, including uniforms.[62] A second company, the Salvation Army Industrial Homes Company, quickly followed in order to raise funds "for the extension and equipment of the Industrial Homes."[63] As early as 1899, the consul and commander claimed that the efficiencies they implemented since their arrival successfully cut NHQ expenditures by $15,000.[64]

Emma and Frederick Booth-Tucker also legally restructured the organization to centralize authority and provide greater security for Army property. Immediately upon taking control, the Booth-Tuckers began the process of incorporating the Salvation Army's assets on behalf of William Booth. The group's second schism in this country could have cost the organization all property then held in Ballington Booth's name. Furthermore, recent court decisions that allowed successful challenges of bequests to the organization finally convinced the British leadership that legal steps must be taken. At the same time, William Booth still vigorously opposed any strategies that placed organizational authority in the hands of a board of trustees over which he had no control.[65]

Assisted by a well-connected law firm, Frederick Booth-Tucker developed a compromise by which five to seven top Salvation Army officers would incorporate an association for the purpose of holding the property of the Salvation Army. These officers would transfer their powers to the president, the presiding general of the Salvation Army. Conveniently, the general would be responsible for appointing the trustees and officers who managed the corporation. "Hence," wrote Booth-Tucker, "all the power remains in the hands of the General, and at the same time he has the power and privileges of the Incorporation behind him." Finally, in April 1899, the New York legislature passed a special act of incorporation for the organization.[66]

The Booth-Tuckers also attempted to reverse a longstanding tradition of local and regional autonomy by shifting power away from the corps and districts to National Headquarters. In addition to efficiency this move may have been motivated by a desire to minimize the power of district officers (DO) to foment insurrection. During the 1896 crisis, seventeen staff officers from the Central Division sent a lengthy cablegram to Britain objecting to the general's decision to reassign Maud and Ballington Booth; by 1898 several members of that division had resigned to join the Volunteers of America.[67] Furthermore, the Booth-Tuckers issued a flood of "Field Orders" which shifted control upward. Some of these directives attempted to bring uniformity to religious services and discourage local innovation. Divisions, they said, must stop printing and selling their own songbooks. Wrote the commanders, "in future . . . no such Song books may be published and . . . [only] the National song Books are to be used throughout the Territory." "Unity in singing will thus be preserved," they explained, "and the issuing of new editions from time to time will ensure the necessary variety."[68]

The consul and commander also minimized local autonomy by centralizing the payment of corps hall rent. By ordering that payments be sent to NHQ and forwarded from there to the landlord, the Booth-Tuckers undermined local control over finances and decisions regarding corps locations. Furthermore, to ensure that corps and divisions released cadets from local duties and possibly to help build individual loyalty to the national organization, the consul and commander gave orders that NHQ rather than the divisions were to pay the training home expenses. And, perhaps in an additional effort to control dissent and local autonomy, the Booth-Tuckers decided to discontinue publication of the Pacific Coast edition of The War Cry, leaving only the New York–based version of the newspaper in operation. While describing the latter as a cost-saving move, by 1902 the Booth-Tuckers insisted that all district or corps publications receive National Headquarters' sanction before they were issued.[69]

Lastly, in 1897 as the social scheme got under way, Commander Booth-

Tucker ordered that no social work be "commenced without his consent in writing."[70] Since its earliest days in the United States, Salvation Army corps, like many evangelical missions, had provided ad hoc and temporary social services to the destitute. Field officers, for example, often allowed the homeless to "sleep in the hall after meetings" and at times provided free food and clothing to "poor and needy families." Salvation Army officers regarded these efforts as part of their "ordinary pastoral work."[71] By 1904, however, Army leadership insisted that, "No officer from this date can enter into any branch of Social Work, even although there may be no Social Institution in the city. Salvage must not be collected, or any operation of a Social character be commenced."[72]

In addition to minimizing autonomy and shifting power upward, the Booth-Tuckers began to separate the administration of the social from the spiritual work. Army leaders confronted the social wing's insatiable appetite for financial resources and the fact that hard-pressed Salvationists would be unlikely to deliver the revenue required to expand those institutions. In the long term the leaders preferred to muster outside sources, including a combination of state subsidies, matching funds from private donations and income "produced by the non-competitive labor of the inmates," to bankroll the social work. Initial expansion of the City Colony, however, required an investment of resources from the Salvation Army's own General Fund.[73] To maximize funds, the consul and commander imposed a program of economic rationalization and efficiency on the corps and districts. These changes, argued the consul, would "not only strengthen our hands here at the centre but . . . very materially assist us in the necessary initial expenditure in the direction of advance throughout the field."[74]

Admonishing officers to "[m]ake religion as cheap as possible to the people" and lecturing them that "a dollar saved is usually better than a dollar begged," the consul and commander imposed a new regime of thrift in 1899. Headquarters suggested a number of ways in which corps could cut costs: by subletting the front of their properties to stores, sharing space with a social institution (albeit with separate entrances), and by encouraging soldiers and officers to live near the corps building in order to save carfare wherever possible. To reduce district expenses, National Headquarters cut the salaries of staff officers and reduced the size of its support staff; NHQ also encouraged other economies such as applying for reduced utility rates and sending letters instead of telegrams.[75]

The economy-drive particularly targeted the districts. Historically, corps provided the main source of financial support for the district, sending 12 to 15 percent of its weekly income to the chief divisional officer (CDO). The Booth-Tuckers pointed out that with an additional 50 percent going toward hall rents, corps engaged in a constant round of "begging" at meetings or soliciting from the well to do. This system, they warned, not only "has a serious tendency to drive away crowds" but also risked alienating outside supporters. Once more undermining local autonomy and decision-making power, the consul and commander issued orders that field officers must limit themselves to one ten-minute round of "begging" at all indoor and outdoor meetings and that they may hold only one special fund-raising service per week.[76]

To further alleviate the economic burden on corps, national leadership provided districts with new sources of income. All CDOs could claim two-thirds of the earnings from "Mercy Boxes," small collection boxes placed in stores around the cities. They also would be entitled to 10 percent of the sales income from Salvation Army publications like *The War Cry, The Young Soldier, Harbor Lights,* and *Social News,* as well as 10 percent of the gross income from the social institutions in each district.[77]

The consul and commander also increased the authority of national headquarters by holding districts accountable for bringing rationality and efficiency to fund-raising to their area. For example, the Booth-Tuckers recommended the establishment of a "Rent League" for each corps to help eliminate "the necessity for ceaseless begging." From among "the leading gentlemen in the city," the CDO would select a treasurer for the league who would solicit contributors, collect, and hold the funds until required for paying rents. In order to "prevent overlapping in the begging amongst the moneyed people," the leaders suggested that the main contributors be "distributed amongst the Corps and Institutions, each being held strictly liable for regularly visiting the places which are entrusted to them."[78]

The efforts of Salvation Army leaders to impose efficiency, rationality, control, and accountability combined with ambivalence toward social work triggered a period of turmoil in the organization. Resentments over centralization sometimes expressed themselves in Anglophobic terms. Beginning in 1898, for example one officer documented growing anti-English sentiments expressed toward British headquarters and the Booth family. In a letter to John Milsaps, an officer who resigned and joined the Volunteers claimed that since the arrival of the Booth-Tuckers all of the new chief divisional officers were British or had been trained in England. Furthermore, he charged that the Booths were also sending field officers to be trained at International Headquarters at American expense. Wrote

Milsaps, "More than one important officer in the United States has said to me and to others that an anti-American policy was being pursued by Gen. Booth and the Booth-Tuckers since the advent of the latter in the U.S. Americans seem to be backseated."[79]

Competition over personnel and finances also fueled a growing sense of alienation between social and spiritual officers, threatening to make administrative divisions even more fundamental. Tensions between social and field officers grew, for example, as the Booth-Tuckers attempted to provide sufficient staff for the social institutions without depleting the pool of qualified field officers. Following the message of their leaders, CDOs treated the social work as an appropriate assignment for men and women who, they felt, failed at spiritual work. As a consequence, managers of social institutions frequently complained not only of being short-handed but also that "the average CDO still cherishes the fallacy that 'anything is good enough for the Social.'" Grumbled one Salvage Brigade officer, "I have been offered some that were too lazy to make a shadow." In frustration, the national social secretary, R. E. Holz, warned the Booth-Tuckers that morale among social officers had plummeted because of the quality of the help they were offered. Moreover, he charged, the policy unfairly stigmatized officers as failures, lazy, or looking for a "soft snap" if they sought appointment to social work. Said Holz, the "transfer from the Field to the Social of dissatisfied officers . . . the airing of their grievances and complaints is anything but helpful to the other Social Officers and . . . it has a tendency to lower the standard of the Social work in the eyes of their comrades of the field."[80]

The distribution of financial resources also generated tensions. Initially, in exchange for "oversight" of the social institutions the Booth-Tuckers gave CDOs permission to collect a 10 percent tax or "centage" from the gross income of the social work. In 1899 an enraged social work staff-captain wrote complaining bitterly about an increase in the centage in his district, charging that it threatened the social's ability to pay its expenses and, moreover, that any surplus should be reserved for expansion of the social institutions.[81] From the perspective of this officer, although the district failed to provide support of any kind, it exploited him and his social work for its own purposes. The district commanders, he said, regarded the social institutions as cash-cows. "It seems to me," he wrote, "that all the CDO wants the Social for is to . . . be a string to pull for cash."[82] Clearly feeling overwhelmed, exploited, and alienated, the same social officer wrote, "To come to cold facts I do not see the fun or fareness [sic] of being a slave and work among rags and dirt to build up a business for the CDO and be despised by the officers whom we are helping to support."[83]

In these early stages of centralization, unhappy social officers found little remedy at NHQ. Initially the national social secretary of the City Colony wielded little power over the operations of the Social Wing. Indeed, National Social Secretary Holz frequently complained that he was merely "a figurehead" ignored by both the district and NHQ.[84] Reflecting the tenacity of local and regional autonomy, Holz wrote, "[E]very Divisional officer looks upon the Social Work in his division as his own affair, and resents any interference on the part of the National Social Secretary." He felt particularly annoyed at his inability to control the staffing of social positions. Each CDO, he said, "looks upon the officers in this particular Division as belonging to him and when I do want to make any change to help out somewhere where there is a great need, a howl goes up at once, and every possible hindrance is placed in the way of such transfers taking place." Holz believed that his lack of authority exacerbated the problem. Although the consul and commander held him responsible for the success of the social work nationwide, they "at the same time vest[ed] only a shadow of authority in me so far as the Social Work in the different Divisions under the C.D.O. is concerned."[85] In 1904, reasoning that "[o]fficers in charge of . . . the spiritual operations . . . should be free to give their whole time to that brand of the service," the Salvation Army strengthened centralized authority, shifting responsibility from the CDOs to the hands of social officers who answered directly to NHQ.[86]

Far from easing tensions, centralization of the social wing increased the resentment of many officers in the spiritual work. Colonel French, leader of the Pacific Coast Province for example, argued that the new arrangement created problems for the Provincial leadership.[87] The decision, he said, created confusing lines of command and threatened his authority internally and externally. "[T]he relieving of the Provincial Officer of the responsibility of the Social," he said, "means his being totally ignored by the officers in the Social Department." Social officers not only "failed to attend Officers' Meetings," he complained, but they refused to provide him with the information he needed "for the purpose of giving the information to the public, as the Army's chief representative on the coast."[88]

Moreover, he argued, the new arrangement jeopardized the financial stability of the province. Changes in the "centage" placed distribution of these monies in the hands of NHQ, which would periodically pay the Provincial Officers 25 percent of the *profits* earned by every institution in their region instead of allowing the PO to claim 10 percent of the *gross income*. Wrote Colonel French, "I hardly see my way clear to relinquish the Social Work . . . at the present time because to do so would simply paralyze us financially." Losing the 10 percent, he argued, would cost the province over $300 per month. Furthermore, revealing his distrust of social officers, French suggested that to avoid having to share with the PO social officers would "be extravagant and . . . swallow up any profits that might remain, in expenses."[89]

Centralization of authority over social work coupled with incessant financial demands left POs in the unenviable position of competing with the Army's own institutions for local funds. To make matters worse, in 1901 NHQ issued orders that gave priority to the Social Wing regarding outside fund-raising. Wrote the consul and commander, "Each branch of the work has an equal right to issue appeals, but if any have a greater right to more consideration it is those branches of Salvation Army work that can be strictly classed as charitable, such as Social, Rescue, Slums, etc."[90] As a consequence, POs at times found themselves contending with poachers from the National Social leadership. In 1906 one PO reportedly discovered that a National Social Secretary had sent officers into his area to collect funds "to clear up the mortgage on the Rescue Home" and that these men "would not report to [the PO] in any way." When he objected to the incursion into his territory, the National Social Secretary in question invited him to NHQ to discuss the matter. Mused the officer, "I do not think anything can be accomplished [by going to NHQ] . . . for they are filled with plausible excuses and they twist out of anything and as they have the power whether ones [*sic*] arguments are clear and right or not their decision settles all."[91]

Provincial/divisional officers were not the only Salvationists to feel squeezed by the expansion of the social work and ceaseless financial demands. In the minds of many staff and field officers, the social scheme actually endangered the lifeblood of the organization, the retention of existing Salvation Army officers and the addition of new members. In Chicago, for example, the number of corps had grown steadily until 1897. Over the next few years, however, as the social programs expanded, the number of regular corps declined from 35 to 21. Indeed, according to the *Disposition of Forces*, between 1897 and 1901 the number of officers associated with the Social Wing increased five times over from 66 to 368 while the number of regular officers increased by only 14 percent.[92] In his letter of resignation, one staff member suggested that recent efforts not only failed to build the group's membership but that the interminable "begging" hurt the cause, "by the discouragement of officers, soldiers, saints and sinners, and the humiliation of all concerned." Moreover, some officers believed the Booth-Tuckers distorted the traditional evangelical measurement of success, that is, the numbers of conversions that resulted from one's labors. Instead, they argued, the "fruits" by which "ye shall know them" had become fund-raising, not soul raising. The same officer in his resignation letter wrote resentfully that the consul and commander increasingly measured his service to the Army and suitability for promotion "more by dollars and cents than by the considerations for which I had chiefly rendered them."[93]

Centralization also prompted internal criticism of NHQ's use of funds. One angry captain who worked as a "money collector" for San Francisco social institutions reportedly marched into Provincial HQ and threatened to quit raising money because her "conscience [wouldn't] let her beg for them" anymore. The incompetent leaders, she felt, were "doing nothing . . . [and] money [was being] misapplied."[94] Others accused the Booths of unseemly materialism and hypocrisy. Said one officer, "[t]here is an extravagant expenditure of the Lord's money (the people's pennies) in connection with the General's and other leaders' travels and entertainment on Army duty, which is entirely inconsistent with their teachings on the subject."[95] In 1906 another officer commented on the extravagantly decorated offices at NHQ which boasted fresh wall paper, parquet floors, a new wardrobe and furnishings all of which used the "most expensive materials." "In view of the pressing appeal for funds that appeared in the War Cry," he remarked, "this hardly looks valid."[96]

Some veteran Salvationists believed that the fiscal demands of the social scheme posed a genuine threat to the spiritual goals of the Army. As the Salvation Army became more deeply involved in "secular money making enterprises," these officers feared that "the religious side of our organization will gradually be pushed to one side and the secular get the upper hand."[97] Dissatisfied officers argued that as the social work grew in importance they became "uneasy for the Salvation Army's future, lest this organization be subverted from the purpose for which God raised it up — soul saving and be turned into a vast money making machine."[98] Two prominent Salvationists in California even prayed that the Lord would "upset the Commander's plans & . . . the Social work if in the Lord's sight they will swamp the soul saving work of the Salvation Army."[99]

In addition to centralizing the administration of the social wing, national leadership tried to assert authority over Army personnel. They did so most effectively with officers in New York at NHQ. After moving from a provincial position to NHQ, one officer noticed, "In name my job is much greater but in many ways I haven't near the power. In Chicago I settled things on the spot and what I said when the P.O. was absent was law and when he was present I was at least consulted re important matters. Here decisions are passed on to me and all matters are referred to C. Or Comdr."[100] Ambitious officers also felt the power of the consul and commander to promote or punish them. After one young officer, Francis Lee, wrote a letter criticizing Commander Booth-Tucker and the way the Army handled its finances, he found himself hanging around headquarters for months without an assignment. He complained that he'd been at NHQ for six months, "yet during all that time I have never been given any position, my name has never been even placed in the 'Dispo.' " Instead, he found himself "going around to H.Q. dailylike . . . looking for a job and nothing for me." He ended his letter by apologizing for his critical remarks: "[L]et me say how deeply I still regret my hasty letter and comments. . . . I cannot express too heartily my sorrow."[101]

Like Francis Lee, more than one officer complained of being put in "the freezer" or exiled to undesirable assignments by the national commanders. Between June 1898 and April 1900, John Milsaps mentioned at least three officers who claimed that "it was customary in the Salvation Army to 'freeze' an officer out when they want to get rid of the same."[102] Another Salvationist suggested that members who returned to the organization after resigning found that they "never advanced beyond the rank that [they] formerly held." "This," he said, "was the Army's mode of punishment."[103] Still others complained that the Booth-Tuckers disciplined officers by "lift[ing] them out of important field commands and put[ting] them into departments, or relegat[ing] them into small divisions." One officer, for example, found himself shipped from National Headquarters to a newly created and very weak southern division.[104]

In spite of the leaders' attempts to assert their authority, the voluntary nature of Salvation Army membership still left officers and soldiers with considerable power. In an organization where autocracy and democracy had always coexisted in continuous tension, Salvation Army officers at the turn of the century continued to vote with their feet. Overworked field officers repeatedly resisted the demands of their leaders by taking "furloughs" without permission. Often these officers had requested permission for time off and when denied simply left without the sanction of their superiors.[105] Others "farewelled" from assignments without permission; Ensign P——, for example, left his local post and just showed up at Divisional Headquarters one day "without permission."[106] An officer's ultimate weapon, of course, was resignation. Some field officers resigned in response to personality conflicts within local corps or because of affronts by superior officers. One captain reportedly resigned "on acct of her CDOs treatment." Others used the threat of resignation to demand transfers. On one occasion a staff officer discovered that a group of "fine young officers of the Central [Division]" sought transfers, "failing in which they will resign."[107]

Field officers also sometimes resisted the myriad fund-raising schemes increasingly thrust upon them by the exigencies of the expanding social work. Corps officers objected to these special fund-raising events because headquarters received so much of the money, the events required tremendous energy, and they tended to drain local resources upon which officers depended for their wages. One District Headquarters officer found himself negotiating with a corps officer who refused to do a Harvest Festival.[108] At last, "after two hours got her to say 'yes' [to his proposal for] her to arrange a Special Meeting sell tickets ½ proceeds go H.Q., other half for Corps debt."[109]

Finally, even staff officers resisted Salvation Army authority. In a revealing portrait, one PO described the qualities and leadership of "the only woman Divisional Officer in the Country." Major B——, he wrote, "is a strong minded woman and one most difficult to move once she has decided a matter to *her own* satisfaction." Among her positive qualities, he mentioned her speaking, her fund-raising skills, and her willingness to send money to Provincial Headquarters "*if she is convinced [they] . . . need it*" [my emphasis]. On the negative side, he indicated that she "likes very much to be left alone"; she refused to send in her itinerary to headquarters, traveling when and where she pleased without permission; and finally she tended to move her officers around without consulting the provincial officer. This successful divisional officer demanded and clearly received considerable autonomy.[110] In yet another instance, an NHQ officer resisted reassignment from the position of field secretary to one that required fund-raising among the wealthy for the Army's Prison Work. He explained that such a transfer would "humiliate [him] before all [his] comrades" but that he would stand it if the commander thought it necessary (and God's will). Taking the hint, she sent him, instead, to command the Atlantic Coast Province.[111]

In addition to centralization and administrative segmentation, implementing the social scheme created critical differences between the social and spiritual work. As we've seen, the Salvation Army, unlike any other religious movements of the period, provided women with a remarkable level of administrative and spiritual authority over both men and women in the field. In contrast, the Salvation Army's social work followed the model established by other rescue, missionary, and evangelical Christian women's groups, rigidly gendering its social work. Female Salvationists performed the Army's equivalent of "woman's work for woman."[112] These officers managed Slum and Rescue work for women, while male officers administered the Industrial Homes and Salvage work for men. The group even renamed the Slum and Rescue Departments the Women's Social, while the City Colony became the Men's Social Department. The Army seems to have particularly focused on expanding social services for men. In the Eastern Territory alone, Industrial Homes, hotels, and employment bureaus meeting men's needs made up nearly 83 percent of the 215 social institutions operating in that region. Programs specifically aimed at women made up only 16 percent of the Eastern Territorial total by the 1920s.[113]

The goals of the Army's social work were also gendered. Men's social work focused almost exclusively on services that provided temporary work or helped men to find jobs. While dedicated to all "people," in reality these programs served mostly men. The Industrial Homes, for example, hired men to sort through the waste paper, lumber, furniture, rags, or clothing collected by the Salvage Brigades and bundle or prepare the materials for sale in Salvation Army Junk Stores. Similarly, in some cities the Salvation Army opened woodyards that compensated the men for collecting, sawing, and delivering wood.[114] In exchange for their labor, the men received room, board, and a small wage until they found regular work. As early as 1898, the National Social Secretary reported that the twenty Industrial Homes operating in the United States gave work to as many as 342 men per day. To assist these and other unemployed men to find work, the Army also opened employment bureaus.[115] The Salvation Army expected the men's industrial work not only to be self-supporting but also to generate "profits" that would assist the organization as a whole.

Salvation Army social efforts on behalf of women tended to focus on redeeming women, "waifs and strays."[116] The group's social rescue work, which began in 1887 "for the reclamation of fallen women," had, like other efforts of its kind by the turn of the century, become institutions to address the physical welfare of women and children, including maternity hospitals for poor and unwed mothers as well as children's homes.[117] Most Salvation Army women's rescue facilities operated some small "home industry," for example, an in-house laundry and/or a sewing workroom and officers often asked able-bodied women to assist with domestic chores. However, in contrast to men's institutions, Rescue Homes did not require women to work in exchange for care.[118] Furthermore, while the group hoped that the rescue work would become "self-supporting," it did not expect to make "profits" from these efforts. Financial support for women's and children's institutions came primarily from donations in cash and kind and "confinement fees" from women who could afford them.[119]

Similarly, early Slum Brigades (1889) combined pastoral and "practical" work by nursing, scrubbing, cleaning, and praying for their neighbors in city slums. By the turn of the century, however, nurseries for working mothers and the distribution of "relief" made up the bulk of Slum Brigade work.[120] Like Rescue Home work, Slum service made no effort to find or provide work for women. Only the Army's newly expanded "Slum Settlements" included work facilities like laundries, "where mothers can either bring their own washing, or do the same character of work with which to earn means to support their family . . . at a nominal sum," and sewing rooms "where mothers can bring their sewing, and earn their living under proper healthful conditions, instead of . . . mak[ing] garments in the crowded tenements."[121] Slum posts like the Rescue Homes did not try to provide paid labor for women and relied upon contributions to sustain the work.

The gendering of Salvation Army social work was not its only difference with the spiritual wing. Although the spiritual and social work of the Salvation Army shared a fundamental religious goal, the Army's own efforts to segment administration helped exclude some fundamental elements of Salvation Army religious culture from all social institutions. Moreover, the leaders' determination not to squander successful spiritual personnel on the social scheme and concerns about critics who viewed the work as a means to establish a new and powerful denomination, ensured that the group would not integrate Salvation Army religious experience and rituals into social work. In 1910 NHQ even prohibited the organization of corps in any social institution except when no other field corps was available.[122]

This is not to minimize the religious foundation of the work, nor the fact that the goal of social service was the salvation of souls. However, traditional forms of Salvation Army religious culture played little or no role in social institutions. While Salvationists often participated in six religious services per week at their local corps, social institutions reported holding only one service weekly. Moreover, religion in social institutions rarely featured boisterous services, rowdy street marches, or inventive special meetings. Indeed, one observer noted that officers expressed spirituality in women's social institutions through "the homelike relations of workers and patients, rather than through direct evangelical work." Furthermore, in men's institutions, where inmates generally stayed only briefly, opportunity for direct religious influence was even less likely. In these circumstances the best that could be hoped for was that the men would "feel the religious interest of Army personnel" rather than experience their religion firsthand.[123] Although the first slum sisters had combined evangelical methods with working-class mutuality expressed as "neighborliness," religion in Salvation Army social services at the turn of the century came to resemble the more diffuse Christianity offered by middle-class institutional churches and settlement houses.

Reinforcing their differences, social officers developed their own rituals and symbols of membership. Female social officers, for example, wore uniforms in the field that distinguished them from spiritual officers. Women attached to hospitals or health facilities dressed in white like nurses, while those in the slum service wore work clothes adopted originally by the Slum Sisters in the late 1880s. Although the men's social workers did not wear distinctive uniforms, they met annually in their own social service councils; received a book of "Special Orders" filled with Army policy and information specific to men's social service; and published their own separate departmental paper, *The Octogram*, to "inform those working in different sections of the department of the activities of the comrades in other sections."[124]

Beginning in 1896, the Booth-Tuckers' implementation of the social scheme in the United States opened fissures between the Salvation Army's social and spiritual branches of Christian service. Their administration, which began with the death of their infant son, ended in October 1903 with another tragedy. As it passed through Missouri on its way to Chicago, a train carrying the consul "ran into an open switch," tearing off the last three cars and sending them crashing "into a steel water tower." Emma Booth-Tucker died as a result of the accident, leaving behind her husband and seven children under the age of thirteen. Her death was widely reported in the press, and funeral services in both Chicago and New York drew thousands of mourners. Although he tried to continue leading the American forces on his own, by November 1904 General Booth permitted Frederick St. George de Lautour Booth-Tucker to return with his family to Britain.[125]

Continuing a policy of nepotism that led some Salvationists to refer to the Army as "family property," William Booth appointed his fourth daughter, Evangeline Booth, national commander of the Salvation Army in the United States.[126] Evangeline had filled a variety of offices and exercised considerable personal autonomy in the Salvation Army. One historian of the movement commented that while still quite young, she "was placed in positions of authority over thousands, in which she was responsible to no one save God and her father (who usually left her to the Former)." At times her father and brother Bramwell had sent her out as their representative to quell rebellions against International Headquarters' authority that broke out periodically around the globe. In London she had also operated a training garrison and served as "Field Commissioner"; between 1896 and 1904 she held the office of national commander in Canada. After her sister Emma's death and the subsequent departure of Frederick Booth-Tucker, her father appointed Evangeline commander over the Salvation Army forces in the United States.[127]

Evangeline Booth moved quickly to consolidate her power base in this country. In spite of the authority her father bestowed upon her, she initially had to contend with a problematic change in the American administrative structure. Dividing the United States at Chicago, the general created a territorial position to administer the western half of the country, leaving Evangeline Booth in charge of the East as well as national policies. Army historians suggest that William Booth decided that the unmarried Evangeline Booth needed an administrative, albeit junior, partner to help her run Army operations in the United States. I would argue, however, a more likely reason lay in William Booth's longtime desire to suppress national identity in the Salvation Army; indeed, by 1914 the organization in the United States was the organization's only remaining national unit.[128] It is a testament to Evangeline Booth's strength that after a period of confusion over the extent of the western territorial commander's authority, she managed to gain thorough control over the entire American organization.[129]

Evangeline Booth, remembered as imperious, condescending, vain, impetuous, and emotional, was a thoroughly effective leader. She surrounded herself with trusted supporters, many of whom she worked with in Canada and London. At the same time, Commander Booth used her considerable flair for the dramatic to promote the Army's work and raise contributions from wealthy evangelical gentlemen like John Wanamaker. Over the course of her thirty-year administration (1904–1934), she built upon the foundation laid by her sister, expanding work that was religiously inspired but not directly evangelical in nature. In the aftermath of

Portrait of Evangeline Booth, National Commander of the United States, 1904–1934. (Courtesy of the Salvation Army National Archives)

the 1906 San Francisco Earthquake and Fire, for example, she launched an Emergency Relief Work for the victims of the disaster. With the United States' entry into World War I, the Salvation Army inaugurated its "war service." On the home front the Army opened hostels near military bases that offered canteens as well as writing, reading, and meeting rooms. Then in August 1917 the Salvation Army, along with agencies like the Red Cross and the YMCA, sent eleven officers, seven men and four women, to France with orders to "mother," as opposed to save the souls of, the troops. In France the Salvationists distributed toilet articles, writing materials and, especially, doughnuts to soldiers. The Army developed a reputation for being the enlisted men's friend because they distributed the supplies for free or gave credit to those who could not pay. The Salvation Army Doughnut Girl became a popular symbol of this ministry that made an important contribution to its public relations in the early twentieth century.[130]

Riding the wave of popularity generated by its emergency relief and war work, in 1919 the Army inaugurated a huge drive to secure financing for its social programs. The successful Home Service Campaign allowed the Salvation Army to limit fund-raising for this work to once a year. In contrast, local corps, the heart of the Army's purely religious mission, continued to face membership and money problems. The Army organized the Home League hoping to increase the participation of families in its religious activities. At the same time Evangeline Booth tried to generate religious enthusiasm within the organization by instituting yearly revivals like "The Siege," beginning in 1905. In spite of these efforts, there is no evidence that the Salvation Army's membership made any significant gains. Moreover, after the war many corps, unable to sustain themselves on the contributions of their soldiers, grew increasingly dependent upon support from the annual Community Chest to stay afloat.[131]

The implementation of William Booth's social scheme profoundly affected the Salvation Army in the United States. First, the widespread promotion and expansion of its social program changed the fundamental identity of the organization in the public's mind from a working-class urban revivalist organization to a social service agency. Centralization of the bureaucracy shifted power upward although Salvationists still struggled to maintain some individual and local autonomy. Meanwhile, internal divisions developed which increasingly separated Salvationists engaged in spiritual work from those performing social service. As we will see in chapter 5, in the early twentieth century the spiritual wing of the Salvation Army would have to adjust to these and other changed circumstances.

Although William Booth insisted that he wielded autocratic control over all aspects of organizational life from ownership of Army property to regulations regarding marriage, officers and soldiers at all levels in the United States exercised considerable autonomy. From Major Moore's fateful decision to incorporate Army holdings in 1884 to soldiers who disciplined their captains by withholding their support, lines of authority in the Salvation Army were never as clear as William Booth imagined.

Indeed, in the Army's first two decades in the United States, the disjuncture between the general's imagined authority and the demands of operating in the American religious marketplace exploded into divisive confrontations during the administrations of both Thomas E. Moore and Ballington Booth. By the 1920s, however, the myth of hierarchical authority more closely resembled reality in the Salvation Army. One study of the group's administration in the United States concluded, all "practical power is in the Commander." Under the leadership of Evangeline Booth the tension between centralized authority and autonomy had been resolved in favor of national authority; individual corps and officers no longer easily operated autonomously.[132]

Only the power struggle between national and international headquarters remained unresolved. That contest would precipitate a dramatic change of leadership at IHQ in 1929 and erode the power of the general's office. Ironically, the outcome also facilitated decentralization in the United States and left the authority of national headquarters irreparably weakened. In their efforts to prevent Bramwell Booth from wielding the autocratic power his father had always claimed to enjoy, Salvation Army "reformers" wrote a final chapter in the group's historic tension between democracy and autocracy.

After 1896 relations between Britain and the United States settled into a relative peace; William Booth apparently trusted his daughters Emma and Evangeline a great deal more than his son Ballington. Moreover, in contrast to Ballington, Evangeline seems to have been particularly effective in persuading her father to overrule orders issued by his second in command, her brother Bramwell Booth. On one occasion, for example, someone gave Evangeline an automobile as a gift. She asked Bramwell for permission to keep it but he refused. Undeterred, Evangeline Booth appealed directly to her father. In response to her argument that "she was tired of being a straphanger," Booth reportedly replied, " 'Accept it and don't break your neck.' "[133]

Eight years after Evangeline became national commander, General William Booth, eighty-three, was "promoted to glory." As provided in the Deed Poll of 1878, the elder Booth selected his successor, Bramwell, as the organization's second general. With her father no longer alive to intervene on her behalf, relations between the new general and his sister Evangeline quickly deteriorated, exacerbating long simmering hostilities between Britain and the United States.

General Bramwell Booth spent more than thirty years of his life in his father's shadow serving as chief administrative officer. As chief of the staff, the eldest Booth sibling handled the bureaucratic operations of the international organization leaving his father free to do what he did best, preach to the masses and inspire the troops. In stark contrast to his father's blood-and-fire preaching and his sister's penchant for drama, however, many people found Bramwell's performances "lackluster." Moreover, unlike his charismatic sibling, "Bramwell was deaf and wore a wobbly pair of pince-nez, which made him appear fussy and uncertain."[134]

While not a strong speaker, the new general was "a thoroughgoing bureaucrat" whom "Ballington had called . . . a 'systems man.'" Even after his ascension to the generalship, Bramwell continued to exercise his authority over daily organizational details. During a 1926 tour of Salvation Army territories around the world, for example, letters to his administrative officer revealed Bramwell Booth's inclination to micromanagement. The nearly daily correspondence reveals the new general's preoccupation with details. Topics in the letters ranged from the height of the king's bust at Mile End Waste (relative to William Booth's), the size of the eagle on the American version of the Salvation Army crest, to the disinclination of Japanese Salvationists to encourage converts through home visits.[135]

Bramwell apparently looked forward to asserting unrestrained international control over the Army, particularly in the United States. Unfortunately, his authoritarian inclinations placed him on a collision course with his sister's desire to maintain her own power as well as the autonomy of the Salvation Army in this country. Bramwell and Evangeline had not always been at odds; early letters reveal a close and loving relationship. In a very expressive letter written in 1888, Bramwell said, "My darling Eva. . . . It seems so sad that I cannot SEE you. . . . Are you soon coming home? . . . I really truly specially personally want to have an hours chat with you and a smal[?] kiss and a look into your dear dark eyes."[136] Evangeline also served as an important ally during the uproar over Ballington Booth's resignation when she rushed to the United States to try and preserve the loyalty of the rank and file.[137]

By the 1920s, however, Bramwell and Evangeline had become locked in mortal combat; like his father before him, Bramwell sought, in the long term, to dismantle the United States as a distinct national unit. The end of World War I provided Bramwell with his first opportunity to make such changes beginning with the establishment of a third territory headquartered in San Francisco. Then, according to a September 1922 article in the *New York World*, the general not only planned to remove his sister from her command in the United States but also intended to eliminate the office of national commander altogether. The United States as a national unit would finally be eradicated, leaving all three territorial commanders reporting directly to General Bramwell Booth at IHQ.[138]

By this time Evangeline had served as commander of the United States forces for sixteen years, making her transfer reasonable enough. The American public, however, which had come to identify Evangeline with the Army and the Army with its very popular social service, emergency relief, and war work, protested vigorously. Organizations like the Benevolent Order of Elks as well as prominent figures, including Herbert Hoover, Thomas R. Marshall, William G. McAdoo, Bishop Manning, and Rabbi Silverman, cabled their protests to Britain.[139] Undoubtedly, Bramwell feared that if he forced the commander's hand she might resign, threaten a schism, or use American newspapers to incite a new public backlash against British autocracy and imperialism.[140] In the face of such pressure the general backed down, telling the *World* in December, "I have had no thought of an immediate farewell."[141]

While his effort to transfer the commander proved unsuccessful, between 1920 and 1924 Bramwell issued orders designed to limit her authority. In addition to the creation of a third territory, the general restricted Evangeline's power to award promotions beyond the rank of staff-captain and/or mid-level management in the territories. He may have taken these steps in an effort to undermine Evangeline's ability to consolidate her power by rewarding her supporters. High-ranking appointments would have to be approved by the general himself. At the same time, however, his inability to successfully oust Evangeline from office "represented a disintegration of the absolute power wielded by William Booth as General."[142]

In the aftermath of their confrontation, Bramwell and Evangeline repeatedly wrestled for power. Not unlike soldiers and officers in the American field who resisted centralization, the commander, when not simply ignoring her brother's orders, apparently contested many of the promotions that he planned. In a letter to his chief of the staff, a frustrated Bramwell said, "We have a telegram from Mapp saying that Eva says she cannot possibly accept McMillan for the States! . . . I have telegraphed him to remember that she objected to Damon, to Sowton and at first very strongly to Rich. . . . I must confess that I do not think that the objection to McMillan . . . is dictated by any genuine desire for the work. It is simply that she wishes to be in opposition and delay and hinder what we do."[143]

In addition to the personal struggle for power between the Booth siblings, the growing importance of social work in the United States also exacerbated tensions between IHQ and NHQ. In contrast to his father, Bramwell Booth had never supported solutions that emphasized amelioration of material conditions. Indeed, he told his father in 1903 that he was "puzzled . . . with respect to our relations with the poor" because he supported more traditional evangelical solutions to privation. Indeed, in 1926 he supported an officer to command the Central Territory in the United States because, said Booth, "I believe he sincerely desires the Army, as we want it, and to get rid of this everlasting charity business."[144] Evangeline like her father, however, recognized that the social work provided the group with legitimacy and public support. Moreover, its fundraising mechanism, the Home Service fund, "made the United States Army the richest and most powerful in the world."[145] From the commander's perspective, American contributions were far too important to the economy and prestige of the Salvation Army to even consider reducing or ending social service work.

Bramwell's inability to comprehend the importance of social work to the Salvation Army in the United States reflected not only his own preference for spiritual solutions but also distinctions in the development of the welfare state in Britain and the United States. Recent research characterized the Salvation Army's social service as an example of the "new philanthropy" which, in the late nineteenth century, sought to "reorganize charity, rather than replace it altogether with state aid" and represented a transitional stage between Christian charity and the welfare state. As a nation's welfare state unfolded, however, "the social services of the . . . churches appear[ed] redundant." In Britain, where IHQ was located, social welfare legislation came much earlier than it did to the United States. England had, by 1911, established a system of social insurance including old-age pensions and workers compensation. By the end of World War II, "British social provision attempted to blend public assistance, social services, and social insurance into a seamless national system of basic protections, creating a uniform floor of protection for all citizens."[146] In contrast, American social provision came more slowly and was never as complete; social security was not even established until 1935. Not fully comprehending these basic differences between the United States and Britain, Bramwell Booth failed to grasp the significance of the "everlasting charity work" in this country. While the growth of the welfare state enabled the Salvation Army in Britain to deemphasize its social welfare work and reemphasize its working-class religious and temperance role, in the American *semi*-welfare state the Army's social and emergency rescue work continue to serve an important public function.[147]

The power struggle between Bramwell and Evangeline energized a reform movement fueled, in part, by smoldering hostilities among American career officers. In March 1925 the conflict began to heat up with the worldwide distribution of an unsigned declaration titled "Manifesto No. 1." This document, and others that followed it over the next several years, inventoried grievances against Bramwell Booth. These included the general's self-serving and autocratic leadership, nepotism (in relation to his children), retaliation against critics ("The General's Freezer"), and his sanction of a biography (referred to as a "bliography — Bios for life and Lios for lies"), which contained some criticisms of his father, his advocacy of evolutionism, his treatment of Evangeline Booth, and the appointment of foreign-born Salvationists to top posts in the United States. These documents demanded democratic reforms to establish, "representative government, autonomy for all self-supporting countries and a joint body for the administration of the Army generally, with the power of appointing successive Generals."[148]

In 1929 the crisis came to a head as Evangeline Booth and the reformers utilized a 1904 amendment to the first Deed Poll to remove an ailing Bramwell Booth from office. The 1904 "supplement" provided that a "High Council," consisting of "the Chief of the Staff, the Secretary for Foreign Affairs, all commissioners not on the retired list, and all officers holding territorial commands regardless of rank," could "remove from office a General judged 'unfit' and elect a successor."[149] By February 1929 the council officially deposed General Bramwell Booth and elected, in his place, not Evangeline Booth, but rather Edward J. Higgins, the former general's chief of the staff. Commander Evangeline apparently misjudged her own popularity. In June, Bramwell Booth died.[150]

The following year General Higgins called a Commissioners' Conference to finally address organizational reforms. The conference strengthened democracy and weakened the authority of the general by allowing the High Council to elect his/her successor. Furthermore, rather than allowing the general to serve as sole trustee of Salvation Army property in England and northern Ireland, a board, not unlike that in the United States, now played that role.[151] Then in 1934 General Higgins voluntarily retired and Evangeline Booth finally achieved what some believed was her primary objective in her support of democratic reform; after five ballots she received the two-thirds vote required to be elected general of the Salvation Army.

Ironically, upon stepping into the now weakened generalship that she helped to create, Evangeline Booth attempted to restore the power of the office at the expense of the National Commander in the United States. While she served in this country she fought tirelessly for American autonomy and the supreme authority of the national commander. As general, however, she accomplished exactly what her brother had tried to do; she gutted the position of national commander and decentralized the American command by making the territories virtually autonomous answering only to IHQ. Indeed, the position of national commander never recovered its stature after she became general. The Army left the position vacant for nine years, and one year after it was restored the organization decided to "rotate the office . . . among the four territorial commanders — each holding the office for a year."[152]

The epic struggle between the center and the periphery plagued the Army since it first came to the United States and intensified after the death of William Booth in 1912. Personified by the battle between Evangeline and Bramwell Booth, the power struggle ultimately eroded the authority of *both* international and national headquarters. Today both the positions of general and national commander are largely ceremonial and spiritual. In contrast to William Booth, who served until his death at eighty-two, each leader serves a five-year term and may only hold office until reaching the mandatory retirement age of sixty-five. Furthermore, every territory associated with the Worldwide Salvation Army operates almost autonomously with the greatest authority in the hands of the individual Territorial Commanders. The battle between autocracy and democracy resolved itself in a model that gave territorial units autonomy and provided that high-ranking officers would participate in the democratic election of the organization's top leader.

CHAPTER FIVE

SALVATIONISM AT THE TURN OF THE CENTURY

Refining Religious Culture,
Reconceiving a Religious Market

Formalism will leave your house cold and freezing; fanaticism will burn your house down. — WILLIAM LOGAN BRENGLE, *Portrait of a Prophet*

B y the turn of the century the curriculum at the Men's Training Garrison included techniques for conducting open-air meetings. "First, light the torch. Get the chair in position. Someone mounts the chair and lines out the first verse of a salvation song, in which all join in singing." After the closing of prayers one after another, "someone climbs up on the chair and either sings or speaks." During a brief pause in the solo, "the flag is stretched out" and a pitch made for contributions. Over the next hour as the singing continues, soldiers, "go out among the crowd with a tambourine and from time to time throw that they have collected on the flag." At the end of the meeting, "a pointed, pungent, earnest appeal is made to the unsaved to get right with God at once."[1]

Fifty years later, Lt. Col. Lyell Rader wrote a small book called *Rediscovering the Open-Air Meeting: A Manual for Salvationist Soul Winning.* His book provided a basic primer on open-air evangelism. Like the script provided for the cadets, Rader's handbook described in great detail all the elements of successful open-air meetings. Testimonies, he said, should be sincere, delivered in a "natural" voice, and "brief." They should describe "[t]he B.C. or Before Christ Life. . . . The R.C. or Receive Christ experience. . . . The L.C. or Living Christ experience." Music at open-airs must be familiar or have a simple, easily learned chorus, and songs must not be "super-sentimental" but rather "virile." Bands must be "tuneful" and all-female "timbrel brigades" well rehearsed. The book even provided detailed instructions for "the physical setup" of a street meeting. The "open-air team" wrote Rader, "should form a ring," not a crescent. Organizers should provide a platform, light, and amplification for the speakers, and literature ought to be provided but tracts not "dump[ed]" on the crowd.[2]

As we have seen, implementation of the social scheme contributed to the transformation of the Salvation Army by the turn of the century. Administrative reorganization discouraged democracy and local autonomy, and the new mission of temporal salvation segmented the group in separate and at times contentious social and spiritual wings. It should not be surprising, then, that during the first half of the twentieth century the Salvation Army's religious culture also changed in significant ways. As the training-school curriculum demonstrates, at the beginning of the century the Army started to ritualize its expressive and spontaneous street meetings by institutionalizing them and creating carefully scripted performances. By mid-century even these ritualized exhibitions disappeared. Salvationists had largely abandoned their "open-air heritage" and no longer performed their spirituality in the streets.[3] Significantly, even Salvationists like Lt. Colonel Rader, who encouraged a renaissance of religious street performance, could imagine only a highly controlled version of the spontaneous and expressive camp-meeting-style demonstrations of the late nineteenth century.

The urban landscape of which the Salvation Army had become a part changed radically during the nineteenth century. Industrialization, urbanization, and immigration transformed the nature of city life, making it more diverse and culturally confusing. Alarmed by, but also attracted to, all that was new and exciting in the cities, urban elites and the emerging middle class sought to limit or gain some control over urban cultural life. "Culture," according to Lawrence Levine, became "one of the mechanisms that made it possible to identify, distinguish, and order this new universe of strangers." Their strategies included separating themselves, imposing their own rules of behavior as well as standards of taste, and encouraging everyone else to accept their cultural preferences.[4]

These tactics served both to segment American culture and to renovate popular culture. The self-appointed cultural leadership isolated transgressive cultural forms that resisted refinement, setting them aside for an exclusively male working-class audience (e.g., burlesque, striptease), while they placed "purified" or sacralized forms of culture (e.g., opera, Shakespeare) in environments where prices and dress requirements excluded all but the most "respectable." Meanwhile, canny entrepreneurs, who imposed limits on both performances and audiences, presented variety acts and films now cleansed of any sexual innuendo and bawdy humor in elegant commercial theaters where middle-class men and women could safely join well-behaved members of the working class.[5]

John Kasson suggests that "the segmentation of society was mirrored by a segmentation of self." The spread of gentility, he argues, created new demands for physical and emotional control. According to this standard, physical behavior (in public as well as private) must be guided, above all, by an effort to remain inconspicuous. As a consequence, "civilized" men and women exerted "strict bodily control" over their walking ("neither hurrying nor sauntering"), "organic processes" (sneezing, coughing, throat clearing, eating, etc.), and "irrepressible noisemaking" (singing, humming, whistling). Similarly, genteel men and women exerted control over all displays of emotion from anger to joy. Resisting these standards of public and private behavior, according to Kasson, created a dilemma for the working classes. Failure to observe the conventions "meant to stigmatize themselves as 'uncivilized' boors unfit to associate with respectable" people, while "[t]o behave themselves meant to accede to their own marginalization."[6]

In the face of a changing public and private cultural landscape, the Salvation Army confronted two choices: embrace its adaptations of rowdy working-class leisure culture and accept outsider status, or refashion its cultural practices and avoid segmentation. In its first two decades in the United States, Salvationists largely rejected cultural refinement. The organization identified itself as a working-class form of religion and defended its rowdy, boisterous, and physically expressive religious culture as both sanctified by God and critical to successfully advertising salvation to the "heathen masses." In the face of pressures to conform to middle-class standards of genteel behavior, the Army argued that its "methods" were essential to reaching its target audience. Wrote one supporter, Salvationists "reach a class of debased, depraved, and sinful men and women, who are attracted by the novelty." And although Salvationists may be "uncouth, noisy, and disagreeable . . . by these very means [they] reach a mass of people which you cannot approach."[7] By 1887 Maud and Ballington Booth sought to balance Salvationists' use of boisterous working-class popular culture for religious purposes with their personal gentility as leaders. New York society embraced the charming young couple as Maud apologized for but still defended the "startling means" they were "necessarily forced to use . . . in order to reach the masses."[8]

Beginning in the late 1890s, a faction within the Army that had been uneasy with expressive religious culture gained new allies from among administrators interested in expanding the social work. In addition, a second generation that no longer needed the alternative world provided by the Army and who were less willing to accept outsider status joined these Salvationists. As a result of their efforts, Salvationism evolved from a camp-meeting-style religion, using the vernacular of urban working-class leisure culture, to a much more decorous religion that combined carefully scripted or choreographed Salvationist rituals, judicious uses of the emerging technologies of middle-class commercial culture, the "refinement of spectacle," and restraint of the audience.[9]

The forces that changed the Army's religious culture at the turn of the century also profoundly affected the Salvation Army's relationship to the American religious marketplace. When experiential and performative religion declined as a means to advertise salvation, the Army's web of Christian social services increasingly supplanted direct evangelical work with the masses. Not all Salvationists supported these transformations, and many veterans expressed their discontent by resigning. Alarmed by the losses, American leaders sought to maintain and cultivate the loyalty of existing Salvationist families. Inadvertently, this decision caused the Army to reconceptualize its market so that by the early twentieth century most of the Army's directly spiritual work targeted already converted Salvation Army soldiers, officers, and their children instead of the unconverted heathen masses.

During the early twentieth century the Salvation Army ceased to be a working-class-dominated religious organization devoted to advertising salvation to others like themselves with lively and boisterous expressions of spirituality. Instead, the organization served an increasingly segmented constituency; its social institutions offered temporal salvation to the poor while its spiritual work ministered to upwardly mobile second and third generations of previously working-class Salvationist families. In contrast to the blood-washed warriors of the nineteenth century, Salvationists in the twentieth century generally regarded themselves as members of a church that sponsored professionalized Christian social services to the downtrodden.

Although the organization's leaders officially defended the group's "methods" against critics, from the beginning a few college-educated Salvationists sought to curb demonstrative, experiential religion, arguing that it concealed a superficial spirituality. Until the late 1890s, however, these men and women found themselves unsuccessful either in convincing the rank and file or in gaining the support of leadership. Not only did the group's concept of corporate holiness sacralize Salvationism's urban camp-meeting style, but also the level of local autonomy and democracy in the group made their task nearly impossible.[10] The only concession that the Salvation Army made to those seeking a less expressive religious culture was the creation of auxiliaries. As an auxiliary member, one could support the goals of the Salvation Army without participating in its religious performances.[11]

By the turn of the century, Salvationists who opposed the Army's expressive religious culture and rowdy public performances began to gain new allies among social-wing administrators. At this time Emma and Frederick Booth-Tucker began to promote the "social scheme" as an alternative means to advertise salvation to the poor and worked assiduously to make allies who could facilitate the implementation of the Army's plans.[12] The Booth-Tuckers not only believed that the social work needed outside resources to successfully expand but also that the programs offered an unprecedented opportunity to raise the entire organization in public esteem.[13] The social work champions soon realized, however, that in a world that enshrined gentility as a standard for public and private behavior, the organization could no longer afford to foster its own marginalization if it meant to achieve its goals.[14] Although there is no indication that the leaders intended to transform Salvation Army religious culture, they clearly recognized the need for public legitimization in order to gain financial assistance from government and industry. As a consequence, the Booth-Tuckers and NHQ administrators took steps to improve the organization's public image by discouraging noisy, confrontational public performances while at the same time providing the public with alternative images of Salvation Army religious culture.

For many administrators, Frederick Booth-Tucker's arrest in 1897 demonstrated precisely why the Army needed to rethink its religious performances. Just one year after the Booth-Tuckers took command of the American forces, authorities in New York City arrested the commander for keeping "an ill-governed and disorderly house." Neighbors of Salvation Army Headquarters complained that on April 13, 1897, the group held a noisy all-night meeting that ran from 8:00 P.M. Tuesday to around 5:00 A.M. the following morning. Prosecution testimony revealed public perceptions that the organization encouraged blatant violations of genteel behavioral standards and highlighted the importance of providing a different picture of Salvation Army religious practice. Defense testimony demonstrated a critical shift in the group's traditional justification of its "methods." Salvationists did not defend "uncouth, noisy, and disagreeable" services but rather provided an alternative account of the nature of the group's religious performances.

The trial began in May 1897. Twelve of the prosecution's thirteen witnesses lived on West Thirteenth Street within 125 feet of the Salvation Army Headquarters on West Fourteenth Street.[15] The People tried to demonstrate that the Army's noisy meetings threatened the peace as well as the property values of what apparently had become a fairly respectable middle-class neighborhood.[16] Nearly all of the landlords testified that over the years the noise generated by Salvation Army services cost them money and/or tenants. "I have had to lower rents in order to keep the tenants in the house," said Mrs. Ahearn. The noise, testified Miss Julia Meade, has injured "my comfort and repose and my business and pocket book in every respect." Her tenants, she said, "come down to breakfast cross and disagreeable, and they say we couldn't sleep last night there was so much noise . . . and they say, 'Miss Meade, what are you going to do about it?'" One family to whom she rented rooms packed up and left after only one month. Another landlord testified that his tenants had "simply moved out. They couldn't stand the noise."[17] Furthermore, a tenant, George Hayes, testified that if he asked friends over for an evening visit, "I am compelled to leave my own rooms and go somewhere else, so that we can pursue our conversation." He went on to complain that "these all-night sessions, they keep me awake."[18]

Two prosecution witnesses, Phineas Smith and Robert Foote, provide a particularly vivid glimpse into negative public opinion about Salvation Army members and their religious performances at the turn of the century. Both men heard the Salvation Army from their homes and went into the hall to observe the proceedings. Said Foote, "I have been [in the hall] the same as I would go to a dime museum, to see the curiosities." Both men expressed shock at Salvationists' violations of genteel injunctions "to remain publicly as inconspicuous as possible."[19] They repeatedly emphasized that the Salvationists and their "rough looking audience" made loud noises by stamping feet, clapping hands, yelling, shouting, beating drums, and playing brass instruments like coronets, trombones, and "shrieking concertinas." Smith was particularly offended by the singing of songs which he considered "vulgar for a church organization" and went on to say that it would be pleasant to hear the Salvation Army sing and pray "if they would only do so at reasonable hours and sing nicely."[20]

Foote seemed most disturbed by the Salvationists' lack of physical and emotional control that manifested itself in extreme expressions of religious feeling that spread from one person to another like a contagion. At various points in his testimony he characterized the Salvationists' verbal exclamations as "hysteric yells of the suddenly overcome," "unearthly yells," and "Comanche Indian yells." He found these voices even more alarming when combined with physical action, "when the first man collapses, perhaps another gets up, and then he goes on for from one to three minutes, and then he collapses, and then that is interlarded with shouts from two or three hundred of the faithful there; the big bass drum gets abanging . . . and then the next man jumps up and that lasts two or three hours." Finally, even the uniforms worn by Salvationists offended Foote's sensibilities. He seems to have felt that Salvationists tried to legitimate their behavior by wearing costumes that resembled Union Army uniforms. He claimed to have said to one officer, "[Y]ou are here with General Grant's uniform on, four stars. There is a law against that too."[21]

A. Oakley Hall, former mayor of New York City and member of the infamous Tweed Ring, served as counsel for the defense.[22] In his opening statement Hall avoided the organization's traditional justification of its methods. Instead, the attorney suggested that whatever sounds the group made must be understood both within their urban context and as a historically legitimate style of worship. Since New York was "a city of noises," argued Hall, any sounds made by the group should be regarded as the "common noise of give and take" characteristic of urban areas. He went on to compare Salvationist services to "the old Mosaic Hebrew style of worship," the "great revivals of 1835, 1836, and 1837," and the more recent work of respected revivalist Dwight Moody.[23]

Hall's second, and more important strategy not only characterized the prosecution testimony as questionable but also argued that it completely misrepresented the character of Salvation Army religious services. To undermine the credibility of the opposition's witnesses, the attorney suggested that they, and not the Salvationists, failed to control their emotions and allowed feelings of ill will to taint their testimony. Targeting Phineas Smith particularly, Hall accused him of failing to control his feelings and lying on the stand. Said Hall, "[t]here is a lie of an hour on the part of Phineas Smith . . . for when men get excited . . . they are apt to magnify, and apt to testify from emotion, and not from judgment, which is the proper mode of testifying."[24]

Furthermore, in contrast to the residents of West Thirteenth Street, whom he characterized as a "coterie" giving "bastard descriptions" of events, Hall argued that the very respectable Salvation Army witnesses would provide the jury with "mental photographs" of the meetings.[25] According to Hall the defendant, Frederick St. George de Lautour Booth-Tucker, had impeccable credentials, being a man "of high family name . . . a name great in the annals of Virginia."[26] The lawyer also claimed that during Booth-Tucker's time in India, as a member of the Civil Service he became a judge. Said Hall, "if I call him hereafter inadvertently, 'Judge', you will know what I mean by that." Finally, the lawyer made it clear that in India, Booth-Tucker had been a man of means having, earned "a salary . . . of seven thousand five hundred dollars a year for life."[27]

Hall called four women and nine men to testify for the defense. Interestingly, only six of them actually belonged to the Salvation Army; two were auxiliary members who, along with five others, attended auxiliary meetings sporadically. None of the witnesses represented the Army's rank and file; among the six Salvationists, three held very high rank while the others held positions of lesser but still significant responsibility.[28] The non-Salvationists included a bank president, a "medical professional," two clergymen, a former lawyer, and a Women's Christian Temperance Union member. Seven witnesses (five of them Salvation Army members) had actually attended the April gathering and so testified about that specific meeting; the court permitted the remaining six witnesses to describe meetings they had attended since January 1897.

The "mental photographs" provided by defense witnesses represented Salvation Army religious performance in terms radically different from the prosecution. While the People portrayed the meetings as noisy and out-of-control physically and emotionally, each Salvation Army witness suggested that order, self-control, and decorum characterized the gatherings. Frederick Booth-Tucker's testimony emphasized that he exercised considerable control over services. "I generally conduct my meetings with my watch in my hand," he said, "and I divide up the meeting into certain sections." While large numbers of Salvationists participated in the meetings, he went on, "there is always an officer in charge who regulates." Far from chaotic, "[o]ne [person] speaks at a time. There may be five or six speakers, and there may be two or three singers, and then there are two or three who will lead in prayer, each separately and in order. But there is always an officer in charge, who is responsible for the conduct of the meeting."[29]

In addition to being orderly, the testimony of Brigadier Alice Lewis, Consul Emma Booth-Tucker's private secretary, suggested that the Salvation Army service in April was quite decorous.[30] Lewis claimed to be "practically the leader of the music . . . that night . . . and so . . . quite au fait with the musical arrangements of that all night of prayer." When asked if there had been yelling that night, she replied "no." Stressing her own credentials as a genteel woman, she went on to explain, "I have been brought up to be an operatic singer, and my musical ear is so trained that I could not stand any yelling, and my voice has been so carefully trained that I would have to leave the hall if there were yelling."[31]

In spite of Oakley Hall's best efforts, the jury found Frederick Booth-Tucker guilty of keeping a public nuisance.[32] In his public response, the commander again failed to cite the Army's traditional justification of its boisterous methods. Instead, in a statement to the press, Booth-Tucker characterized the verdict as a threat against "religious liberty" and argued that the decision favored the upper crust because it barred working men from meeting to pray during precisely the same hours in which rich men danced the night away.[33]

Although we have no way of knowing exactly what went on at the all-night of prayer in April 1897, the trial provides important insight into the Salvation Army's representation of its membership and religious culture by the late 1890s. Not only did they decide to ask dignified officers and respectable auxiliary members to testify at the trial, but they also chose not to defend the group's traditional use of rowdy and boisterous methods. Instead, each of the witnesses suggested that while Salvationism was spiritually powerful it was also orderly, dignified, devotional, and decorous. I would argue that the Army's defense at the 1897 trial represented a desire to reject segmentation, to put a new, more refined face on Salvation Army religious performances, to inform the public, and, perhaps, to educate its own rank-and-file members.

While social-work advocates and the Salvation Army's top leadership began to put a more dignified face on Salvation Army public religious performances, different attitudes toward open-airs began forming among rank-and-file officers and soldiers. Throughout the late nineteenth century, Salvationists argued that open-air marches provided the most effective means to advertise salvation to working-class men and women. Indeed, local officers suggested that the survival of the Army's spiritual work depended on open-airs as a means to save souls, attract an audience, and collect money. As one captain argued, "If we can't have open airs then you just as well close this business up, for officers can't even live. The weather is getting so now, the people stay on the st. [street] and don't come to our building around in a back court, so if we can't go to them then we can't stay here."[34]

Given the centrality of open-air work to the survival of local corps, officers persisted in using the streets even when they risked arrest. Indeed, until the turn of the century, Salvationists regarded being confined as a "jailbird for Jesus" a meaningful and heroic form of public religious performance.[35] All around the country the Army's "blood washed warriors" adroitly turned arrest and incarceration into a sequel to their street demonstrations. In 1885, for example, a police officer apprehended Lt. Lizzie Franks and her squad of twenty-one hardy Salvation Army soldiers as they marched through the streets of Portland, Maine. Without missing a beat, Franks ordered the soldiers to "keep in rank" and led the troops, single file, into the police station, where they "marched around a long table . . . stopped and . . . went on [their] knees and gave praise to God" before twenty-five startled police officers. Even after authorities confined the men in cells and the women in the lodging room, *The Portland Press* reported that "[t]he members of the Army . . . spent the evening singing their songs and praying fervently."[36]

Faced with fines ranging from five to twenty-five dollars, officers like "Jail-Bird Smith" often refused to pay, electing, instead, to go to jail.[37] In recognition of their sacrifices, the Salvation Army hailed these men and women as "Our Jail Birds! for Christ's Sake and the Gospel's." Indeed, one edition of *The War Cry* in 1889 devoted its entire front cover to these heroes with a drawing of a jail cell surrounded by small portraits of the men and women "Imprisoned for Jesus" with shackles decorating the upper left and right corners of the page.[38]

Although field officers continued to believe in the centrality of the open-air, by the turn of the century most felt unwilling either to make the Christian sacrifice of arrest and confinement like "Jail-Bird Smith" or, like Lizzie Franks, to turn these occasions into another religious performance. Instead, field officers increasingly insisted that as Americans they had the *right* to hold open-air demonstrations unmolested. After local authorities in Schenectady threatened to arrest him, for example, one captain wrote, "I feel the injustice of this business and I do not feel prepared to put up with such nonsense."[39] Said another officer, "I want my rights that is all." From Pen Yan, New York, to Hutchinson, Kansas, officers wrote indignantly to the Army's Legal Department asking for assistance in protecting the open-air work and fighting "this compromise of our Constitutional rights."[40]

On one hand, the decision of local officers to seek support from NHQ suggests that the Booth-Tuckers successfully centralized authority in the Salvation Army at the turn of the century. At the same time, however, it demonstrates that Salvationists expected something in return, in this case legal and financial support to fight for their rights as American

Open-air meeting, Guthrie, Oklahoma, 1897.
(Courtesy of the Salvation Army National Archives)

citizens to march in the streets. In 1898, "village trustees" threatened to arrest Captain Harrington of Potsdam, New York, if he continued to play music in the street. The captain asked his superior, "shall I take my drum on the street[?] . . . Please answer immediately." Staff-Captain Madison Ferris, head of the Salvation Army's newly created Legal Department, advised Harrington's superior officer against a confrontation. Wrote Ferris, "[T]ell him not to do anything to bring on a conflict between him and the authorities." Hoping to settle the issue "amicably," the lawyer went on to say that "[i]n all the instances that have come before me where trouble has ensued, excepting three cases, I have been able to settle them without a fight"[41]

While its leadership began to redefine appropriate public performances of religion, Salvation Army administrators promoted new levels of restraint by encouraging compromise with local authorities and discouraging use of the drum. As Ferris wrote to one local officer, "Is it really necessary that you should have a drum there. . . . Why can't you hold your open-air meetings and do away with the drum for the present?"[42] He later expressed his personal disapproval of noisy street performances to an administrative officer: "[T]here is an awful lot of indiscreet thumping on the drum, and an unnecessary pounding. . . . [T]here are times when I believe we ourselves are really at fault."[43]

Before joining the staff of the Army's Property and Legal Department in 1896, Madison J. H. Ferris had worked as an attorney for Tammeny Hall. In addition to taking charge of Salvation Army legal matters, Ferris took on private cases, advertising himself as the "Poor Man's Lawyer." Between 1908 and 1916, he became a major and served as the Salvation Army's Legal Secretary.[44] Ferris represented a growing segment of Salvationists concerned about cultivating public support for the Salvation Army who found boisterous public performances of religion counterproductive. In contrast to earlier injunctions to use the streets to "attract attention," he believed that overzealous field officers threatened community relations by seeking out confrontations. "Many of our officers," the lawyer complained, "rather court trouble to make some sort of an excitement whereby to get a crowd, and Headquarters has to stand the brunt of the conflict after all; and no real good result accrues from it, and bad feelings exist for a long while in those localities . . . indiscretion on the part of our own people, have been instrumental in making bad feelings."[45]

Reaction to the tactics of the venerable Salvation Army warrior Joe the Turk illustrates the growing gap between local officers and administrators like Ferris. Since the 1880s, Joe, with his colorful costume, electrified umbrella, drum, and coronet, had been jailed for Jesus in countless cities around the country. Every officer knew that Joe specialized in deliberately disobeying local ordinances in order to publicize violations of Salvationists' rights. When local authorities in Wilkes-Barre, Pennsylvania, refused to permit the corps to use their drums on the streets even though "wagons with drums inside advertising . . . ballgames . . . have not been molested," one ensign begged his superiors to "let me have the services of 'Joe the Turk' for a week or two[.] I'm sure he would be a great help to me and to the Army in Wilkes-Barre, and I'm sure he could settle this difficulty as he has many others."[46] Two weeks later, the officer again wrote, "i [sic] should like very much if you could arrange for 'Joe the Turk' to come: it would create some excitement and would no doubt finish up the case."[47]

By the late 1890s, however, administrators and opponents of rowdy religious street theater regarded Joe's confrontational methods as a threat to cordial relations with local authorities. Although NHQ apparently declined to send Joe, he showed up in Wilkes-Barre anyway. In response to the news that Joe had invaded the city and exacerbated the already tense situation by getting arrested while leading a street parade, one frustrated administrator wrote, "There seems no alternative now but to fight the case."[48] Ferris replied sardonically, "Yours of Oct. 21st, announcing the pleasing information that Joe had at last been able to again see the inside of a prison cell, and to be instrumental in winning to his side fourteen other victims — duly received."[49] The growing reluctance of Army leadership to characterize "Jailbirds for Jesus" as heroes may have contributed to the reluctance of local officers to accept arrest and confinement as an appropriate form of Christian sacrifice.

In addition to the long-term impact of arrests on relations with the community, cost-conscious Army bureaucrats also expressed alarm at the expense associated with appeals. Wrote one brigadier wistfully, "I almost wish they hadn't bothered with this Appeal business at all. They could have got the victory far easier by paying no fine, and going to jail in the old-fashioned way."[50] According to Ferris, each Salvation Army division faced several choices, "incur the expense of the trial and an appeal," abandon the field, or make concessions and avoid "antagoniz[ing] the officials."[51]

While persuading the public of the decorousness of the Army's religious culture and discouraging traditional forms of street performances, Emma and Frederick Booth-Tucker offered refined alternatives that adapted the forms, venues, and technologies of urban middle-class commercial culture. Rather than appearing in the streets, at the local corps hall, in a circus-like tent, or on the stage of Harry Hill's Variety Theater, the Booth-Tuckers took their extravaganzas to new more elegant theaters. These venues had been designed, not for the typical Salvation Army crowd, but for a predominantly middle-class family audience. Furthermore, instead of performances modeled on minstrel shows or spectacles that burned the devil in effigy, the leaders took a cue from vaudeville entrepreneurs and offered lavish productions cleansed of unseemly violations of gentility. For their productions, wrote Commander Booth-Tucker, "[a] suitable party was selected and carefully trained. ... Some of The Army's sweetest-voiced and most effective soloists enhanced the charm of the Lecture with their heart-moving songs. The instrumental music was planned to add its powerful appeal."[52]

Hoping to "increase [its] popularity and attract the outside crowd," the Booth-Tuckers created an elaborate performance piece consisting of a lecture, stereoptican slides, and "living tableaux, in which actual scenes from The Army's work should be depicted on the platform, and some touching stories from actual life retold." On a Sunday afternoon early in 1899, the Army inaugurated this "unique crusade for souls" at the Bijou Theater in Pittsburgh, Pennsylvania.[53] The special program, entitled *Dra-*

matic Scenes of Love and Sorrow, featured Emma Booth-Tucker, looking like an "Eastern Joan of Arc" in an Indian sari. The consul, reported one newspaper, "swayed that vast audience and carried them in imagination, now to the attic of drunken widow and the mother, and again the Army ministrations amongst the poor."[54]

As she spoke, stereoptican or lantern-slide images of "the drunkard, surrounded with all the habiliments and harrows of a drunkard's home . . . kneeling with the criminal upon the stone flooring of the prison cell . . . with the Magdalene, the would-be suicide at the waters brink," appeared on the screen.[55] Then after each series of slides, the screen rose to reveal a group of Salvationists arranged in various tableaux against a painted sheet of scenery. A scene depicting the Army's work in the slums, for example, showed "an attic room where a dying mother was leaving her two babies to a Salvationist's tender care."[56] Reported a press account of the first lecture, "The Madonna of the Slums, with her baby burden, sings her tale of sorrow. . . . Child-life in sorrow is beautifully illustrated, while the happy possibilities of the Army's efforts in this field are refreshingly and vividly portrayed. 'Home, Sweet Home,' is touchingly rendered, with cornet and piano accompaniment, while the Colonist's Cottage home, with its creeper growths and sunny surroundings, is thrown upon the canvas, and touches a chord in every heart."[57]

Evangeline Booth, over the course of her thirty-year tenure as commander of the Salvation Army, continued to perform refined spectacles in venues like the Academy of Music in Philadelphia. Her shows, "The Commander in Rags," "The Shepherd," "My Father," and "The World's Greatest Romance," included costumes, props, lantern slides, scenery, lights, music, and singing by the "Red Knights," a special Salvation Army musical group.[58]

In addition to representing Salvation Army religious practice as orderly and providing refined examples for the "outside crowd," the Booth-Tuckers called on Samuel Brengle to help deliver the message to the rank and file. Since his earliest years as a field officer, Brengle opposed physically and emotionally expressive religious performances; indeed, in the 1880s his attempts to instruct the soldiers accordingly made his tenure as a field captain so difficult that he spent most of the next decade as an administrator. In 1897, however, the Booth-Tuckers relieved him of his staff position and appointed him "National Spiritual Special . . . 'a kind of holiness evangelist to The Army.' " With their blessing, Brengle toured the United States over the next seven years, teaching the "little people," as he called them, that salvation and holiness must be achieved without "fanatacism." Emotion, he claimed, could be "a fire, warming and useful when correctly applied, but destructive and demoralizing when out of control." As a consequence, his own preaching did not "excite a fever of enthusiasm," but rather aimed "to incite to earnest heart-scrutiny . . . deep penitence and soul satisfaction." Emotional and expressive religion, he argued, led the "little people" into a shallow spiritual experience.[59]

Along with Brengle's intramural spiritual work, the Army increasingly focused energy and attention on the cultivation of its second generation. Ad hoc efforts in the 1880s and early 1890s gave way in 1898 to more organized campaigns. Regularizing the effort, the Booth-Tuckers created a separate Junior Soldier Department, with its own field secretary, and ordered that each division appoint a staff secretary to oversee the work of its junior corps.[60]

The second generation of Salvationists provided the final critical element in the transformation of Salvation Army religious culture and reconceptualization of its religious market. As I have suggested, the first generation of Salvationists re-created the frontier camp meeting in the city and gave it urban working-class cultural expression. These men and women, who shared so many characteristics with southern plain folk, created an alternative world in which they accomplished things that would otherwise have been impossible from their marginalized position in secular society. In contrast to their parents, second-generation Salvationists moved from the margins to the middle of American society. A study of the Canadian Salvation Army, for example, found that in the twentieth century growing numbers of children began to "ris[e] in social rank" and become members of the middle class. As a result, "congregations did not remain the 'poor and outcast' nor 'unchurched,'" but, rather, nearly all corps had "a distinct air of middle-class respectability."[61] Like Canadians, second-generation Salvationists in the United States became "skilled workers, craftsmen, tradesmen, or white-collar and professional people."[62] All five of Edward and Eva Parker's children, for example, completed high school and four went on to college. One son became a dentist, another a professional photographer, a third worked in his father-in-law's lumber company, and a fourth went into the insurance business. Their daughter, the only child to become a Salvation Army officer, attended Boston School of Physical Education.[63]

It is especially intriguing to note that the Army's decision to advertise salvation through social work contributed to the impulse for higher education among Salvationists and, hence, the second generation's movement into the middle class. As social work in the United States became increasingly professionalized in the early twentieth century, the Army needed to ensure that its institutions met the standards and could provide the trained personnel now demanded by the field.[64] Consequently, Social Wing leaders encouraged young officers to attend college and get the appropriate training. One officer recalled that when the Army considered "enter[ing] into work with retarded children," social officers recommended that his daughter complete a suitable master's degree at Columbia University.[65]

Second-generation Salvationists placed great value on their respectability and middle-class status. One child of Army officers clearly remembered feeling embarrassed by her connection to the organization. As she confessed, "I guess I was a little ashamed. Those were the early days when people didn't think too much of The Salvation Army."[66] As they advertised salvation, first-generation Salvationists had created the enduring impression that *all* their members were redeemed members of the "depraved classes."[67] By the early twentieth century, however, many Salvationists' children challenged that notion openly. During a street meeting in 1924, for example, a group of young cadets demonstrated their unwillingness to accept public perceptions of Salvation Army members as redeemed sinners from "the lowest classes." Frustrated by the audience's expressions of pity for the "poor Salvation Army lassies as though they had been rescued from lives of sin," the officer in charge asked all those from Christian families to step forward. "Almost without exception," reported an observer, "the group represented families which belonged either to the Salvation Army or to other religious denominations."[68]

After the turn of the century, the Salvation Army shed many features of its urban frontier camp-meeting past. Instead, Salvationism began to resemble the more respectable Methodist holiness camp meetings of the late nineteenth century. Like second-generation Salvationists, many late-nineteenth-century Methodists had secured their place in the ranks of the middle class. At the same time, their religious services had become more structured and formal. Indeed, according to Charles H. Lippy, "[w]hile the emphasis on some inner experience of the presence of Christ remained strong, the enthusiasm and spontaneity that marked much of earlier Methodism seemed muted."[69] Similarly, in the early twentieth century, upwardly mobile second-generation Salvationists helped to naturalize a much more formal and less expressive form of Salvation Army religious culture. They no longer "respond[ed] to the 'novelty of expression and worship' that attracted their forbears."[70] A study of the

Salvation Army in Chicago found that by the turn of the century "the period of experimentation and innovation seemed to be over."[71]

Religious rituals gradually became steeped in tradition. Salvation Army meetings in the twentieth century ceased to be "the oasis of anti-traditionalism, of revivalistic evangelism, of 'free-and-easy' worship."[72] Instead, services took on a "traditional ritual and form . . . consist[ing] of a call to worship, some offertory, band and songster special numbers, and a message, followed by an alter call."[73] As the training-school curriculum suggests, open-airs became less spontaneous and more ritualized as the century proceeded. By the 1930s those meetings had become so re-hearsed and uninspired that one slightly irascible eighty-four-year-old retired officer observed that they typically consisted of nothing more than officers who "line[d] up on the curb, maybe in a crescent, and just threaten[ed] the crowd with a pincers movement."[74]

Salvation Army street parades also lost their inventiveness and sponta-neous exuberance.[75] "Marches," according to one source, "degenerated into parades of bands." In 1912, for example, an officer requested a permit to hold a parade in New York City. He wrote, "We will have . . . [the] Staff Band out. We will be playing National Airs and old familiar hymns."[76] Moreover, the Army's bands became increasingly profession-alized. In contrast to early "bands" which might include a "hallelujah organ, [a] bass drum, two other small drums, a pair of cymbals and two timbrels," by 1903 one band was "equipped with a new seven hundred dollar set of silver-plated instruments."[77]

By the early twentieth century Salvation Army bands, like American musical culture more generally, took on "a disciplined professionalism" that led to the development of highly trained "staff bands" playing care-fully planned and executed musical programs.[78] Soon well-trained Salva-tion Army bands began to take their place in civic street demonstrations like Armistice Day Parades and the Tournament of Roses in Pasadena, California. Indeed, participation in the Rose Parade marks an especially important milestone in the remodeling of Salvation Army street perfor-mance. The Pasadena elite, who served on the Tournament of Roses committee, rigorously screened applications to participate in the parade; by 1920 the Salvation Army apparently met their exacting standards of respectability.[79]

In addition to formalizing its religious traditions and professionalizing its musical culture, the Salvation Army followed the Booth-Tuckers' lead and developed refined modes of performance that used the new technologies of mass culture. Around 1898, the Army began to incorporate stereoptican or lantern slides, gramophones, and, later, film into their special meetings. One officer reported showing stereoptican slides of his work in the Philippines. Another recalled that the group used the gramophone, "to give recorded speeches of General William Booth and other great Army leaders in outlying communities." In the 1930s an officer modernized a Dwight Moody–style "Gospel Wagon" by adding a microphone and stereo speakers to his "Glory Wagon," a narrow platform mounted on small wheels. Years later, a corps in Philadelphia "dolled up" the Glory Wagon "like a church-on-wheels . . . [with] posh ropes . . . brass stanchions and . . . [a] pulpit." Over the next years others joined the effort by giving "illustrated lectures" on "The Problems of the Poor."[80] One officer's two-part program combined colored lantern slides and motion pictures; the first part "showed the dire need which existed in our great cities . . . while part two illustrated the Army's efforts to solve the problems of the poor."[81]

As the Army developed refined alternatives to its older forms of spectacular display, it also took steps to restrain spectators. In its early years the audiences played an active role in services through spontaneous testimonies, shouts of "Hallelujah," stamping feet, clapping hands, waving handkerchiefs, "hallelujah joy-jigs," "hallelujah cartwheels," and other expressions of the spirit. Performances in elegant commercial theaters or at lavish Salvation Army "Temples" and "Citadels" (that replaced disreputable "barracks" and "salvation factories") discouraged physical displays of religious feeling.[82] Moreover, just as Booth-Tucker envisioned at his 1897 trial, the officer in charge, like the conductor of an orchestra, exerted greater control and became master of the proceedings in which the congregation now played a passive role. Even the venerable William Booth had sought ways to exert discipline over the audience. In a handwritten memo, the general demanded that the following poster be prepared for all of his meetings, "No person may leave the meeting while the General is speaking!"[83]

The taming of Salvation Army religious performance in the twentieth century resembles the "Disciplining of Spectatorship," which John Kasson observed in "[i]nstitutions of the performing arts" in the late nineteenth century. In addition to segmenting cultural forms and spectators, "the arbiters of culture" exerted discipline both on the stage and the audience by professionalizing the former and restraining the latter. In exchange for sacrificing spontaneity and free expression, audiences found themselves in elegant theaters quietly watching lavish performances.[84]

Pamphlet, "Problems of the Poor."
(Courtesy of the Salvation Army National Archives)

Although Lawrence Levine suggested that sports and religion provide exceptions, I would argue that after the turn of the century changes in Army religious culture actually corresponded to this model.[85]

As the Salvation Army confronts another turn of the century, its religious performances continue to adapt the forms and technologies of mass culture. Evangelical Christians have increasingly co-opted rock music. Young, well-trained Salvation Army musicians, for example, have left brass bands behind to create rock bands that "bring honor to the Lord." While the inclusion of rock music represents a departure for the Salvation Army, it does *not* reflect a significant shift in its religious culture. Whether Salvationists play traditional Salvation Army songs or praise music written by an "admitted Eddie Van Halen 'fanatic,'" they do so under the watchful eye of the officer-in-charge with a well-rehearsed musical program and carefully guided audience participation. Recently at a corps in Tustin, California, while the band rocked on, "[t]he faithful, 100 strong, sway[ed] and [sang] to words beamed above the band with an overhead projector." A newspaper astutely called the activity "karaoke for the soul."[86]

In addition to the transformation of its religious culture, changes in the Salvation Army by the twentieth century also reconfigured its religious mission. In the nineteenth century, the Army's central goal, like that of frontier camp meetings and gospel missions, was "conversion of the lost." In the twentieth century, however, conversion of the heathen masses became the purview of the social work and was no longer rigorously evangelical. At the same time, Salvation Army spiritual work increasingly focused on "those already converted and . . . those who were being nurtured in the faith." Like the late-nineteenth-century holiness camp meetings, Salvationists in the twentieth century began "'preaching to the choir.'"[87]

Although Salvationist leaders intended the social work to serve simply as an *additional* way to advertise salvation, its introduction not only created administrative specialization (i.e., separate social and spiritual branches) but also effectively segmented the Salvation Army's congregation.[88] As the programs proliferated, instead of attracting the "heathen masses" to open-air or corps meetings, the Army increasingly ministered to them in its social institutions. Because the leadership structured social work to facilitate temporal salvation but not to proselytize, its religious effect was indirect when clients experienced the Christian love motivating Army officers. Furthermore, there is little evidence that contact with Salvation Army social programs led men and women to join the organization.

Indeed, the success of the social work in attracting (but not converting) the poor provided a disincentive to traditional forms of Army evangelism through which it historically gained new members.

As a result, by the early twentieth century the Army's rate of growth dropped significantly. While Salvation Army membership increased by 1,562 soldiers per year between 1880 and 1896, in the sixteen years between 1897 and 1913 membership increased by only 419 persons each year, a 73 percent decline.[89] Furthermore, in 1900 an officer noted sadly that circulation of the Pacific Coast's version of *The War Cry* had dwindled significantly during the summer. "It is hard to keep our circulation up," he said, "on account of scarcity of officers." Indeed, the shortage of officers was so grave that seven Pacific Coast Division corps closed that summer, while only one opened. The officer feared that, "the S.A. w[ould] die out for lack of officers and soldiers."[90]

By 1905 even Commander Evangeline Booth had become concerned about the losses. "The leakage between the penitent-form and the roll-book," she said, "is appalling. . . . [H]undreds of our converts who have found salvation under the Flag, and who by every sacred right belong to The Army, drift away."[91] Historically, men and women like "Happy Bill" and "Hallelujah Annie" joined the Salvation Army after getting saved at a boisterous indoor or open-air meeting. After 1900, neither the more refined Salvation Army religious culture nor the indirect forms of religious influence found in the social wing apparently attracted the interest of the Army's traditional working-class constituency.[92]

Faced with expanding social services and declining evangelical campaigns, many seasoned officers objected to, but were powerless to stop, the changes taking place around them. One officer wrote poignantly that he missed the single-minded sense of mission he experienced during the early days of millennial revivalism. "I long for the days of yore," he said, "when I was a private marching the streets . . . for dear Jesus' sake, or a humble field Captain toiling, enduring and sacrificing without a murmur. My enthusiasm was at fever heat in those happy blessed years."[93] For these veteran warriors, the Salvation Army was God's instrument to bring the perishing masses to Christ.

In her campaign to stop the "leakage" of potential Salvationists, Evangeline Booth chose not to recall the evangelistic techniques of the late nineteenth century in which public testimony and ecstatic religious performance aroused converts, soldiers, and officers. Instead, the "Siege" introduced a model based on the fund-raising efficiencies inaugurated by Emma and Frederick Booth-Tucker. The commander set a national target for the number of new soldiers enlisted (instead of the number of dollars raised) which was divided among the provinces, divisions, field officers, and, finally, individual soldiers. "[N]o soldier's target," said Commander Evangeline Booth, should "be less than the winning of one soul and the making of one soldier through his own individual effort during the Siege."[94]

While concerned about bringing new souls into the Salvation Army, Commander Booth found the "leakage" among long-time soldiers and officers even more alarming. Many veterans who refused to accept the Army's changes protested by resigning from the organization. Leaving the Army was, according to one officer, "the hardest thing I ever did. I think I felt at the time that the Army had been leaving me."[95] As a result, only one year after the first siege, Commander Booth admonished district officers that keeping officers required "the strengthening of their character, and the confirming of their hold on God and their calling."[96]

In the face of its new social mission and refined religious culture, the Army found itself scrambling to maintain the religious commitment of its own officers. As a result, the group reconceptualized its religious market and increasingly focused its spiritual energies inward, toward preserving its own membership, rather than outward, advertising salvation to the masses. Because the Army was "being supplied more and more by the children of Salvationists," said one long-time officer, the directly spiritual work of the Salvation Army increasingly served the needs of its own Salvation Army families after the turn of the century.[97]

In the late twentieth and early twenty-first centuries, the Salvation Army has followed the lead of nineteenth-century holiness camp meetings. The goals of its new spiritual mission are to bring holiness to already converted Salvationists and to sustain their children by nurturing them in the faith. These upwardly mobile children, in contrast to their working-class parents, do not see themselves as the vanguard of the millennium. As Richard Niebuhr pointed out, "Rarely does a second generation hold the convictions it has inherited with the fervor equal to that of its fathers [and mothers], who fashioned those convictions in the heat of conflict and at the risk of martyrdom."[98] Instead, most second-generation Salvationists regard the organization as their church, providing them with "a place of Sunday worship."[99] Recalled one woman, when growing up she did not "know too much about The Army except that I went to Sunday School there."[100] Today, when the Army organizes spectacular religious performances, including precision timbrel drill teams and highly choreographed extravaganzas, they are not designed to evangelize the unconverted but rather to "thrill" Salvationists "and cause them to make a deeper commitment of their personal calling to the Gospel of Jesus Christ."[101]

Two questions remain. First, could the free-and-easy, spontaneous, democratic Salvation Army religious culture of the nineteenth century have competed successfully with new forms of commercial entertainment in the early twentieth century? The decline of other forms of spectacular public display, notably political parades, owed much to its inability to compete with the emerging leisure and consumer culture, according to Michael McGerr. Moreover, there is evidence that cheap neighborhood movie houses competed successfully with saloons for working-class (men's) leisure dollars by the early twentieth century. According to a 1910 study of working-class leisure, among the men questioned, "60 percent patronized the movies, whereas only 30 percent frequented the saloon."[102] It must be recalled, however, that the Salvation Army had *always* faced stiff competition from popular entertainment. Indeed, the group relied on the audience's familiarity with and attraction to these forms. Although the group never displaced working-class forms of popular entertainment, they did successfully attract thousands of Americans to their meetings through the years.

Second, would the Army's exuberant, physically expressive performances have continued to attract working-class men and women in the twentieth century? While new leisure forms like movies captured an increasing proportion of the working-class entertainment dollar in the early twentieth century, it is also clear that "[w]orking-class movie theater conduct built on a long tradition of crowd behavior that could be found at a variety of earlier popular amusements from melodramas to saloons to July Fourth picnics to working-class parks." Eating, drinking, sleeping, necking, informal sociability, and group singing created a boisterous atmosphere in which patrons interacted with each other and the movie.[103] These behaviors would not change until theater buildings grew more lavish and came "under the control of theatrical chains and the direction of professional theater managers."[104] Furthermore, although entrepreneurs refined older forms of expressive culture, the working class either "satisfied their aesthetic cravings" through new forms—blues, jazz, and musical comedy—or took their entertainment in "particular theatrical spaces devoted to them exclusively," for example, working-class and lower-middle-class men attending burlesque houses.[105]

There is also evidence that after the turn of the century other popular religious movements, notably the Pentecostals, successfully used "exuberant religious services" to evangelize the masses. At the Azuza Street Mission in Los Angeles, for example, observers called the services "unstructured," spontaneous, and disorderly and noted that although "[h]undreds were present, yet none seemed in charge." Religious performances at the mission featured speaking in tongues, as well as "chattering, jabbering, wind-sucking, and jerking fits." Similarly, the Pillar of Fire, a holiness group, featured expressive forms of worship, including "'people going through every form of gymnastic exercise . . . [and] students playing leap-frog while in prayer.'"[106]

By the turn of the century the terms under which the Salvation Army sought to escape segmentation meant modifying the more physically and emotionally expressive elements of its religious culture. On the one hand, that choice allowed the organization to gain broad public support which enhanced its ability to finance its expanding social programs. Moreover, the decision probably ensured that succeeding generations of economically and socially mobile Salvationists remained committed to the organization as their "church." At the same time, however, by adopting a more controlled and decorous religious culture and leaving conversion of sinners to the social wing, Salvationism no longer attracted its traditional constituency and capitulated to the marginalization of its uniquely working-class form of religious expression. "That the movement had departed from its original work there could be no question," wrote one ex-Salvationist. By the turn of the century the Salvation Army was no longer a working-class-dominated vanguard of the millennium. Instead, it had become a church which "found its place, in the great stream of philanthropic endeavor . . . to become the great go-between, the national distributor, of the country's wealth, to the country's poor and needy."[107]

{ CONCLUSION }

The Salvation Army is a romance geographically. A ring around a London lamppost expands until it encircles the world.

It is a romance numerically. William and Catherine Booth . . . sacrificing the promise of a most successful church ministry start a procession of two along a road in East London with a story to tell, a faith to proclaim, and the procession increases until its train numbers tens of hundreds of thousands.

It is a romance financially. A poverty stricken mission begging its bread from door to door to keep its disciples alive grows into an organization which can appeal to the financial world for the millions necessary to do the work the world is asking it to do.

But above all it is a romance spiritually. The young man, our founder, standing on the slum curb telling the wretched . . . of Jesus Christ the sinner's friend becomes a leader of an army of hosts of men and women who cry in all the languages of the earth, "Behold the Lamb of God who taketh away the sin of the world."

So perhaps it is not too much to say that the Salvation Army is the world's greatest romance.

— GENERAL EVANGELINE BOOTH, "The World's Greatest Romance"

In 1986, the High Council elected Eva Burrows general of the Salvation Army. Burrows was the eleventh general selected by that body and only the second woman to hold the top "spiritual, inspirational and administrative" post in the organization. She was also the first female general who was not related to the founders, William and Catherine Booth. The college-educated Salvationist was born in Australia and had held a variety of powerful administrative positions before rising to the highest office in the organization at the age of fifty-seven. Her official portrait shows a woman in full uniform. In contrast to the power suits and dresses of late-twentieth-century top executives, her dark blue Army tunic sports epaulets and a high, tight collar with a large "S" displayed on each side of the neck. Her hat is the modern equivalent of the original "poke bonnet," complete with "The Salvation Army" embroidered in yellow and a huge ribbon tied on the side.[1]

During its first fifty years in the United States, the Salvation Army experienced a profound transformation. In the late nineteenth century, working-class men and women created an autonomous, democratic, heterosocial alternative world in which they could express and share their spirituality using the vernacular culture of the northern urban working class. By the twentieth century, the Army lost many of the qualities that made it a vibrant working-class-dominated institution. It had become, instead, a highly centralized organization with a complex bureaucracy. In place of its inventive alternative world, the Army had become a stable church complete with ritualized religious culture. In place of street performances designed to share the keys to the kingdom with the masses, it operated increasingly professionalized social services that offered the needy only "as much religion as anyone wants."[2] At the same time, however, the portrait of General Burrows illustrates that there have been important continuities over those five decades. Whether barely literate working-class men and women in the nineteenth century or college-educated middle-class men and women in the twentieth, Salvationists share an identity that continues to make them unique.

The Salvation Army's transformation also reveals what American society lost because the group failed to sustain its alternative world. The decision to implement a broad program of social services required extensive reorganization in order to satisfy modern institutional standards. As a consequence, the group's leadership encouraged centralization while discouraging democracy and autonomy. The process of bureaucratization and decline of democracy in the Salvation Army at the turn of the century foreshadowed what other emphatically working-class organizations like industrial unions would forfeit by the 1940s.

The urban "plain folk" who joined the Salvation Army took democratic elements from both the frontier camp meeting and the saloon and created an autonomous religious culture in the late nineteenth century. Together with a small number of college-educated men and women, the group built a sacred community in which its members found moral authority as well as opportunities for usefulness and leadership. Although they adapted the values and popular culture of the working-class experience, however, Salvationists set themselves apart from it by rejecting alcohol, "manly sports," and the sexuality associated with saloons and music halls. Moreover, in contrast to the male-centered culture of the saloon and workshop, Salvation Army religious culture included both men and women; and, unlike the male-dominated middle-class public sphere, the Army accepted the spiritual and administrative authority of women. Finally, Salvationists set themselves apart from both the working and middle class by wearing the uniform and performing distinctive rituals of membership.

The forces that came together at the turn of the century changed the Salvation Army significantly. The children of working-class Salvationists found opportunities in the expanding American economy and moved into the ranks of the middle class. Along with administrators and early opponents of expressive religion, the second generation embraced refinement of the self and of their religious culture. Having successfully negotiated the mainstream, they did not mourn the loss of the Army's alternative world but rather embraced the organization as their church in which they expressed Christian usefulness largely through social service.

While the Army began to conform to middle-class standards in some ways, by the twentieth century American society also changed, making the group appear less unique. This is particularly noticeable in relation to gender equality and heterosociality. By the turn of the century entrepreneurs of mass culture worked diligently to attract a mixed audience of middle-class men and women and turned commercial leisure, from amusement parks to vaudeville theaters, into a heterosocial experience. Moreover, as the twentieth century proceeded, more and more jobs and career opportunities opened to women. At the same time, although women in the Salvation Army continued to wield considerable authority, the gendering of its social work and the tendency of officers' wives to withdraw from active service minimized the group's contrast with mainstream culture on issues relating to equal opportunity for women.

Although the Salvation Army and middle-class American society became more alike, twentieth-century Salvationists still set themselves apart from others of their class in a number of ways. First, they rejected the enthusiastic consumerism and materialism integral to the middle-class experience. From gold watches to automobiles, the Army has been selective in its relationship to consumer goods, rejecting them unless useful to the work. Moreover, although accusations of excess have surfaced periodically, the Salvation Army's notoriously low salaries and internal socialization discourage freewheeling engagement in consumer culture.

In addition, the Army's rituals of membership continued to reinforce a Salvationist identity that was different from other middle-class Americans. Indeed, some young officers struggled to accept the way in which the uniform so thoroughly set them apart. Walking alone on the streets wearing her uniform for the first time, a young cadet recalled, "I just knew everybody in New York was looking at me because I was so self-conscious with this uniform on." When she arrived at Carnegie Hall, however, she felt more at ease because "plenty of other people . . . had uniforms on."[3] The Salvationists' story is in part about change and continuity. Although it has grown more like middle-class American society, now as they did in the beginning, Salvationists stand apart.

The Army's transformation is significant not only for what makes the Salvationists unique but also because it demonstrates what American society lost when the group failed to sustain its autonomous and democratic working-class-dominated alternative world. Moreover, it foreshadows a similar transformation identified by labor historians in industrial unions by the 1940s. Notable increases of rank-and-file militancy in the 1930s not only helped union leaders like John L. Lewis rebuild the UMW but also encouraged significant levels of democracy and local autonomy. By the 1940s, however, leaders not only created bureaucratic divisions within the union but also exerted increasing levels of control over the rank and file.[4]

Although the impulses for greater centralized control in industrial unions are quite different from those that drove bureaucratization in the Army, the consequences for democracy are disconcertingly similar. For new industrial unions, argued James R. Green, "[g]overnment labor policy assured . . . growth and stability . . . but it also created internal tension. In outlawing the strike and emphasizing arbitration and other bureaucratic procedures, the state stressed the role of the international officers as disciplinarians, and placed penalties on 'local union initiative and rank and file militancy.' "[5] Similarly, by embracing an elaborate system of social service that required broad public and private financial support, the Salvation Army's leadership made itself responsible for disciplining and controlling the behavior of rank-and-file Salvationists. As Madison Ferris pointed out, no good could come from local corps initiatives that antagonized private business donors or political authorities that could provide public money. For industrial unions, as for the Salvation Army, the exercise of greater centralized control created internal tensions that facilitated the decline of democracy and local autonomy in both of these working-class organizations.

TABLE 1

Percentages of Married and Single Field Officers in Selected Years

Marital Status	N*	1888	1893	1898	1903
Single male	1,559	38.5%	33.5%	46.6%	58.7%
Single female	1,563	45.5	47.5	46.4	41.3
Married officers	317	16	19	7	0
Total	3,439	100	100	100	100

Source: *Disposition of Forces*, January issues for years 1888, 1893, 1898, and 1903 (New York: Salvation Army, 1888–1920).

Notes: While the Army did not keep a total count of male and female officers, it did print female officers' names in italics. It was therefore possible to get a rough count of male versus female officers for each year by counting the names of officers printed in italics and those in regular print, which appeared in that year's January *Disposition of Forces*. Married officers' names appeared as Captain and Mrs. ———.

*In this and all the tables to follow, N represents the total number of officers in my sample for each category.

TABLE 2

Percentages of Married and Single People Entering Officer Training, 1880–1924

Marital Status	N	1880–1899	1900–1914	1915–1924
Single	355	65.8%	27.4%	42.9%
Married	263	32.2	72.6	57.1
Divorced	2	.5	0	0
Widow(er)	7	1.6	0	0
Total	627	100	100	100
Missing cases = 431				

Sources: Data for Tables 2–8 compiled from Officer Career Sheets and Training School Rosters, RG 1.6, 1.8, 2.7, SAA, and biographical sketches published in *The War Cry* between 1880 and 1888.

Note: In this and the following tables, "missing cases" refers to the number of Salvationists in my database for whom there was no information on a particular variable (e.g., marital status).

TABLE 3

Officers' Ages When Entering Training
(Percentage of Officers within Each Age Group)

Age	N	1880–1899	1900–1914	1915–1924
14–22	554	48.3%	53.7%	62.3%
23–27	252	26.5	21.1	24.6
28–32	109	13.4	14.7	7.6
33–37	54	6.7	6.3	3.9
38–44	20	2.7	1.1	1.5
45–53	10	1.6	3.2	0
54–68	4	.9	0	0
Total	1,003	100	100	100
Missing cases = 55				

TABLE 4

Nationality of Officers Entering Training, 1880–1924
(Percentage of Officers within Each Nationality)

Nationality	N	1880–1899	1900–1914	1915–1924
Canada	42	4.4%	3.3%	4.1%
United States	631	56.9	55.4	70.5
England	120	15.7	10.9	8.5
Germany	44	5.5	7.6	2.6
Scandinavia	37	11.2	15.2	9.9
Other	128	6.3	7.6	4.4
Total	1,002	100	100	100

Missing cases = 56

Notes: For the United States category, 8 cases indicated "German-American." It is not possible to determine whether or not the other "Americans" were the children of native or foreign-born parents. Category "Scandinavia" includes men and women from Norway, Sweden, Denmark, and Finland.

TABLE 5

Men and Women Entering Training, 1880–1924
(Percentage of Each Sex within Each Time Period)

Year	N	Female	Male
1880–99	497	35%	60.8%
1900–1914	95	10.8	7.2
1915–24	458	54.2	32.1
Total	1,050	100	100

Missing cases = 8

TABLE 6

Percentage of Salvation Army Men and Women in Various Occupations, 1880–1924

Occupation	N (% of all jobs)	Female	Male
Clerk	39 (6.4)	6%	6.8%
Stenographer	44 (7.2)	11.7	1.8
Factory hand	133 (21.8)	9.9	35.8
Domestic service	117 (19.1)	33.1	2.5
Professional*	23 (3.8)	3.6	3.9
Salvation Army worker	99 (16.2)	18.7	13.3
Sales	26 (4.3)	3.3	5.4
Agriculture	27 (4.4)	.6	9
Transportation	11 (1.8)	0	3.9
Garment worker	31 (5.1)	9	.4
Other	61 (10)	3.9	17.2
Total	611 (100)	100	100

Missing cases = 447

Note: Nearly 63 percent of the men and women who said they worked for the Salvation Army prior to becoming officers were women. Most of them entered training between 1911 and 1920 (1916, 1917, and 1918 were the peak years). The data do not indicate what specific jobs they performed.

*In the category "Professional" I have included teachers, librarians, doctors, newspaper reporters, and evangelists.

TABLE 7

Percentage of Women in Various Occupations, by Year

Occupation	N	1880–1899	1900–1914	1915–1924
Clerk	20	0%	8.8%	6%
Stenographer	39	0	8.8	12.7
Factory hand	33	20	14.7	8.8
Domestic service	110	0	41.2	33.9
Salvation Army worker	62	6.7	2.9	3.2
Sales	11	0	2.9	3.5
Agriculture	2	13.3	0	0
Garment worker	30	6.7	2.9	9.9
Other	13	40	0	2.5
Total	320	100	100	100

Missing cases = 223

Note: The data available to me showed that of the 549 women who became officers during this period, 35 percent joined between 1880 and 1899, and nearly 65 percent joined after 1900. Of the 332 cases for which there was any occupational data, 95 percent appeared in the later period. This is a reflection of lack of attention or interest in record keeping and preservation in the Army's early period. Nevertheless, the significant proportion of women who performed factory and domestic service work after the turn of the century reinforces the early descriptive literature on the class background of Salvation Army female officers.

TABLE 8

Percentage of Men in Various Occupations, by Year

Occupation	N	1880–1899	1900–1914	1915–1924
Clerk	19	1%	12%	9.7%
Stenographer	5	0	4	2.6
Factory hand	100	26	52	39.6
Domestic service	7	1	4	3.2
Professional	13	10	0	1.9
Salvation Army worker	37	0	20	20.8
Sales	13	4	0	5.8
Agriculture	25	18	0	4.5
Teamster	11	5	0	3.9
Garment worker	1	0	0	.6
Other	48	35	8	7.1
Total	279	100	100	100

Missing cases = 223

Note: As for women, the data available to me showed that of the 502 men who became officers during this period, 60.8 percent joined between 1880 and 1899, and nearly 40 percent joined after 1900. Of the 279 cases for which there was any occupational data, 64 percent appeared in the later period. Still, the significant proportion of men who performed factory work after the turn of the century reinforces the early descriptive literature on the class background of Salvation Army male officers.

{ NOTES }

Abbreviations

ACC	Acquisition number
ARC	Microfilm collection
AWC	*The War Cry* (American edition)
BB	Book collection
LWC	*The War Cry* (London edition)
RG	Record Group
SAA	Salvation Army Archives and Research Center, Alexandria, Virginia
SAWTM	Salvation Army Western Territorial Museum, Rancho Palos Verdes, California
SFOT	School for Officers' Training, Suffern, New York
VF	Vertical Files

Introduction

1. The home was called "Ivy House." It was originally designed to care for children born at the Rescue Home and Hospital in Philadelphia while their mothers went to work. By 1921, children were being placed in the home by "private application or by direction of the court." In 1947 it moved to the location at 4050 Conshohocken Avenue, where I first came into contact with the home. Summary, Ivy House, RG 16.2, SAA.

2. In 1979, Ivy House closed down "due to lack of funds and the changing needs of dependent and neglected children" (ibid.).

3. Lt. Col. Edith MacLachlan, "Bird's Eye View of the Women's Social, 1886–1978," unpublished paper, Salvation Army Territorial Historical Commission Meeting, 1984, 1–2.

4. Clarke A. Chambers, "Toward a Redefinition of Welfare History," *Journal of American History* 73 (September 1986): 420–21, 432.

5. In addition, each Territory (East, Central, West, and South) also supports a Territorial Museum. While I do not know about all of the territorial museums, the Western Territorial Museum is not set up to accommodate researchers. However, when I made a specific request—e.g., for letters, diaries, and memoirs—the director, Frances Dingman, kindly took the time to make copies of what she had and sent them along to me.

6. Some of this material is restricted and requires the permission of family members, the national commander, International Headquarters, and/or the chief archivist. They have now added a computerized database.

7. On my most recent research trip, I mentioned that my daughter was born at

Booth Memorial Hospital in Philadelphia. To my surprise I was able to locate my daughter's birth records, complete with tiny footprints.

8. I chose not to include information from the U.S. Census of Religious Bodies, since these data rely on reports gathered from the religious institutions themselves and there is evidence that Salvationists, like so many other groups, regularly exaggerated their numbers. Officers sometimes complained that people's names had been kept on soldiers' rolls long after they had stopped attending meetings. See, for example, unpublished letter from Captain Geo. Smith to Major R. E. Holz, Syracuse, N.Y., 1 September 1890, R. E. Holz Papers, RG 20.60, 62/5, SAA.

9. These works include: Aaron I. Abell, *The Urban Impact on American Protestantism, 1865–1900* (Cambridge, Mass.: Harvard University Press, 1943); Sydney E. Ahlstrom, *A Religious History of the American People* (New Haven, Conn.: Yale University Press, 1972); Charles H. Hopkins, *The Rise of the Social Gospel in American Protestantism, 1865–1915* (New Haven, Conn.: Yale University Press, 1940); and Robert H. Bremner, *From the Depths: The Discovery of Poverty in the United States* (New York: New York University Press, 1956). I have drawn the term "gospel welfare" from Norris A. Magnuson, *Salvation in the Slums: Evangelical Social Welfare Work, 1865–1920*, (Metuchen, N.J.: Scarecrow Press, 1977), x.

10. Ken Fones-Wolf, *Trade Union Gospel: Christianity and Labor in Industrial Philadelphia, 1865–1915* (Philadelphia: Temple University Press, 1989), xvii (quotation on p. xx). See also Herbert Gutman, "Protestantism and the American Labor Movement: The Christian Spirit in the Gilded Age," in his *Work, Culture and Society in Industrializing America* (New York: Vintage Books, 1977), 79–117; R. Laurence Moore, "Religion, Secularization, and the Shaping of the Culture Industry in Antebellum America," *American Quarterly* 41, no. 2 (1989): 235; and John Bodner, *The Transplanted: A History of Immigrants in Urban America* (Bloomington: Indiana University Press, 1985), 146 ("mutual assistance" quote on p. 148). Bodner also points out that immigrant churches were frequently sites of "discord and division" among which were the issues of class conflict and ethnic nationalism versus religious doctrine, and laymen against clerics, 166. On the "cleavages between the working-class," see Bruce C. Nelson, "Revival and Upheaval: Religion, Irreligion, and Chicago's Working Class in 1886," *Journal of Social History* 25, no. 2 (1991): 233. According to Bruce Laurie, "revivalists" advocated the strict moral behaviors encouraged by evangelical Christianity, while "traditionalists" refused to give up the old ways. Bruce Laurie, *Working People of Philadelphia, 1800–1850* (Philadelphia: Temple University Press, 1980), passim.

11. An important exception to the inattention to working-class religion is the excellent work of Robert A. Orsi, whose books *The Madonna of 115th Street: Faith and Community in Italian Harlem, 1880–1950* (New Haven, Conn.: Yale University Press, 1985), and *Thank You, St. Jude: Women's Devotion to the Patron Saint of Hopeless Causes* (New Haven, Conn.: Yale University Press, 1996), provide one of the few scholarly discussions of Catholic immigrant religious experience and performance in the nineteenth century.

12. Sarah Deutsch, in her article "Learning to Talk More Like a Man: Boston Women's Class-Bridging Organizations, 1870–1940," coined the term "class-bridging," which she uses in lieu of "cross-class," "to acknowledge the middle-class dominance" of many organizations. I have used "cross-class" because working-class culture and personnel dominated the Salvation Army particularly in its earliest days in the United States. *American Historical Review* 97 (1992): 381, n. 10.

13. Nathan Hatch, in *The Democratization of American Christianity* (New Haven, Conn.: Yale University Press, 1989), 16, discusses what he calls the "free market economy in religion." See also R. Stephen Warner, "Work in Progress toward a New Paradigm for the Sociological Study of Religion in the United States," *American Journal of Sociology* 98, no. 5 (1993): 1044–93; Roger Finke and Rodney Stark, *The Churching of America, 1776–1990: Winners and Losers in Our Religious Economy* (New Brunswick, N.J.: Rutgers University Press, 1997); R. Laurence Moore, "Religion, Secularization, and the Shaping of the Culture Industry in Antebellum America," *American Quarterly* 41, no. 2 (1989), 216–42; R. Laurence Moore, *Selling God: American Religion in the Marketplace of Culture* (New York: Oxford University Press, 1994); and Rodney Stark and Laurence R. Iannaccone, "A Supply-Side Reinterpretation of the 'Secularization' of Europe," *Journal for the Scientific Study of Religion* 33, no. 3 (1994): 230–52.

14. Charles Edwin Jones, *Perfectionist Persuasion: The Holiness Movement and American Methodism, 1867–1936* (Metuchen, N.J.: Scarecrow Press, 1974), 53–54.

15. Richard Wightman Fox, "The Culture of Liberal Protestant Progressivism, 1875–1925," *Journal of Interdisciplinary History* 23, no. 3 (1993): 640.

16. A number of scholars have noted that many antimodernist middle-class Americans in the late nineteenth century demonstrated a "craving for intense religious experience." David G. Hackett, "Gender and Religion in American Culture, 1870–1930," *Religion and American Culture* 5, no. 1 (1995): 132; see also T. J. Jackson Lears, *No Place of Grace: Antimodernism and the Transformation of American Culture, 1880–1920* (New York: Pantheon Books, 1981). For many middle-class men, the rituals associated with fraternal organizations satisfied that longing. Mark C. Carnes, *Secret Ritual and Manhood in Victorian America* (New Haven, Conn.: Yale University Press, 1989). For more on fraternal organizations, see Mary Ann Clawson, *Constructing Brotherhood: Class, Gender and Fraternalism* (Princeton, N.J.: Princeton University Press, 1984).

17. Edward H. McKinley, *Marching to Glory: The History of the Salvation Army in the United States of America, 1880–1980* (San Francisco: Harper and Row, 1980); Diane Winston, *Red Hot and Righteous: The Urban Religion of the Salvation Army* (Cambridge, Mass.: Harvard University Press, 1999). While the work on the Salvation Army in the United States is very limited, there has been some excellent research on the organization in both Canada and Great Britain. In her article "The Knights of Labor and the Salvation Army: Religion and Working-Class Culture in Ontario, 1882–1890," Lynne Marks looks at "working-class values, beliefs and culture" in the Knights of Labor and the Salvation Army, *Labour/Le Travail* 28 (Fall 1991): 89–127. Pamela J. Walker has studied the organization in Britain. In several excellent articles and a forthcoming book, Walker has looked at the working-class nature of the Salvation Army and the ways in which Salvationists redefined gender in Britain in the nineteenth century. See Walker, " 'I live but not yet I for Christ liveth in me': Men and Masculinity in the Salvation Army, 1865–1890," in *Manful Assertions: Masculinities in Britain since 1800*, ed. Michael Roper and John Tosh (London: Routledge, 1991), 92–112, and *Pulling the Devil's Kingdom Down: The Salvation Army in Victorian England* (Berkeley: University of California Press, 2001).

18. Virginia Lieson Brereton, *From Sin to Salvation: Stories of Women's Conversions, 1800 to the Present* (Bloomington: Indiana University Press, 1991), xi, xiii.

19. Regenia Gagnier, "Social Atoms: Working-Class Autobiography, Subjectivity, and Gender," *Victorian Studies* 30, no. 3 (Spring 1987): 346–47.

20. Susan Juster, " 'In a Different Voice': Male and Female Narratives of Religious Conversion in Post-Revolutionary America," *American Quarterly* 441, no. 1 (1989): 35, 36, 57.

21. Natalie Zemon Davis, *Fiction in the Archives: Pardon Tales and Their Tellers in Sixteenth-Century France* (Stanford, Calif.: Stanford University Press, 1987), 7.

22. Pamela Jane Walker, "Pulling the Devil's Kingdom Down: Gender and Popular Culture in the Salvation Army, 1865–1895" (Ph.D. diss., Rutgers University, 1992), 75–76.

23. Although issues of class do not enter Juster's argument, she does look at gender and suggest that "the very existence of sexual distinctiveness in the natural state . . . is the precondition for the sexual leveling achieved in the regenerate state" (Juster, " 'In a Different Voice,' " 37). As I show in chapter 2, the class differences in conversion narratives are even more pronounced than gender differences. Working-class men and women concern themselves largely with sins of the flesh — drinking, which exposes them to sexual danger or violence. Middle-class men and women both fear that they have become "half-hearted Christian[s]" used to comfortable, self-indulgent lives. "Mrs. Fannie McAbee," *AWC*, 6 July 1889, 3. The nature of agency also demonstrated class differences. To working-class men and women, it gave the moral authority to preach to others; to middle-class men and women, submission to God's will served as a call to action and imparted a vigor and "manliness" to their Christian service.

Chapter One

1. *Chicago Tribune*, 2 March 1885, 8, cited in Allan Whitworth Bosch, "The Salvation Army in Chicago, 1885–1914" (Ph.D. diss., University of Chicago, 1965), 15–16. Even before 1885, newspapers paid attention to Salvationists' accents. In Philadelphia in 1879, for example, a *News* reporter noted the absence of aspirates in Eliza Shirley's speech when he quoted her comment to a recent convert, "And thee has already taken the feathers out of thy 'at' " and " 'Now let's 'ave a praying band.' " On another occasion, a report on a sermon noted that the Salvation Army officer spoke "in rude, uncultivated language. . . . the King's English was unmercifully slaughtered, with a dreadful mingling of her h's." St. John Ervine, *God's Soldier: General William Booth*, vol. 2 (New York: Macmillian, 1935), 484, 491.

2. Robert Toll, *Blacking Up: The Minstrel Show in Nineteenth-Century America* (New York: Oxford University Press, 1974), 169.

3. During his tenure as editor of the *Atlantic Monthly*, Howells published stories by many authors who also used dialect in their stories. Those authors included Mark Twain, Bret Harte, Sarah Orne Jewett, Charles Egbert Craddock, Constance Fenimore Woolson, John DeForest, Harriet Beecher Stowe, and Rose Terry Cooke. Elsa Nettels, "William Dean Howells and the American Language," *New England Quarterly* 52 (1980): 314.

4. In English literature, "cockneys are frequently portrayed as racially 'mongrelized' (note that Jewish characters like Fagin in *Oliver Twist* have cockney speech affectations)." Moreover, characters of Irish ancestry often appear as cockneys. The association of Jews and Irish (Catholics) with cockneys also sug-

gests the existence of a negative view of nonofficial British religions. Thanks to Carol Siegel for the above ideas on cockney accents provided in an e-mail message on 27 June 1996.

5. George Bernard Shaw, in his play "Pygmalion," illustrated that dialect can represent a person's social station (and indeed his future success). In an early scene Henry Higgins demonstrated his ability to detect a person's birthplace by her accent. Higgins not only correctly identified Eliza Doolittle's Lisson Grove accent but went on to point out that what he called her "kerbstone English [would] . . . keep her in the gutter to the end of her days." As Shaw represented it, an important quality of this accent was the dropped "h" as in "Ow, eez ye-ooa san, is e?" (Oh, he's your son, is he?). Coming to terms with Higgins's assessment of her future, Eliza sought him out so that he could teach her to "talk more genteel." Of particular importance in speaking "more genteel" is the appropriate use of the aspirate. At Higgins's mother's "at-home day," Eliza demonstrated a measure of success when she took special pains to pronounce the "H's" in "How do you do, Mrs. Higgins?" Shaw, *The Complete Plays of Bernard Shaw* (London: Paul Hamlyn, 1965), 715, 717.

6. The working-class background of Salvationists will be addressed in chapter 2.

7. Sydney E. Ahlstrom, *A Religious History of the American People* (New Haven, Conn.: Yale University Press, 1972), 737–38; Paul Boyer, *Urban Masses and Moral Order in America, 1820–1920* (Cambridge, Mass.: Harvard University Press, 1978), 132.

8. Samuel Loomis, *Modern Cities*, quoted in Bruce C. Nelson, "Revival and Upheaval: Religion and Irreligion and Chicago's Working Class in 1886," *Journal of Social History* 25, no. 2 (1991): 236; other middle-class Americans expressing concern included Harriet Beecher Stowe and Josiah Strong. Boyer, *Urban Masses and Moral Order*, 132–33. Religious communities in Britain also perceived a breakdown of relations "between 'the classes' and 'the masses'" and worried about "the 'spiritual destitution' of the lower orders." K. S. Inglis, *Churches and the Working Classes in Victorian England* (London: Routledge and Kegan Paul, 1963), 3; see also Henry F. May, *Protestant Churches and Industrial America* (New York: Harper and Brothers, 1949), 119–20, 189–90, 221–23; Gutman, *Work, Culture and Society*, 83; and Aaron I. Abell, *The Urban Impact on American Protestantism, 1865–1900* (Cambridge, Mass.: Harvard University Press, 1943), 61.

9. Nelson, "Revival and Upheaval," 237.

10. Norman H. Murdoch, "The Salvation Army: An Anglo-American Revivalist Social Mission" (Ph.D. diss., University of Cincinnati, 1985), 235–36. Bruce C. Nelson points out that in Chicago alone by 1890 "Catholics outnumbered . . . Protestants more than 2-to-1" and its "Jewish community became the second largest in the country." Nelson, "Revival and Upheaval," 234. Cultural imperialism or the assertion of "Western value systems" was a critical current in all late-nineteenth-century Anglo-American missionary efforts. See Ian Tyrrell, *Woman's World, Woman's Empire: The Women's Christian Temperance Union in International Perspective, 1880–1930* (Chapel Hill: University of North Carolina Press, 1991), 5. For more on foreign missionary movements, see Patricia Hill, *The World Their Household: The American Woman's Foreign Mission Movement and Cultural Transition, 1870–1920* (Ann Arbor: University of Michigan Press, 1985).

11. Quoted in Richard P. Poethig, "Urban/Metropolitan Mission Policies—An Historical Overview," *Journal of Presbyterian History* 57 (1979): 315.

12. Quote re doctrinal elements in Boyer, *Urban Masses and Moral Order*, 138; quote re soup kitchens in Paul T. Phillips, *Kingdom on Earth: Anglo-American Social Christianity, 1880–1940* (University Park: Pennsylvania State University Press, 1996), 70.

13. Boyer, *Urban Masses and Moral Order*, 139.

14. Ahlstrom, *A Religious History of the American People*, 741; Boyer, *Urban Masses and Moral Order*, 133.

15. Quote from Ahlstrom, *A Religious History of the American People*, 743. These techniques that combined elements of commercial popular culture with revival Protestantism and at the turn of the century, would be adapted, with more or less success, by men like Sam Jones, Rodney "Gipsy" Smith, and Billy Sunday. Boyer, *Urban Masses and Moral Order*, 134; James Gilbert, *Perfect Cities: Chicago's Utopias of 1893* (Chicago: University of Chicago Press, 1991), 178. For more on Moody, see also William McLoughlin Jr., *Modern Revivalism: Charles Grandison Finney to Billy Graham* (New York: Ronald Press, 1959), 166–281; and Bernard A. Weisberger, *They Gathered at the River: The Story of the Great Revivalists and Their Impact upon Religion in America* (Boston: Little, Brown, 1958), 160–219.

16. Among the denominations were the Congregationalists, Methodists, Baptists, and Presbyterians. Boyer, *Urban Masses and Moral Order*, 134. The Presbyterian Board of Home Missions distinguished between home missions (i.e., church planting) directed at "the existing Christian population" and city evangelization, i.e., "rescue work among the neglected multitudes" in city slums. Poethig, "Urban/Metropolitan Mission Policies," 315. Holiness and Pentecostal missions included the Heavenly Recruits (Philadelphia, 1882) and the Peniel Missions (Los Angeles, 1886). Jones argues that the home mission experience proved instrumental in the eventual institutionalization of Holiness and Pentecostal churches. Charles Edwin Jones, *Perfectionist Persuasion: The Holiness Movement and American Methodism, 1867–1936* (Metuchen, N.J.: Scarecrow Press, 1974), 69–71, 107. Nondenominational missions included Jerry McAuley's Water Street Mission in New York, first established in 1872. Boyer, ibid., 135.

17. Murdoch, "The Salvation Army," 103.

18. Ibid., 380–81.

19. *The Christian at Work*, quoted in *AWC*, 19 July 1883, 1.

20. In his recent book, R. Laurence Moore examined the commodification of religion and suggested that the "effort to create a demand for religion committed revivalism to a market logic and . . . market strategies." R. Laurence Moore, *Selling God: American Religion in the Marketplace of Culture* (New York: Oxford University Press, 1994), 6, 10.

21. The resurgence of holiness was, in part, a response to the role of liberal Protestant churches in "mediating Christianity to the modern world." Ahlstrom, *A Religious History of the American People*, 738, 805–6. Modernist ideas included "evolution, comparative religion, and higher criticism of the Scriptures . . . [that] were absorbed with relative ease and seemed only mildly threatening to most fin de siecle church goers." Ferenc Morton Szasz, *The Divided Mind of Protestant America, 1880–1930* (Alabama: University of Alabama Press, 1982), 1. See also Richard Wightman Fox, "The Culture of Liberal Protestant Progressivism, 1875–1925," *Journal of Interdisciplinary History* 23, no. 3 (1993): 640.

22. Officially, the Salvation Army in California remained under the direct command of London until 1886, when control of the Pacific Coast Division was taken

over by National Headquarters in New York. John Milsaps Diary, Vol. 4, Old Series, RG 20.54, SAA; Edward H. McKinley, *Marching to Glory: The History of the Salvation Army in the United States of America, 1880–1980* (San Francisco: Harper and Row, 1980), 23.

23. George M. Marsden, *Fundamentalism and American Culture: The Shaping of Twentieth-Century Evangelicalism, 1870–1925* (Oxford: Oxford University Press, 1980), 45–46.

24. Melvin Easterday Deiter, *The Holiness Revival of the Nineteenth Century* (Metuchen, N.J.: Scarecrow Press, 1980), 60.

25. Virginia Lieson Brereton. *From Sin to Salvation: Stories of Women's Conversions, 1800 to the Present* (Bloomington: Indiana University Press, 1991), 63. Phoebe Palmer took her evangelical message to Europe between 1859 and 1863. It was during that time that Catherine and William Booth came in contact with her particular interpretation of holiness. For more on the religious influences on the Salvation Army and Salvationist theology, see Murdoch, "The Salvation Army," 1–102, and Roger Green, "The Theology of William Booth" (Ph.D. diss., Boston College, 1980). See also Timothy L. Smith, *Revivalism and Social Reform: American Protestantism on the Eve of the Civil War* (Baltimore, Md.: Johns Hopkins University Press, 1957), 140–41, 170; and Deiter, *Holiness Revival,* 27.

26. Dieter, *Holiness Revival,* 36, 42 (quotation on p. 36).

27. By 1850, Palmer had helped to found the Five Points Mission which began "Protestant institutional work in the slums." Smith, *Revivalism,* 170.

28. Jones indicates that, as the sponsors of the first camp meeting devoted entirely to holiness were "well-established urban middle-class people, the meeting attracted listeners similarly situated." Jones argues that the success of the Vineland, New Jersey, meeting and the ensuing formation of the National Camp Meeting Association "mark[ed] the formal opening of a new phase of activity and influence for the movement" which ultimately led to the organization of separate churches, e.g., the Church of the Nazarene. Jones, *Perfectionist Persuasion,* 20; Dieter, *Holiness Revival,* 107.

29. Jones, *Perfectionist Persuasion,* 85–87.

30. The General [William Booth], *Orders and Regulations for Solders of the Salvation Army* (London: International Headquarters, 1899), chapter 3, section 1, #3.

31. "The Salvationists," *New York Times,* 2 February 1892, 4. Pamela Walker, who studies the group in Britain, agrees with the *New York Times*'s evaluation. "The Salvation Army," she wrote, "did not provide a route to bourgeois respectability." Walker, " 'I Live but Not Yet I for Christ Liveth in Me': Men and Masculinity in the Salvation Army, 1865–1890," in *Manful Assertions: Masculinities in Britain since 1800,* ed. Michael Roper and John Tosh (London: Routledge, 1991), 95.

32. Robert C. Allen, *Horrible Prettiness: Burlesque and American Culture* (Chapel Hill: University of North Carolina Press, 1991), 73–74; Moore, *Selling God,* 182. For more on concert saloons, dance halls, and music saloons, see Kathy Peiss, *Cheap Amusements: Leisure in Turn-of-the-Century New York* (Philadelphia: Temple University Press, 1986), 141–42; "Capt. Daniel E. Smith a Grand Life Record," *AWC,* 1 January 1890, 1; "Capt. Ed. Fellers of Wheeling, Va.," *AWC,* 24 May 1890, 14; "Adjutant John Bovil," *AWC,* 29 March 1890, 7; "Almost Drowned but God Had Need of Him: Life of Capt. Hunton," *AWC,* 31 May 1890, 1; and "A Printer's Devil Gets Saved and Develops into a Salvation Army Officer," *AWC,* 24 May 1890, 15.

33. Marsden, *Fundamentalism*, 38, 51. See also Edith Waldvogel Blumhofer, *Restoring the Faith: The Assemblies of God, Penecostalism, and American Culture* (Urbana: University of Illinois Press, 1993), 11–13.

34. Marsden, *Fundamentalism*, 49.

35. Green, "Theology of William Booth," 82.

36. As we will see in ensuing chapters, the Army used the concept of corporate holiness in a number of different ways to justify behaviors that frequently offended mainstream Christians.

37. William Booth, "The General's Address at Exeter Hall on Monday Evening," quoted in Green, "Theology of William Booth," 90.

38. He was the third of five children born to the couple. Their only other son, Henry, died when he was two years old. Their daughters were Ann, Emma, and Mary, none of whom seem to have been associated with the Salvation Army. Indeed, there is no indication that Booth felt a very strong connection to any members of his natal family. His wife, children, and the Salvation Army seem to have functioned as his "family."

39. Murdoch, "The Salvation Army," 51–52. With the exception of the brief period while he "studied" for the ministry, this was the limit of William Booth's education.

40. Ibid., 55.

41. The Salvation Army would use the term "knee drill" when referring to such group prayers. At this time, although most British Methodists were familiar with American "new measures," few of their churches actually used the call to the altar. Richard Carwardine, *Trans-atlantic Revivalism: Popular Evangelism in Britain and America, 1790–1865* (Westport, Conn.: Greenwood Press, 1978), 118–20. Booth not only would imitate Caughey's preaching style and his methods but would go on to institutionalize and pass on the "new measures" techniques in the training of his Salvation Army officer/ministers.

42. Beginning in 1847 as an unpaid local preacher for Wesleyan Methodists, Booth associated himself during the next fourteen years with the Wesleyan Reformers, the Congregational Church, and finally the Methodist New Connexion. He resigned from the latter group in 1861 when the New Connexion conference assigned him for a second time to regular pastoral work instead of itinerancy, which he preferred. Murdoch, "The Salvation Army," 56, 60, 66, 88.

43. Ibid., 13–20.

44. Ibid., 21.

45. Catherine Booth, *Female Ministry: Woman's Right to Preach the Gospel* (New York: Salvation Army Supplies Printing and Publishing Department, 1859, 1975), 22. Catherine Mumford wrote a letter to the minister of a Congregationalist church she was attending to explain her position on the intellectual capacities of women. Ideas about the importance of meaningful education for women were not unique to Catherine Booth. As early as 1792, Mary Wollstonecraft argued that there is no way to know if women's "want of understanding . . . arise[s] from a physical or accidental weakness of faculties," or the "false system of education" to which they have been limited. "[M]en of genius have started out of a class, in which women have never yet been placed." *Vindication of the Rights of Women*, ed. Carol H. Poston (New York: W. W. Norton, 1975), 77. There is a huge literature on women and reform; see, for example, Ruth Bordin, *Woman and Temperance: The*

Quest for Power and Liberty, 1873–1900 (Philadelphia: Temple University Press, 1981); Nancy Schrom Dye, *As Equals and as Sisters: Feminism, the Labor Movement, and the Women's Trade Union League of New York* (Columbia: University of Missouri Press, 1980); Gerda Lerner, *The Grimke Sisters from South Carolina: Pioneers for Women's Rights and Abolition* (Boston: Houghton Mifflin, 1967); Wendy Hamand Venet, *Neither Ballots nor Bullets: Women Abolitionists and the Civil War* (Charlottesville: University Press of Virginia, 1991); Nancy A. Hewitt, *Women's Activism and Social Change: Rochester, New York, 1822–1872* (Ithaca, N.Y.: Cornell University Press, 1984); and Lori D. Ginzburg, *Women and the Work of Benevolence: Morality, Politics and Class in the Nineteenth Century* (New Haven, Conn.: Yale University Press, 1990).

46. For an excellent discussion of Catherine Booth, see Pamela J. Walker's book, *Pulling the Devil's Kingdom Down: The Salvation Army in Victorian England* (Berkeley: University of California Press, 2001), and her dissertation, "Pulling the Devil's Kingdom Down: Gender and Popular Culture in the Salvation Army, 1865–1895" (Ph.D. diss., Rutgers University, 1992), 42–43.

47. "'The Salvation Army' in London," *New York Evangelist*, 1 April 1880, 1; and "A Famous Woman Preacher in London," ibid., 27 May 1880, 1.

48. By 1862, the Booths had five children, ranging in age from 6 months to 6 years. A sixth child would be born in 1864. There would be eight Booth children in all.

49. Murdoch, "The Salvation Army," 103, 107, 134.

50. Ervine, *God's Soldier*, 313. The council complained that Booth failed to consult them before taking on projects that created large debts. The projects that particularly disturbed the council were the soup kitchen, designed to provide low-cost meals to the poor (along with prayer), and the purchase of a permanent building, the People's Market, for the mission's work.

51. Between 1865 and 1868, these missions would be variously known as the Christian Revival Association, the East London Revival Association, and the East London Christian Mission. Between 1868 and 1878, the group would call itself the Christian Mission. Murdoch, "The Salvation Army," 103, 189.

52. Quoted in ibid., 194–95. Recent research suggests that a similar access to spiritual authority also characterized the experience of women in "Penecostal, Holiness and other proto-fundamentalist movements" at least for a time in the early twentieth century. David G. Hackett, "Gender and Religion in American Culture, 1870–1930," *Religion and American Culture* 5, no. 2 (1995): 130. Among the Disciples of Christ between 1870 and 1890, male leaders took a strong stand against expressions of female spiritual and moral authority. Although they allowed women to exhort or lecture in public, they condemned women preaching. Women, they argued, could speak publicly for "'the edification and comfort of saints, and for the conversion of sinners.'" They could also promote a cause, like temperance or a denominational mission. Disciple women must not, however, "preach on a biblical text and exert institutional authority," since that would "indicate a desire to rule over the man." Even when the Disciples began ordaining women, they seldom filled pulpits on a permanent basis. Glenn Michael Zuber, "'Mainline Women Ministers: One Beginning Point' — Women Missionary and Temperance Organizers Become 'Disciples of Christ' Ministers, 1888–1908," *Mid-America: An Historical Review* 78 (Summer 1996): 112–13, 133.

53. Stuart McConnell, "Reading the Flag: A Reconsideration of the Patriotic Cults of the 1890s," *Bonds of Affection: Americans Define Their Patriotism*, ed. John Bodner (Princeton, N.J.: Princeton University Press, 1996), 115.

54. For a more extensive discussion, see T. J. Jackson Lears, *No Place of Grace: Antimodernism and the Transformation of American Culture, 1880–1920* (New York: Pantheon Books, 1981); Susan Curtis, *A Consuming Faith: The Social Gospel and Modern American Culture* (Baltimore, Md.: Johns Hopkins University Press, 1991); Allen Warren, "Popular Manliness: Baden-Powell, Scouting, and the Development of Manly Character," in *Manliness and Morality: Middle-class Masculinity in Britain and America, 1800–1940*, ed. J. Managan and James Walvin, (New York: St. Martin's Press, 1987), 199–216; George M. Fredrickson, *The Inner Civil War: Northern Intellectuals and the Crisis of the Union* (New York: Harper Torchbooks, 1965); and Olive Anderson, "The Growth of Christian Militarism in Mid-Victorian Britain," *English Historical Review* 86 (January 1971): 46–72. Norman Murdoch's discussion of the Salvation Army's use of military imagery argues that William Booth co-opted the spirit of militarism which "lay near the surface of Victorian society and religion." Murdoch, "The Salvation Army," 293. Stuart McConnell associates interest in the military to expressions of patriotism in the late nineteenth century. He suggests that, in contrast to the groups like the Sons and Daughters of the American Revolution in which kinship defined one's connection to the nation, "military obligation was a form of national loyalty" in which even immigrants could participate. McConnell, "Reading the Flag," 115.

55. James Alan Patterson, "The Kingdom and the Great Commission: Social Gospel Impulses and American Protestant Missionary Leaders, 1890–1920," *fides et historia* 25 (1993): 54–55.

56. Over the years there has been a considerable number of changes in the titles used and the authority they confer. Titles like "marachele," "marshal," and "consul" were used only once, each time for a Booth offspring in command of a nation or territory. "Adjutant," "ensign," and "brigadier" went out of favor, and the rank of lieutenant colonel appeared in the twentieth century. As the bureaucracy grew, certain ranks were reserved for the "field" — that is, corps work — and others reserved for "staff" or headquarters, district, territorial, or national. See McKinley, *Marching to Glory*, 224–25; and Murdoch, "The Salvation Army," 182.

57. Brother J. C. Watson, "Chronicle of the War," *AWC*, 12 March 1887, 11.

58. Many organizations in the late nineteenth century co-opted military jargon. Protestant youth groups especially "adopted military organizational models and described their activities in military language." For none of these groups, however, did militiary imagery so completely occupy the day-to-day lives of its members as it did for Salvationists. Lears, *No Place of Grace*, 109.

59. Commissioner Edward Carey, "Mission Flag Hoisted in Cleveland," *AWC*, 9 February 1980, 10.

60. Most histories of the Salvation Army in the United States do not focus much attention on the early efforts of Jermy or the Shirleys, who came to this country in 1878. The Salvation Army's own "Court histories" date the beginning of the work in the United States from the arrival of the "official" representatives of the organization, George Scott Railton and the seven women who accompanied him, in 1880. Ibid.

61. Ervine, *God's Soldier*, 480. See also Carey, "Mission Flag Hoisted."

62. The location of the first Christian Mission in Cleveland — around East 9th Street and Superior — places this mission in the section of the city that was becoming home to various immigrant groups and very close to the area that formed the core of what would become "Cleveland's first black ghetto." Broadway, which also runs through this section of town, was the site of a third Christian Mission station; it opened in 1873. Dorothy Hitzka, "The James Jermy Story, or the Earliest Inception of the Salvation Army in America," unpublished Historical Research Report for the Salvation Army Divisional Headquarters (n.d.); Kenneth L. Kusmer, *A Ghetto Takes Shape* (Urbana: University of Illinois Press, 1980), 37–41.

63. Little is known about the preacher for this congregation, James Fackler. There is some speculation that he was associated with the African Methodist Episcopal Church and may have been African American. Furthermore, when illness forced him to abandon the work in Cleveland, he returned home to the South. Hitzka, "The James Jermy Story," 6.

64. Ervine, *God's Soldier*, 480.

65. Ibid., 481.

66. Carey, "Mission Flag Hoisted," 11.

67. Ervine, *God's Soldier*, 481. According to Dorothy Hitzka, the Christian Mission could not be found in the Cleveland City Directory beyond 1876. Charles Edwin Jones has pointed out that missions were often "short lived." See especially section on the Peniel Mission in Jones, *Perfectionist Persuasion*, 77.

68. Murdoch, "The Salvation Army," 122.

69. John Bodner, *The Transplanted: A History of Immigrants in Urban America* (Bloomington: Indiana University Press, 1985), 146, 148 (n. 57).

70. See George Scott Railton to William Booth, quoted in Ervine, *God's Soldier*, 502.

71. Among these were Reverend James E. Irvine, a revival minister who had held revival meetings at some of the Christian Mission's Stations in East London in 1874 (some sources spell his name Ervine), and his wife, the former Mary C. Billups, who had at one time been a member of the Booth household.

72. McKinley calls those who participated in this early effort "pioneer officers." McKinley, *Marching to Glory*, 7.

73. Ervine, *God's Soldier*, 481–82.

74. Herbert A. Wisbey Jr., *Soldiers Without Swords* (New York: Macmillan, 1956), 12.

75. McKinley, *Marching to Glory*, 5.

76. See David Montgomery, "The Shuttle and the Cross: Weavers and Artisans in the Kensington Riots of 1844," in *Journal of Social History* 5, no. 4 (1972): 411–46.

77. Ervine, *God's Soldier*, 482–83. The Peniel Mission in Los Angeles used some of the same methods as the Salvation Army, including street-corner meetings followed by parades back to the mission hall. Jones, *Perfectionist Persuasion*, 75–76.

78. Nels Erikson, "Research Notes, 1879–80, the Shirleys," RG 20.57, Box 61/12, SAA.

79. *LWC*, 31 January 1880, 1. *The War Cry* is the name of the Salvation Army's official newspaper. McKinley, *Marching to Glory*, 9.

80. *AWC*, 9 July 1881, 1. The year 1898 was the group's peak. The following year the number of corps dropped into the six hundred range and remained there for some time. At the turn of the century a state might have only one or two corps, as in the case of Colorado, or as many as thirty-two, as did Ohio. See also

Disposition of United States Forces (New York: Salvation Army, 1888–1920), microfilm, SAA. The Army first published the *Disposition of Forces* in 1888. It provided a (not entirely reliable) list of the locations and personnel attached to each Salvation Army location in the United States.

81. Peak years for openings were between 1884 and 1891 when there were an average of fifty openings per year. Wisbey, *Soldiers Without Swords*, 33–34; unpublished list of corps and opening dates provided by the Salvation Army Archives and Research Center, Alexandria, Va.; *Disposition of Forces*. While the Army opened many new corps, quite a few of these did not last very long. The frenetic pace of their geographical mobility and the lack of record keeping makes it very difficult for the researcher to reconcile openings and closures in any period.

82. Lt. Col. A. M. Damon, Provincial Officer, to Colonel R. E. Holz, "Brief on the Atlantic Coast Province," 1 July 1908, unpublished report, ACC 89-35, SAA.

83. Wisbey, *Soldiers Without Swords*, 122. After the turn of the century, that growth slowed considerably. By 1913, the number of soldiers had only grown by 6,700 to 31,703.

84. Four thousand people paid admission to see the celebration of the third anniversary of Cmdr. George Scott Railton's arrival in the United States. When Gen. William Booth visited the United States in 1886, he addressed more than 180,000 people in the course of 198 hours of preaching. In 1894, Booth held 340 meetings where he spoke to 437,000 people. Wisbey, Jr., *Soldiers Without Swords*, 42, 66, 87.

85. Similarly, there were 104 corps reported in 1884 but only 17 in 1885. Another boom period, 1887, showed 312 Salvation Army corps followed by a sharp drop in 1888 to 246 corps. These figures are gathered from Wisbey, *Soldiers Without Swords*; McKinley, *Marching to Glory*; and *Disposition of Forces*.

86. For more on these schisms, see McKinley, *Marching to Glory*, 27–31, 74–79.

87. The "parent organization" was quite literally a parent. Three of the national leaders in the United States between 1886 and 1934 were the children of William and Catherine Booth, Ballington and Maud Booth (son and daughter-in-law), Emma and Frederick St. George De Lautour Booth-Tucker (daughter and son-in-law), and Evangeline Booth (daughter), who headed the Army in the United States from 1904 to 1934, after which she became general of the entire international organization.

88. McKinley, *Marching to Glory*, 1; Ervine, *God's Soldier*, 327.

89. Ervine says that Railton had "nervous energy almost to excess." Ervine, *God's Soldier*, 334, 497; McKinley, *Marching to Glory*, 9. As we will see in later chapters, Railton's rapid promotion through the organization was very characteristic of the experience of the few educated, middle-class men and women who joined the Salvation Army.

90. McKinley, *Marching to Glory*, 9.

91. The Hallelujah Lasses were Rachel Evans, Clara Price, Mary Ann Coleman, Elizabeth Pearson, Annie Shaw, and Emma Eliza Florence Morris. Robert Sandall, *The History of the Salvation Army*, vol. 2 (New York: The Salvation Army Supplies and Purchasing Department, 1950), 231.

92. Ervine, *God's Soldier*, 485; McKinley, *Marching to Glory*, 10. Throughout the nineteenth and twentieth centuries in the United States, the sexual division of authority would improve upon the 7 to 1 ratio established by the first "official" contingent. Among staff officers, who served either headquarters, provinces, or

districts in administrative or supervisory capacities, men tended to outnumber women by more than 2 to 1. In the field, among officers who operated the corps on a day-to-day basis, women officers tended to outnumber men by as much as 33 percent. *Disposition of Forces.* The experience of women in the Salvation Army will be addressed at length in chapter 2.

93. Ervine, *God's Soldier,* 487–88.

94. The reporter may have mistaken the crown on the flag for a sun. "The Salvation Army. Arrival of the Pioneer Band in the Country—Their Peculiarities," *New York Times,* 11 March 1880, 5.

95. "Fighting for the Lord: The Movements and Plans of the 'Salvation Army' in This City," *New York Times,* 16 March 1880, 8; "An Attack on the Outworks of Satan in Water-Street," ibid., 19 March 1880, 8.

96. "Fighting for the Lord," *New York Times,* 16 March 1880, 8.

97. "The Salvation Army," *New York Evangelist,* 18 March 1880, 4.

98. Ibid.; see also "The Salvation Army," *New York Evangelist,* 26 February 1880, 1; and "The Salvation Army," *New York Evangelist,* 29 April 1880, 3.

99. According to the mayor, "The public policy appears to be against street preaching and the ordinance only allows it in exceptional cases, that is where clergymen or ministers are to officiate." "Fighting for the Lord," *New York Times,* 16 March 1880, 8.

100. "The American Campaign: How the Soldiers Conduct a Siege," *LWC,* 17; "The American Expedition," *LWC,* 3 April 1880, 4.

101. In 1874, workers in New York held a peaceful labor demonstration at which they demanded that the city provide public-works jobs to desperate workers hit hard by the depression that began in 1873. In a desire to protect themselves, middle-class residents called on city authorities to break up this demonstration and prevent others. At Thompkins Square, police stepped in and violence ensued. Martin Shefter, "Trade Unions and Political Machines: The Organization and Disorganization of the American Working-Class in the Late Nineteenth Century," in *Working-Class Formation: Nineteenth-Century Patterns in Western Europe and the United States,* ed. Ira Katz-Nelson and Aristide Zolberg (Princeton, N.J.: Princeton University Press, 1986), 241–42, 245–46. Diane Winston suggests that the New York ordinances dated from 1810, when an outdoor revival "ended in mob violence." I would speculate, however, that the city refused to exempt Railton from the ordinance because they associated him with the workers and immigrants involved in more recent street violence. Diane Winston, *Red Hot and Righteous: The Urban Religion of the Salvation Army* (Cambridge, Mass.: Harvard University Press, 1999), 27.

102. He left behind Capt. Emma Westbrook to carry on the thankless work in New York City. By the end of the summer the resourceful captain had found a new hall with a porch on which to hold open-air meetings. Wisbey, *Soldiers Without Swords,* 25.

103. Ervine, *God's Soldier,* 502.

104. John D. Waldron, ed. *G. S. R.: Selections from Published and Unpublished Writings of George Scott Railton* (Oakville, Canada: The Salvation Army, 1981), 77–78.

105. Ervine, *God's Soldier,* 493–94.

106. McKinley, *Marching to Glory,* 16.

107. As the story is told, unable to rent a meeting hall (because Salvation Army

services attracted "men who spat on the floor [and] also broke up the seats") and forbidden by authorities to preach in the streets, Railton took to the iced-over Mississippi River singing and preaching to skaters, beyond the reach of city powers. Wisbey, *Soldiers Without Swords*, 17–18; McKinley *Marching to Glory*, 18.

108. Philadelphia apparently had a very large appetite for city missions, and its streets must have been crowded with preachers. In 1882, several years after the Shirleys inaugurated the Salvation Army in that city, a group of preachers "began preaching on the streets of Philadelphia." They rented a hall and "in 1885 incorporated as the Heavenly Recruit Association of Philadelphia." Jones, *Perfectionist Persuasion*, 70.

109. *LWC*, 4 April 1880, 4.

110. *LWC*, 29 May 1880, 4.

111. Moore spent eight years in the United States while he was in his twenties; later, leaving his wife and family in London, he returned for three more years. Murdoch, "The Salvation Army," 396.

112. Although Murdoch has Moore taking over the Salvation Army in the United States in 1882, articles in the 1881 editions of *The War Cry* place him in the United States late in that year. Murdoch, "The Salvation Army," 394; *AWC*, 13 October 1881, 1.

113. In its evaluation of Catherine Booth's preaching, the *New York Evangelist* revealed evangelicals' rationale for quantifying success. "Many conversions are rewarding her labors. . . . God is putting the seal of His approval upon the preaching of Mrs. Booth. 'By their fruits ye shall know them,' was Christ's own test." *New York Evangelist*, 27 May 1880, 1.

114. *AWC*, 13 October 1881, 1. In the late 1870s and the 1880s, various Holiness Associations also published their own periodicals. These, according to Jones, "helped to unite the regional associations and provide necessary direction." They included the *Banner of Holiness* (Western Association), *The Highway* (Iowa Association), *The Good Way* (Southwestern Association), and the *Pacific Herald of Holiness* (Pacific Coast Association). Jones, *Perfectionist Persuasion*, 47. Mainline Protestant denominations also had their own periodicals such as the Presbyterian *New York Evangelist*.

115. "Massachusetts" and "Who Gets the Money," *AWC*, 5 June 1884, 4; "Capture of the Eagle," ibid., 6 February 1883, 4; "Hallelujah Wedding," ibid., 15 May 1884, 3.

116. Emphasis in original. "Promotions," *AWC*, 30 November 1881, 1; "General on Charity," ibid., 5 June 1884, 1; "Notice," ibid., 3 June 1881, 4; "How to Improve the War Cry," ibid., 4 September 1884, 3; Murdoch, "The Salvation Army," 396. Initially *The War Cry* sold for two cents. In late December 1884, the price rose to five cents.

117. The property issue would soon become critical to the first schism that affected the Salvation Army in the United States. Murdoch, "The Salvation Army," 396; McKinley, *Marching to Glory*, 25.

118. Wisbey, *Soldiers Without Swords*, 118–19.

119. In contrast, before wealthy audiences, neither slum-wear nor standard-issue Army attire would do. Instead, Maud Booth wore a uniform "of fine material" and a bonnet "trimmed with a broad silk ribbon" so as not "to shock the sensitive or cultivated nature." Harry B. Wilson, "Contrasting Methods of Salvation Army Warfare," *Harper's Weekly* 38 (1894): 1219.

120. In addition to William and Catherine Booth, there were seven brothers and sisters active in the organization. They not only held key posts in the Salvation Army but were often dispatched as their father's representatives.

121. McKinley, *Marching to Glory*, 28.

122. By this time, Moore had moved the Salvation Army headquarters to Brooklyn, New York.

123. Thomas Moore, "Attention! Attention! Eyes Front!" *AWC*, 30 October 1884, 4.

124. Moore announced in *The War Cry*, "We have . . . taken what appears to us to be the only wise step that is, to incorporate in the name of the Salvation Army, and the property will henceforth be held by a Board of Trustees, with a board of seven Directors which will be composed of the Mayor and staff, thus preserving to the Army the freedom of spiritual direction and showing to our people the proper use of the moneys and property of the Army" (ibid.). See also McKinley, *Marching to Glory*, 28.

125. The two groups would be reunited in 1889. McKinley, *Marching to Glory*, 25–31.

126. Ibid., 28.

127. Frank Smith, *The Salvation War in America for 1885* (New York: Salvation Army Printing and Publishing Department, 1885), 13.

128. *AWC*, quoted in T. E. Moore, *All About the Salvation Army and the Holy Revolution of 1884* (Brooklyn: The Salvation Army of America, n.d.), 13, BB1094, SAA.

129. As indicated, Moore had moved his headquarters to Brooklyn. Smith, meanwhile, set up shop in New York City.

130. "The Hallelujah Octopus," *New York Times*, 20 March 1885, 2; quotation in "A Salvation Army Captain," ibid., 21 March 1885, 8.

131. Moore told the reporter that when he tried to explain to General Booth that he (Booth) could not hold title to "all property acquired in America" but that since Moore had become a naturalized citizen he'd had "all deeds, leases etc executed to himself," the general was displeased. Said Moore, "At 'ome in the hold country he 'olds everything in 'is hone name." "Salvation Army Rebels: General Moore Speaks Very Bitterly about General Booth of England," New York *World*, 25 March 1885, 8.

132. Moore, *All About the Salvation Army*.

133. *Positive Facts Regarding the Salvation Army of America* (Atlanta: Salvation Army Southern Headquarters, n.d.), 1, in Archives of Atlanta Historical Society, Atlanta, Georgia, BB1282.

134. Frank Smith, *The Salvation War in America*, 147; Murdoch, "The Salvation Army," 400.

135. Norman H. Murdoch, "Salvationist-Socialist Frank Smith, M.P.: Father of Salvation Army Social Work," paper presented to the Salvation Army Historical Conference, New York City, 13 September 1978, 2.

136. The Pacific Coast Branch had never been under Moore's jurisdiction but, rather, had answered directly to England.

137. Why being called a "curly headed white man" was a sign of affection is not clear. It seems to have been as much a description of Pugmire as a sign of regard.

138. Smith, *Salvation War*, 136. In 1885, Pugmire wrote a hymn (in minstrel-show dialect) published in *The War Cry* entitled "Southern Colored Work" to the

tune of "When de Stars ob de Elements Are Falling." One stanza summarized the Salvation Army's evangelical Christian basis for advertising salvation to African Americans. "It does not matter wedder / We are black or white / Blessed be de name ob de Lord! / For God says, 'Whoever,' / Can come and be put right." *AWC*, 26 December 1885, 7.

139. Murdoch, "The Salvation Army," 396. The numbers of corps Smith opened during his tenure is not absolutely clear. Some sources suggest that as many as 300 new corps opened by 1886. As Smith himself reported, however, many of his corps opened and closed quickly. Indeed, he characterized the work as being "of a somewhat guerrilla character in certain localities." That is, the Army would "form flying columns, and . . . deliver sharp and rapid strokes upon the slumbering conscience of one city after another." Smith, *The Salvation War*, 74.

140. Murdoch, "The Salvation Army," 400; McKinley, *Marching to Glory*, 25–28, 30, 82–83.

141. Bosch, "The Salvation Army in Chicago," 66; "Salvation Army Funeral," *Dover Daily Republican*, reprinted in *AWC*, 4 April 1884, 2.

142. The earlier definition had been based on "sameness" provided by the notion of republicanism and obligation "mediated through such local institutions as the town, family or the regiment." He defines republicanism as sameness, "socially in their standing as actual or potential owners of property and politically in their standing as independent voters." In the 1890s several new models of "American" emerged, including nationalization of "small group loyalties" (e.g., hereditary groups like the DAR), and the statist model of national loyalty, which defined the nation along narrow class and ethnic boundaries. McConnell, "Reading the Flag," 116–17.

143. Frank Smith, "The Cause of Estrangement between Major Moore and the General Was Not Incorporation, but Mismanagement and Insubordination," *AWC*, 22 November 1884, 4.

144. The General, "Weekly Letter," *AWC*, 13 December 1884, 1.

145. His son Herbert would visit two years later. Booth would visit the United States again in 1894.

146. *Chicago Tribune*, 31 October 1886, 9, and 1 November 1886, 3; *Advance*, 4 November 1886, quoted in Bosch, "The Salvation Army in Chicago," 36.

147. "Salvation Army Meetings," *New York Times*, 11 September 1886, 2.

148. William Booth gave all of his children special titles. For example, son Ballington was "Marshall," while daughters Emma and Catherine were the "Consul" and "Marechale," respectively. McKinley, *Marching to Glory*, passim; Flora Larson, *My Best Men Are Women* (London: Hodder and Stoughton, Ltd. 1974), 9.

149. Ballington and Maud would be replaced by Emma and Frederick St. George de Lautour Booth-Tucker. After Emma Booth-Tucker's death in 1904, Evangeline Booth was sent to lead the United States. She held that position until 1934, when she was selected to be general of the International Salvation Army.

150. McKinley, *Marching to Glory*, 70–76. In practice, of course, Booth was thoroughly British, from the flying of Union Jacks from his automobile in the early twentieth century to his advocacy of social imperialism in his book *In Darkest England*.

151. "Pine Knots from Michigan," *AWC*, 1 December 1888, 5.

152. Wisbey, *Soldiers Without Swords*, 76–77.

153. For more on Maud Charlesworth and the significance of her experience in Britain, see Pamela J. Walker, *Pulling the Devil's Kingdom Down: The Salvation Army in Victorian Britain* (Berkeley: University of California, forthcoming). Many thanks to Pamela Walker for generously sharing chapter 5 of her manuscript with me.

154. "Mrs. Ballington Booth," *New York Times*, 13 February 1889, 8.

155. Patterson, "The Kingdom and the Great Commission," 49.

156. Walker, *Pulling the Devil's Kingdom Down*, 14–15.

157. "By 1900 there were rescue homes in Los Angeles, Spokane, Portland . . . St. Louis, Chicago, Omaha, Philadelphia, Des Moines, St. Paul, San Diego, and Louisville." Lt. Col. Edith MacLachlan, "Bird's Eye View of the Women's Social, 1886–1978," paper presented at the Salvation Army Territorial Historical Commission Meeting, 8 June 1984. See also McKinley, *Marching to Glory*, 55.

158. "Victorian rhetoric" quotation in Peggy Pasco, *Relations of Rescue: The Search for Female Moral Authority in the American West, 1874–1939* (New York: Oxford University Press, 1990), 6; "Rescue Morris Cottage," *AWC*, 23 October 1886, 1. For more on female moral reform, see Carol Smith-Rosenberg, "Beauty, the Beast, and the Militant Woman: A Case Study in Sex Roles and Social Stress in Jacksonian America," *American Quarterly* 23 (October 1971): 562–84; and Mary P. Ryan, "The Power of Women's Networks: A Case Study of Female Moral Reform in Antebellum America," *Feminist Studies* 5 (Spring 1979): 66–86. On the slum nursery, see McKinley, *Marching to Glory*, 55.

159. Bosch, "The Salvation Army in Chicago," 106. Because the uniform failed to afford female Salvationists with protection among the "masses," the Lasses in this branch of the Army dressed like their neighbors, in "old calico frocks, aprons and shawls . . . fastened at the throat with an old wire hairpin." Julia Hayes Percy, "In the Vilest Slums," New York *World*, quoted in *AWC*, 1 March 1890, 2. For more on working-class understandings of mutual aid and neighborliness, see Christine Stansell, *City of Women: Sex and Class in New York, 1789–1860* (Urbana: University of Illinois Press, 1987), 55. The Army operated a similar work in Britain called the Cellar, Gutter and Garret Brigade, inaugurated in 1884.

160. "A Great Newspaper's Opinion on the Salvation Army," *New York Sun*, quoted in *AWC*, 16 March 1889, 9.

161. William Halpin, "Some Salvation Army 'High Spots' in the United States, 1879–1904," unpublished paper, ACC 86-37, SAA. McKinley, *Marching to Glory*, 61. Maud also spoke before audiences at the University of Chicago, the Presbyterian Social Union, and the World's Congress of Representative Women. Bosch, "The Salvation Army in Chicago," 77–78, 81.

162. "Charmed with Mrs. Booth," *New York Times*, 2 February 1889, 8; "Mrs. Ballington Booth," 13 February 1889, 8.

163. "Mrs. Booth's Magnetism," *New York Times*, 15 February 1889, 8. Similarly, at a 1892 Continental Congress, the boxes in the Music Hall were "filled with fashionably-dressed men and women, leaders in denominational church work, who had been especially invited." "Rally of Salvationists," *New York Times*, 22 November 1892, 2.

164. "Mrs. Ballington Booth," *New York Times*, 13 February 1889, 8. Maud's position was reiterated in *AWC*. "As the meeting is strictly for the class Mrs. Booth has lately been reaching in her drawingroom meetings. . . . the invitations will be restricted to them alone." Quoted in Wisbey, *Soldiers Without Swords*, 94.

165. Quotation in "Flattery in the New York Press," *AWC*, 16 February 1889, 8. Between 1887 and 1896, prominent members of the clergy like Josiah Strong and Lyman Abbott became league members. See Josiah Strong's *Religious Movements for Social Betterment* (New York: Baker and Taylor, 1900).

166. The Auxiliary League first appeared in 1883 but was apparently not very successful and petered out during the confusion of the schism in 1884.

167. McKinley, *Marching to Glory*, 61; Ballington Booth, "Salvation Army Auxiliary Force of the United States," *AWC*, 20 August 1887, 9.

168. Harry B. Wilson, "Contrasting Methods of Salvation Army Warfare," *Harper's Weekly* 38 (12 December 1894): 1219.

169. Herbert A. Wisbey Jr., interview with Commissioner Edward J. Parker, 9 August 1948, Wisbey Collection, Interviews, RG 20.53, Box 51/19, SAA.

170. In 1896, there were 6,000 auxiliaries; in 1898, there were 735 local corps.

171. The nature of the Social Scheme and its impact on the Salvation Army will be addressed in chapter 4.

172. Private memorandum by the Chief of the Staff to the Field Commissioner on her visit to New York, February 1896, Evangeline Cory Booth, RG 20.40, Box 28/5, SAA; "Ballington Booth's Suppressed Farewell Letter," *New York Times*, Sunday ed., 25 August 1912, 5.

173. "Ballington Booth's Suppressed Farewell Letter." Warren C. Platt suggests that "questions of local autonomy and the permitted degree of assimilation to the larger society and conformity to its values" were the roots of the disagreement. "The Volunteers of America: The Origins and Development of Its Ideology," *Journal of Religious History* 16 (June 1990): 35.

174. McKinley, *Marching to Glory*, 70–76.

175. *Chicago Tribune*, 31 March 1896, 6.

176. "Alarm in the Salvation Army," *New York Times*, 15 January 1896, 7. See also in ibid., "Salvationists in Doubt," 16 January 1896, 4; and "Loyal to Old Leaders," 23 February 1896, 4.

177. "Keep the Booths Here," *New York Times*, 25 January 1896, 4. See also "To Commend the Army Leaders," ibid., 31 January 1896, 8.

178. The couple went on to form the Volunteers of America, a movement very similar to the Salvation Army in organization and mission.

179. Quote from *Living Church*, 29 February 1896, 899. *Advance*, 12 March 1896, 368. See also *Chicago Tribune*, 2 March 1896, 6, and 15 March 1896, 34.

180. *Chicago Daily News*, 4 February 1896, 7.

181. Ibid.

182. Some of these Salvationists had only returned to the fold in 1889, when Ballington Booth reconciled with the Salvation Army of America then under the leadership of Colonel Richard Holz. Under the agreement, most officers from Moore's incorporated Army "returned to the Booth ranks." These men and women may have been particularly reluctant to leave a second time. The reconciliation did not spell the end of the American Salvation Army. Twenty-five loyal posts remained with the Army, which reorganized first under the new leadership of General Duffin. Ultimately, Booth's Army used American courts to force Duffin's organization to change its name; the group became the American Rescue Workers in 1913. The Worldwide Salvation Army in the United States did not incorporate until 1899. Until that time, Ballington Booth was legal owner of all Army property in the United States. When he split with his father in 1896 and left

the organization to start the Volunteers of America, he could have taken all Army property with him, but did not. McKinley, *Marching to Glory*, 82, 237 (n. 47).

183. At Booth's insistence, all of the sons-in-law added the Booth name to their own. The general also saw to it that each of his daughters held "rank and authority independent of, and only grudgingly subordinate to, that of their husbands." McKinley, *Marching to Glory*, 80.

184. *AWC*, 14 March 1896, 13.

185. "Miss Booth Victorious," *New York Times*, 2 March 1896, 4.

186. Bramwell Booth to Chief, 7 October 1926, Bramwell Booth, RG 20.111 Box 125/5, SAA.

Chapter Two

1. According to Jackson, "wheelers would go along the face of the coal where the various miners worked and take as many boxes [of dirt and slate] as we could push and push them to what we called the 'road head' where there was a flat piece of sheet iron on which we turned the boxes and took them out [to] the entry. . . ." The Jackson family had moved to Higginsville after illness forced them to sell their farm in Lafayette County and crop failures plagued them on rented land. In Higginsville, he said, "there appeared to be plenty of work available for [my father] and my older brothers." Lt. Col. Arthur Jackson, "Reminiscences of Lt. Colonel Arthur Jackson," unpublished manuscript, 1939, SAA.

2. Ibid.

3. "Life of Lieut. Nellie Upham," *AWC*, 26 March 1887, 1.

4. Brig. Eileen Douglas, *Elizabeth Swift Brengle* (London: Salvationist Publishing and Supplies, 1922), 29. Susan Swift later quit the Army to join a Catholic order. Sally Chesham, *Born to Battle: The Salvation Army in America* (New York: The Salvation Army, 1965), 76; Susan Swift, "The Conversion of Susan Swift," unpublished manuscript, 1897, RG 20.11, Box 209/19, SAA.

5. Clarence W. Hall, *Samuel Logan Brengle: Portrait of a Prophet* (Chicago: The Salvation Army Supply and Purchasing Department, 1933), 33, 54, 99. Other Brengle biographies include: Eric Coward, *Brick and the Book* (London: Salvationist Publishing and Supplies, 1948); William Clark, *Logan Brengle: Teacher of Holiness* (London: Hodder and Stoughton, 1980); Sallie Chesham, *Like a River* (Atlanta: The Salvation Army Supplies and Purchasing Department, 1981). I have relied most heavily on Hall's biography since all of the others offer little additional information.

6. Norman H. Murdoch, "Female Ministry in the Thought and Work of Catherine Booth," *Church History* 53 (September 1984): 357. See also Winston for a discussion of the "attraction the Army held for middle- and upper-class women." Because she deals almost exclusively with images constructed by the Army's newspaper and the popular press, however, I believe that Winston overemphasizes the centrality of middle- and upper-class women in the organization. Diane Winston, *Red Hot and Righteous: The Urban Religion of the Salvation Army* (Cambridge, Mass.: Harvard University Press, 1999), 62–67 (quotation on p. 51).

7. Data on soldiers can be found in Corps Roll Book, White Plains, N.Y., RG 4.18, Box 209/23; Corps Roll Book, Yorkville, N.Y., RG 4.7, Box 207/3,5,7,8, 9,10,11; Corps Roll Book, Somerville, MA, Eastern Territorial Corps, RG 4.8, Box 208/6,7,8,9; Corps Roll Book, Mt. Vernon Corps Roll, RG 9.10, Box 209/9,10;

Corps Roll Book, St. Thomas, Virgin Islands, RG 4.14, Box 209/4, SAA. Field officers organized, financed, and preached at local corps. Field staff officers, who served at provincial and district headquarters, tended to include more married couples. In 1893, 34 married couples, 20 single males, and 3 single females were field staff officers. By 1903, 50 married couples, 22 single male, and 19 single female officers held staff positions.

8. For the more than 30 percent of Salvation Army officers who were foreign born, memoirs suggest that many (especially the English, Canadians, and Swedes) had either belonged to or been familiar with the Army before emigrating to the United States. The evidence suggests that, particularly for the Swedes, who joined in such large numbers that they formed their own "Scandinavian" Corps, the Army may have played a role similar to that of other immigrant churches, that is, assisting in the adjustment to a new environment. These Corps used the Swedish language for services and published their own Swedish language version of *The War Cry*.

9. Richard D. Shiels, "The Feminization of American Congregationalism, 1730–1835," *American Quarterly* 3, no. 1 (Spring 1981): 48.

10. The data also do not permit me to determine with certainty the relative proportions of working- and middle-class women. None of the documents provided information on paternal occupation, and there is no way to be sure that the men and women for whom I have no occupation were never employed. Indeed, given the youth of the sample, it seems more likely that a larger number of the women had performed wage work at some time prior to joining the Salvation Army.

11. Winston concluded that "[r]ecruits were the daughters of farmers or small businessmen" and rarely worked outside of the home. Winston, *Red Hot and Righteous*, 80, 81. My data suggests, however, that most female Salvation Army officers not only worked but had done so in jobs typically found in urban areas.

12. Of the 1,058 cases I had, 549 were women. Of this number I had occupational data on 332. Age and marital status determined the rate of overall female participation in the labor force with the highest level among unmarried women between the ages of fifteen and twenty-four. Rosalyn Baxandall et al., eds., *America's Working Women: A Documentary History, 1600 to the Present* (New York: Vintage Books, 1976), 405, and Julie A. Matthaei, *An Economic History of Women in America: Women's Work and Sexual Division of Labor, and the Development of Capitalism* (New York: Schocken Books, 1982), 142–43.

13. Officership entitled Salvationists to a salary, and they were not expected to hold down outside jobs. However, in the early years, wages were taken out of the often meager monies collected locally, and Army policy dictated that all Corps bills be paid prior to any salaries. Very often, officers who faced near starvation were forced to moonlight.

14. The dearth of self-employed Salvationists may also be a factor of age, since nearly 45 percent of male Salvationists were between the ages of 17 and 22 and therefore unlikely to have become self-employed. Still, as their memoirs suggest, few of these men had any expectations of becoming proprietors.

15. Evelyn Nakano Glenn and Roslyn L. Feldberg, "Degraded and Deskilled: The Proletarianization of Clerical Work," in Rachel Kahn-Hut et al., *Women and Work: Problems and Perspectives* (New York: Oxford University Press, 1982); Olivier Zunz, *Making America Corporate, 1870–1920* (Chicago: University of Chicago

Press, 1990), chap. 5, passim. See also Alice Kessler-Harris, *Out to Work* (Oxford: Oxford University Press, 1982); and Cindy Sondik Aron, *Ladies and Gentlemen of the Civil Service: Middle-Class Workers in Victorian America* (New York: Oxford University Press, 1987).

16. Without information on paternal occupation, for the purposes of this discussion, I have adopted college education as a sign of middle-class status.

17. Most had been members of the Methodist church, but some had been Episcopalians. Murdoch, "Female Ministry," 357; Hall, *Samuel Logan Brengle*, 46–51; "Mrs. Fannie McAbee," *AWC*, 6 July 1889, 3. My sources reveal that several of their fathers or grandfathers had served in the Union army. Samuel Brengle's father died after being wounded in the Battle of Vicksburg. Fannie Lawson's father had served in the Forty-fifth Illinois Volunteer Infantry Regiment. And Charles McAbee's grandfather had served in the United States army as a noncommissioned officer. Hall, ibid., 19–20; McAbee Letters, SAWTM, 112; "Adjutant Charles McAbee," *AWC*, 6 July 1889, 2. The dearth of information about middle-class Salvationists may reflect the Army's desire to foster an image of success among the "lower" classes. It is also likely that middle-class women and men felt put off by the organization's religious culture and the uneducated working-class officers who held positions of authority in the organization. Their small numbers may also reflect the tendency of middle-class men and women after the mid-1880s to join the Auxiliary League rather than the organization proper. For more on the Auxiliary League, see chapter 1.

18. By 1908, the Atlantic Coast Province included most of Pennsylvania (with thirty-five corps), Delaware, Maryland, Virginia, and North Carolina. Lt. Col. A. M. Damon, Provincial Officer, to Col. R. E. Holz, "Brief on the Atlantic Coast Province," 1 July 1908, unpublished report, ACC 89-35, SAA.

19. Most of the Scandinavian Salvationists were Swedish; smaller numbers were Norwegian.

20. The Scandinavian corps could be found in New Hampshire, Massachusetts, Rhode Island, Connecticut, New York, New Jersey, Pennsylvania, and Ohio. The Italian corps was in New York City and the Chinese corps were in Oakland and San Francisco. Damon Brief; Colonel and Mrs. R. E. Holz, Provincial Officers, "Brief on Ohio, Pittsburgh and Southern Province," 1908, unpublished report, ACC 82-75, SAA; Edward H. McKinley, *Marching to Glory: The History of the Salvation Army in the United States of America, 1880–1980* (San Francisco: Harper and Row, 1980), 50, 104.

21. *AWC*, 18 July 1885, 1.

22. George B. Evans and wife, Cadet Anderson, "White and Colored Troops Unite," *AWC*, 28 September 1889, 3.

23. James E. Beane, "Early Black Salvationists in America," unpublished manuscript presented at the Territorial Historical Commission Conference, 14–15 September 1974, 3, RG 20.65, Box 69/7, SAA. "Wanted, men and women, with colored skins, and white hearts," read an article in *AWC*, "ready to endure hatred and hardships for Jesus." "Wanted for the Southern Expedition," *AWC*, 12 December 1885, 1.

24. *AWC*, 18 July 1885, 1. In the 1898 edition of *Orders and Regulations for Social Officers*, the Army wrote, "none shall be debarred from any of its benefits [social service] . . . because they are of any particular nationality, race, or color." Beane, "Early Black Salvationists," 2, 6.

25. Although the evidence is very sketchy, it seems that not all African Americans joined in segregated corps. Corps in Brooklyn, Manhattan, Philadelphia, and Washington, D.C., appear to have been sparsely integrated. It does seem, however, that through the early twentieth century the Army assigned black officers to exclusively African American corps; since there were so few the Army discouraged blacks from seeking commissions, "because there were no appointments to give them." Sr. Major Lambert Bailey (R), Biographical Material on Individual Black Salvationists, RG 20.65, Box 69/1, SAA.

26. There is, of course, an extensive literature on the disruptive conditions caused by large-scale industrialization during the late nineteenth and early twentieth centuries. Melvin Dubofsky, *Industrialism and the American Worker* (Arlington Heights: Harlan Davidson, Inc., 1975), 3, 16. See also David M. Gordon, Richard Edwards, and Michael Reich, *Segmented Work, Divided Workers: The Historical Transformation of Labor in the United States* (Cambridge: Cambridge University Press, 1982), 112; David Brody, *Steelworkers in America: The Non-Union Era* (New York: Harper Torchbooks, 1960), 32; Alan Trachtenberg, *The Incorporation of America: Culture and Society in the Gilded Age*. New York: Hill and Wang, 1982; Herbert G. Gutman, *Work, Culture and Society in Industrializing America* (New York: Vintage Books, 1977).

27. Stephan Thernstrom, *The Other Bostonians: Poverty and Progress in the American Metropolis, 1880–1970* (Cambridge, Mass.: Harvard University Press, 1973), 143, 121.

28. Since the data do not permit me to determine whether the native-born Americans in my sample are the children of native-born parents, it is possible I have overestimated the Yankeeness of my sample. However, if some of the native-born Salvationists were actually second generation, they may also have felt dissatisfaction with their progress particularly relative to Yankees. Furthermore, Thernstrom found that even second-generation youth who had begun in nonmanual labor were "less able to carve out a secure niche in the white collar world." These young white-collar workers experienced a relatively high (22 percent) rate of downward mobility in the late nineteenth century. Ibid., 119, 121–23.

29. In his home state of Texas, Milsaps had opened a small grocery store and then tried to operate a photography business. In 1877 he set out for the Black Hills of Dakota to prospect for gold, only to discover that the heyday of the individual gold miner had passed. By the late nineteenth century, only large corporations could command the capital equipment required to mine gold, and would-be prospectors usually ended up working for wages. Writing in his diary, Milsaps noted that there was "little gold in the Hills that can be worked and no work to be got there as the country is overcrowded with poor men." John Milsaps Diary, vol. 2, Old Series, RG 20.54, SAA.

30. John Milsaps Diary, vol. 3, Old Series, RG 20.54, SAA. Similar personal stories can be found in other Salvation Army officers' memoirs. From his early years in a spool factory to lumber camps where he performed brute labor, James Price, like John Milsaps, believed that "somehow, somewhere, life held something different for me." James Price, "Random Reminiscences, 1889–1899," RG 20.27, SAA. See also Jackson, "Reminiscences."

31. Joseph F. Kett, *Rites of Passage: Adolescence in America, 1790 to the Present* (New York: Basic Books, 1977), 146–50.

32. Ibid., 151–53.

33. Jackson, "Reminiscences"; John Milsaps Diary, vol. 1, Old Series, RG 20.54, SAA.

34. George Cunningham to his parents, 3 February 1888, RG 20.16, Box 211/5, SAA.

35. Major Mrs. Henry L. Stephen, "A Resume of My 73 Years as a Salvation Army Officer," ACC 84-51, SAA; for the impact of industrialization on women's labor, see Kessler-Harris, *Out to Work*, 110, 113; Nancy Woloch, *Women and the American Experience* (New York: Alfred A. Knopf, 1984), 220; Joanne J. Meyerowitz, *Women Adrift: Independent Wage Earners in Chicago, 1880–1930* (Chicago: University of Chicago Press, 1988); and Lynn Y. Weiner, *From Working Girl to Working Mother: The Female Labor Force in the United States, 1820–1980* (Chapel Hill: University of North Carolina Press, 1985). See also Susan Porter Benson, *Counter Cultures: Saleswomen, Managers and Customers in American Department Stores, 1890–1940* (Urbana: University of Illinois Press, 1986), for a thorough look at the world of the department store and the saleswoman's world of work.

36. Eva Thompson to Ensign E. Parker, 22 August 1891, SAA; Commissioner Edward Justus Parker, *My Fifty-Eight Years* (New York: Salvation Army Printing and Publishing Department, 1943), 96.

37. H. Knott, "Captain May Harris," *AWC*, 22 March 1890, 1.

38. Matthaei, *An Economic History*, chap. 9, passim; Gordon, Edwards, and Reich, *Segmented Work*, 93–94; Kessler-Harris, *Out to Work*, 123.

39. Meyerowitz, *Women Adrift*, 20. Sara M. Evans, *Born for Liberty: A History of Women in America* (New York: The Free Press, 1989), 135.

40. Susan Curtis, *A Consuming Faith: The Social Gospel and Modern American Culture* (Baltimore, Md.: Johns Hopkins University Press, 1991), 16.

41. Aron, *Ladies and Gentlemen*, 39. Quote from Kett, *Rites of Passage*, 161.

42. Curtis, *A Consuming Faith*, 75.

43. Brengle's biographer suggests that he rejected the pulpit in South Bend because he "felt a definite call to evangelistic work." He may also have rejected the Studebaker offer because of a concern that he would not be free to preach as he saw fit. During his time in seminary, Brengle had come to advocate the controversial doctrine of holiness which, as a friend pointed out to him, was a "doctrine that split[ ] churches." Hall, *Samuel Logan Brengle*, 53. His rejection of the opportunity may also reflect a reluctance to leave the larger and more cosmopolitan environment of Boston for a provincial South Bend pulpit.

44. It is interesting to note that in 1855, William Booth had become a hired preacher for a well-to-do boot manufacturer, Edward Rabbits. Three months later, Booth left this post feeling that Rabbits and his congregation were "denying the Minister . . . his proper authority . . . speaking of him in public and in private as their 'hired' preacher." Norman H. Murdoch, "The Salvation Army: An Anglo-American Revivalist Social Mission" (Ph.D. diss., University of Cincinnati, 1985), 49; St. John Ervine, *God's Soldier: General William Booth*, vol. 1 (New York: Macmillian, 1935), 61–62.

45. Hall, *Samuel Logan Brengle*, 118.

46. There is a vast literature on women and the domestic sphere. Among the works are: Nancy F. Cott, *The Bonds of Womanhood: "Women's Sphere" in New England, 1780–1835* (New Haven, Conn.: Yale University Press, 1977); Kathryn

Kish Sklar, *Catherine Beecher: A Study in American Domesticity* (New York: W. W. Norton, 1973); and Mary Ryan, *Cradle of the Middle Class: The Family in Oneida County, New York, 1790–1865* (Cambridge: Cambridge University Press, 1981).

47. See Ryan, *Cradle of the Middle Class*, passim; Mark Carnes, in his article "Middle-Class Men and the Solace of Fraternal Ritual" suggests that men may not have "pliantly changed in response to maternal preachments." While this may be the case, both middle-class men and women regarded such training as women's responsibility, and it is from that belief that women drew much of their moral authority in this era. Mark C. Carnes and Clyde Griffen, eds., *Meanings for Manhood: Constructions of Masculinity in Victorian America* (Chicago: University of Chicago Press, 1990), 37–38.

48. T. J. Jackson Lears, *No Place of Grace: Antimodernism and the Transformation of American Culture, 1880–1920* (New York: Pantheon, 1981), 16.

49. Mary Ann Clawson, *Constructing Brotherhood: Class, Gender and Fraternalism* (Princeton, N.J.: Princeton University Press, 1989), 186–87 (quotation on p. 185).

50. S. F. Swift, "Emancipated: Story of a Danish Girl," *AWC*, 26 April 1890, 14. The expansion of the domestic sphere earlier in the century had drawn increasing numbers of young, single, middle-class women into college. Allen F. Davis, *American Heroine: The Life and Legend of Jane Addams* (London: Oxford University Press, 1973), 10.

51. While 90 percent of late-nineteenth-century women married, only 63 percent of college-educated women married during the same period. Woloch, *Women and the American Experience*, 282–87. Anonymous, *Elizabeth Swift Brengle: A Girl Collegiate*, (London: Salvationist Publishing and Supplies, 1930), 12; William Clark, *Samuel Logan Brengle: Teacher of Holiness* (London: Hodder and Stoughton, 1980), 39; Susan Swift, "The Conversion of Susan Swift," unpublished manuscript, 1897, RG 20.11, Box 209/19, SAA; Ensign E. M. Clark, "Brigadier Susie Swift," *The Conqueror* (November 1896): 513–15. For more on college-educated women in the late nineteenth century, see Woloch, *Women and the American Experience*, 278–79, 282–87; Davis, *American Heroine*, 24–37; and Curtis, *A Consuming Faith*, chap. 2, passim.

52. Susan Juster, "'In a Different Voice': Male and Female Narratives of Religious Conversion in Post-Revolutionary America," *American Quarterly* 441, no. 1 (1989): 36.

53. John Milsaps Diary, vol. 2, Old Series, RG 20.54, SAA.

54. While the rejection of alcohol may appear to mimic the concerns of bourgeois evangelicals, as we will see in chapter 3, and although Salvationists rejected liquor and the violence and risky sexual behavior it encouraged, they did not reject the sociability, camaraderie, and mutuality of saloon culture. Among men's conversion stories published in *The War Cry* between 1885 and 1890, nearly half cited drink as the cause of their degraded position. Of 48 stories, 23 mentioned the impact of drink. Men also discussed the impact of drink in other terms. Married men or young men with drunken fathers considered the consequences of drinking in language similar to that of female temperance reformers; that is, they stressed the threat of alcohol to the family economy and the physical welfare of women. See, for example, "A Thrilling Story," *AWC*, 5 February 1887, 4. For a discussion of the ways in which women temperance reformers framed the debate about drinking, see Ruth Bordin, *Women and Temperance: The Quest for Power and*

Liberty, 1873–1900 (Philadelphia: Temple University Press, 1980); Barbara L. Epstein, *The Politics of Domesticity: Women, Evangelism, and Temperance in Nineteenth Century America* (Middletown, Conn.: Wesleyan University Press, 1981); Ian Tyrrell, *Woman's World, Woman's Empire: The Woman's Christian Temperance Union in International Perspective, 1880–1930* (Chapel Hill: University of North Carolina Press, 1991); and Ryan, *Cradle of the Middle Class.*

55. Elliott Gorn, in his article " 'Good-Bye Boys, I Die a True American': Homicide, Nativism, and Working-Class Culture in Antebellum New York City," points out that bachelor culture in nineteenth-century cities "was an oppositional culture, a living refutation of bourgeois and evangelical verities . . . [m]utuality, deep loyalties, and elaborate rituals of friendship on the one hand, fierce hatreds among rival cliques and intense competition for status on the other." It was also "a culture with a high potential for violence, because working-class existence encourages callousness as one response to pain." *Journal of American History* 74 (1987): 406–7.

56. "A Printer's Devil Gets Saved," *AWC*, 24 May 1890, 15.

57. Charles Buckley, "A Few Notes Extracted from a Burglar's Diary," *AWC*, 26 December 1885, 2.

58. Kathy Peiss, *Cheap Amusements: Leisure in Turn-of-the-Century New York* (Philadelphia: Temple University Press, 1986), 95, 100, 105.

59. "Life of Lieut. Nellie Upham."

60. Throughout the seventeenth and eighteenth centuries, Americans had also warned each other about the corrupting influences of wealth and "luxury." This concern was often discussed in gendered terms: "emasculation by luxury," "effeminate European society." However, as John Higham has noted, in the 1890s even women were "more manly." Clyde Griffen, "Reconstructing Masculinity from the Evangelical Revival to the Waning of Progressivism: A Speculative Synthesis," in *Meanings for Manhood: Constructions of Masculinity in Victorian America*, ed. Mark C. Carnes and Clyde Griffen (Chicago: University of Chicago Press, 1990), 189; John Higham, *Writing American History: Essays on Modern Scholarship* (Bloomington: Indiana University Press, 1970), 83.

61. Anthony Rotundo argues that a physical ideal of manhood emerged in the first half of the nineteenth century. The ideal man had great physical strength and "primitive energy," which he sought to use for "civilized ends." He traces this ideal, in part, to the rise of individualism (which focused on the person over the community) and changes in middle-class life. "Body and Soul: Changing Ideals of American Middle-Class Manhood, 1770–1920," *Journal of Social History* 16, no. 4 (1983): 26–33.

62. Richard L. Bushman, *From Puritan to Yankee: Character and the Social Order in Connecticut, 1690–1795* (New York: W. W. Norton, 1967), 23–24; Lears, *No Place of Grace*, 26–32; Lears, "From Salvation to Self-Realization: Advertising and the Therapeutic Roots of the Consumer Culture, 1880–1930," in *The Culture of Consumption*, ed. Lears and Richard Wightman Fox (New York: Pantheon, 1983), 7.

63. Swift, "Conversion."

64. These feelings have also been found in young women during the revivals of the Second Great Awakening. They focused less on specific kinds of sinful behavior and more on a general sense of guilt over their state of rebellion against God, which made them unable to live out their faith. Quotation in Epstein, *The Politics of Domesticity*, 55.

65. Lears, *No Place of Grace*, 98; Rotundo, "Body and Soul," 27–28.

66. "Life of Mrs. Capt. Sandy," *AWC*, 7 June 1890, 15; "Capt. De Long Relates Her Experience," *AWC*, 31 May 1890, 10; "Life of Capt. B. H. Shadduck," *AWC*, 18 October 1890, 14.

67. Henry F. May, *Protestant Churches and Industrial America* (New York: Harper Brothers Publishers, 1949), 73, 71; K. S. Inglis, *Churches and the Working Classes in Victorian England* (London: Routledge and Kegan Paul, 1963), 1, 13.

68. Lynne Marks, "The Knights of Labor and the Salvation Army: Religion and Working-Class Culture in Ontario, 1882–1980," *Labour/Le Travail* 28 (Fall 1991): 115. See also Kenneth Fones-Wolf, *Trade Union Gospel: Christianity and Labor in Industrial Philadelphia, 1865–1915* (Philadelphia: Temple University Press, 1989).

69. Sydney E. Ahlstrom, *A Religious History of the American People* (New Haven, Conn.: Yale University Press, 1972), 738. See also Richard Wightman Fox, "The Culture of Liberal Protestant Progressivism, 1875–1925," *Journal of Interdisciplinary History* 23, no. 3 (1993): 640, and Ferenc Morton Szasz, *The Divided Mind of Protestant America, 1880–1930* (University: University of Alabama Press, 1982), 1.

70. Josiah Strong quoted in Susan Curtis, "The Son of Man and God the Father: The Social Gospel and Victorian Masculinity," in *Meanings for Manhood: Constructions of Masculinity in Victorian America*, ed. Mark C. Carnes and Clyde Griffen (Chicago: University of Chicago Press, 1990), 68.

71. A volume entitled *Orders and Regulations for Field Officers of the Salvation Army* was later joined by a similar book for sergeants (1889), soldiers (1899), and staff officers (1904).

72. William Booth, *Orders and Regulations for Field Officers of the Salvation Army* (London: International Headquarters of the Salvation Army, 1888), 44–45. As we will see in chapter 3, however, Salvationists created a religious culture and public religious performance that was far from decorous.

73. Booth, *Orders and Regulations for Field Officers*, 54. In addition to these regulations, during her tenure as co-commander of the Salvation Army in the United States, Maud Booth published "Health Tips" and even issued a letter to corps captains in which she warned them to watch out for "women Officers . . . addicted to tight-lacing." Tight-lacing refers to the tendency of some women to try and achieve a very small waist by pulling their corset laces *very* tight. "Tight-lacing," she said, "is as bad as cigarette-smoking in a man." Officers must make women understand that tight-lacing "is ruination to the health" and makes a mockery of efforts to preach against "self conceit and the follies of fashion." Maud Booth to "My Dear Comrade," n.d., RG 20.97, Box 89/30, SAA.

74. "Life of Lieut. Nellie Upham"; Jackson, "Reminiscences."

75. Special William Day ("Happy Bill"), Pacific Coast, "Sold Out to God," *The Conqueror* (August 1892): 200–205.

76. Rosabeth Moss Kanter, *Commitment and Community: Communes and Utopias in Sociological Perspective* (Cambridge, Mass.: Harvard University Press, 1972), 73–74.

77. Although Salvationists rejected the moral dangers of "worldly amusements," they adapted much of the culture into their own religious performances. For more on Salvation Army religious performance and working-class popular culture, see Lillian Taiz, "Applying the Devil's Works in a Holy Cause: Working-

Class Popular Culture and the Salvation Army in the United States, 1879–1900," *Religion and American Culture* 7, no. 2 (1997): 195–223.

78. The General, "To Recruits," *AWC*, 5 April 1890, 14.

79. The Salvation Army shared much in common with the Methodist and Baptist churches of the early nineteenth century, which Charles Sellers describes in his book *The Market Revolution*. Like these Protestant churches, the Army embraced the "values of love, community and equality," adopted an experience of holiness that provided spiritual intensity, and depended on the discipline or "the watchful care of their intense, lifelong, come-outer communities to sustain their newborn resistance to temptation." Sellers, *The Market Revolution: Jacksonian America, 1815–1846* (New York: Oxford University Press, 1991), 157–61.

80. Knott, "Captain May Harris." The Army moved officers for a number of reasons: a chronic shortage of personnel, special skills an officer might bring to opening or building up corps, an officer's lack of skills, etc. See also "Adjutant Charles McAbee," *AWC*, 6 July 1889, 2.

81. Information on Fannie Lawson found in letter from Fannie Lawson to Maryanne Lawson, 21 August 1877, McAbee Letters, SAWTM. Information on Charles McAbee found in notes at end of letter from Fannie Lawson to Charles McAbee, 16 August 1888, McAbee Letters, SAWTM; and in "Adjutant Charles McAbee"; Murdoch, "Female Ministry," 357.

82. Philip Gerringer, "Diary," RG 20.22, Box 212/14, SAA.

83. Price, "Random Reminiscences," 78; George Scott Railton, "Our War Memories," *LWC*, 19 June 1880, 4.

84. "Captain Lilly Kline," *AWC*, 12 May 1890, 6.

85. Religious performance will be addressed in greater detail in chapter 3's discussion of Salvation Army religious culture.

86. "The Eventful Life of Capt. Dixon," *AWC*, 8 February 1890, 1.

87. Diary of Deziah Conrad, 1 January 1893–29 December 1893, SAWTM.

88. "Lives of Little Shaw and Williams, Apart and Together," *AWC*, 7 June 1890, 1. Notes (n.d.) attached to letter from Frank McAbee to Charles McAbee, 7 October 1889, McAbee Letters, SAWTM; "Adjutant Charles McAbee."

89. Mrs. Higgins, Brief, "Slum Department," 1903, RG 2.7, Fldr. 21-8, 39, 41, SAA. There is some very scant and scattered mention in *The War Cry* that male officers were occasionally "teamed."

90. "My Boy Jack," *AWC*, 7 August 1886, 1; "The Young Man Away from Home," ibid., 19 February 1887, 15. Another theme is the obligation of drunken fathers to their children. See "What Will Become of Him!," 26 December 1885, 4. Adopting the title used by cofounder Catherine Booth, mother of the Salvation Army, Maud Booth frequently signed her articles in *The War Cry* "Your Mother in the War." Ibid., 30 June 1888, 5; 7 July 1888, 5.

91. "Protestant Jesuits," *New York Times*, 7 March 1883, 4. This article also made reference to the Salvation Army's role in the estrangement between Maud Booth and her father Samuel Charlesworth over her connection to the Salvation Army. There is also evidence that family illnesses or financial need frequently took officers away from their work for the Army. Mrs. Higgins Brief, 57; Damon Brief, ACC 89-35, SAA.

92. The General, *Orders and Regulations for Soldiers of the Salvation Army* (London, E.C.: International Headquarters, 1899), 121; The General, "Twenty Thousand

Souls: How to Keep Them," *AWC*, 8 March 1890. For more on the notion of family in evangelical societies, see Melvin Easterday Deiter, *The Holiness Revival of the Nineteenth Century* (Metuchen, N.J.: Scarecrow Press, 1980), 46; and Charles Edwin Jones, *Perfectionist Persuasion: The Holiness Movement and American Methodism, 1867–1936* (Metuchen, N.J.: Scarecrow Press, 1974), 70, 87–88. In his discussion of New Lights, Charles Sellers suggests that the "intensification of communal bonds was its essence" (Sellers, *The Market Revolution*, 159).

93. "Holz Brief for the Atlantic Coast Province," Holz Manuscript Collection, July 1, 1908, SAA. Mrs. Ballington Booth, "My Mother or My God," *AWC*, 5 October 1886.

94. Notes, McAbee Letters, 29 May 1896, 211.

95. *Orders and Regulations for Soldiers*, 59. It should be noted, however, that while there were pages of rules and directives regulating Salvation Army marriages, they were frequently observed in the breech. Soldiers and officers would sometimes resign, marry, and then rejoin the group to get around the rules. Damon Brief.

96. Typically, working-class wives lacked the authority to question how much or on what a man spent what he considered his discretionary money. If a man subtracted from his pay money for drink, tobacco, or gambling, his wife had to make do on what remained. Susan J. Kleinberg, "Technology and Women's Work: The Lives of Working-Class Women in Pittsburgh, 1870–1900," *Labor History* 17, no. 1 (1976): 66–67.

97. The General, *Orders and Regulations*, 68.

98. See Ruth Hallidin, "Memories," 1914–41, ACC 86-76; Damon Diaries, RG 20.38; Phillipson Personal Papers, RG 20.41; and Parker Correspondence, RG 20.12, all at SAA. See also *AWC* passim, coverage of "Hallelujah Weddings."

99. *AWC*, 27 December 1884, 3; 18 July 1885, 1.

100. For a discussion of denominational limitations on women's right to preach, see Martha Tomhave Blauvelt, "Women and Revivalism," 1–9, and Barbara Brown Zikmund, "The Struggle for the Right to Preach," 194, both in *Women and Religion in America: The Nineteenth Century: A Documentary History*, vol. 1, ed. Rosemary Radford Ruether and Rosemary Skinner Keller (San Francisco: Harper and Row, 1981). See also Barbara Welter, "The Feminization of American Religion: 1800–1860," in *Clio's Consciousness Raised*, ed. Mary Hartman and Lois Banner (New York: Harper and Row, 1974), 139; Mary Agnes Theresa Dougherty, "The Methodist Deaconess, 1885–1918: A Study in Religious Feminism" (Ph.D. diss., University of California–Davis, 1979), x; and Glenn Michael Zuber, " 'Mainline Women Ministers: One Beginning Point': Women Missionary and Temperance Organizers Become 'Disciples of Christ' Ministers, 1888–1908," *Mid-America* 78 (Summer 1996): 109–37.

101. Roger Joseph Green, "Spirit Filled and Fighting Fit: Women in the Salvation Army," paper presented to the Salvation Army Territorial Historical Commission Meeting, June 1984, 8–9.

102. Sir Walter Besant, *London in the Nineteenth Century*, quoted in ibid., 9. See also Murdoch, "Female Ministry." In 1930, Evangeline Booth became the Army's fourth general and the first female to hold that rank. The Grange was one of the few organizations that opened membership and office to men and women. Women generally exercised organizational authority only in groups that were

restricted to or dominated by women, such as the WCTU, women's clubs, and suffrage organizations.

103. May Wright Sewall, ed., *The World's Congress of Representative Women* (Chicago: Rand, McNally, 1894), 371–72, quoted in Alan Whitworth Bosch, "The Salvation Army in Chicago, 1885–1914" (Ph.D. diss., University of Chicago, 1965), 78.

104. "The Eventful Life of Captain Dixon" and "Mrs. Major Brewer," *AWC*, 12 May 1888.

105. Knott, "Captain May Harris."

106. "Interesting to Our Women Officers," *AWC*, 31 March 1890.

107. Married men earned more than single men and were given additional "children's allowances."

108. Reportedly, William Booth discouraged his daughter Evangeline from marrying by arguing, "I am not sure that if you married you would be given every opportunity to use your many talents for the Lord." Quoted in Margaret Troutt, *The General Was a Lady* (Nashville: A. J. Holman, 1980), 78.

109. In 1926, the Army clarified the officer status of the couple in a ruling about "Officers Wives Commissions." After the usual twelve-month probationary period, "the wife and husband *each* receive a Commission as fully accredited Officers of The Salvation Army, but following that all appointments and promotions are to 'Captain and Mrs.' jointly, not individually." Field Activities, RG 1.17, SAA. When the group's rescue and slum work expanded in the late 1880s, married middle-class women frequently became administrators of rescue homes.

110. In spite of this attempt to insure that marriage would not result in the loss of skilled officers, the reality is that many wives left active service in order to raise their children. Eva Parker, according to her daughter Mildred Fahey, "did what she could while raising a family . . . but she was more or less in the background." Nicki Tanner, "The Salvation Army Oral History Interview with Mrs. Brigadier John Fahey," unpublished typescript, 1987, 12, SAA.

111. The Army also frequently placed middle-class men with business experience in administrative positions at the district level immediately after training. Douglas, *Elizabeth Swift Brengle*, 41; Murdoch, "Female Ministry," 357; Price, "Random Reminiscences," 140.

112. McKinley, *Marching to Glory*, 172–73.

113. For more perceptions of working-class women's sexuality, see Christine Stansell, *City of Women: Sex and Class in New York, 1789–1860* (Urbana: University of Illinois Press, 1987).

114. Stansel, *City of Women*, 55. Since working-class men found mutuality in institutions like the saloon, it is significant that the Army adapted that culture as part of their religious performance. Roy Rosenzweig, *Eight Hours for What We Will: Workers and Leisure in an Industrial City, 1870–1920* (Cambridge: Cambridge University Press, 1983), 56.

115. Murdoch, "The Salvation Army," 442.

116. Curtis, *A Consuming Faith*, 27.

117. Virginia Lieson Brereton, *From Sin to Salvation: Stories of Women's Conversions, 1800 to the Present* (Bloomington: Indiana University Press, 1991), 3–4, 57. See also Timothy L. Smith, *Revivalism and Social Reform: American Protestantism on the Eve of the Civil War* (Baltimore, Md.: Johns Hopkins University Press, 1957);

Carroll Smith-Rosenberg, *Religion and the Rise of the American City* (Ithaca, N.Y.: Cornell University Press, 1971); and McKinley, *Marching to Glory*, 61.

118. Letter to Capt. M.[ary] Hartelius, 19 June 1889, R.O.E. Lodge, RG 20.8, SAA; Debra Campbell, "Hannah Whitall Smith (1832–1911): Theology of the Mother-hearted God," *Signs* 15, no. 1 (1989): 90–91.

119. Letters to Capt. M.[ary] Hartelius, 19 June 1889 and 9 July 1887, RG 20.8, SAA; see also Clark, "Susie Swift," 513.

120. Lodge to Hartelius, 9 August 1888, RG 20.8, SAA.

121. The Army's regulations on the responsibilities of husbands and wives reinforced this construction of manhood and womanhood by asking men to assist in household duties so that women could remain active in Army work. Winston also takes up Maud Booth's construction of womanhood, and to a lesser extent manhood, in chapter 2 of her book, *Red Hot and Righteous*.

122. Commissioner Richard E. Holz, "Bringing Them to the Street Corner: Early Day Music of the S.A.," paper presented to the Salvation Army Historical Commission Biennial Meeting, 8 June 1984, SAA, 9.

123. Ironically, William Booth suffered from chronic dyspepsia and other physical complaints for most of his life.

124. Hall, *Samuel Logan Brengle*, 56. According to E. Anthony Rotundo, as the middle class became more preoccupied with men's bodies, they also concerned themselves with the personal "vigor that a man brought to his tasks." Many believed that "a man who lacked power of personality was . . . deficient as a man." Richard Fox has also pointed out the value that many late-nineteenth-century Americans placed on "personality." Men like Henry Beecher understood personality as individuality. Beecher felt, according to Fox, that "personality was indispensable because, in addition to promoting individual vitality, it permitted what he called 'spiritual engineering.' Charismatic preachers empowered by their own individuality could discipline the selfish and awaken the somnolent by sweeping them up in a flurry of feeling." William Booth (and most of the Booth family, three of whom would become national leaders in the United States) seems to have had a wealth of "personality" which enabled him to evoke a strong emotional response from Brengle and many others. E. Anthony Rotundo, "Learning about Manhood: Gender Ideals and the Middle-Class Family in Nineteenth-Century America," in *Manliness and Morality: Middle-Class Masculinity in Britain and America, 1800–1840*, ed. J. A. Mangan and James Walvin (New York: St. Martin's Press, 1887), 41; Richard Wightman Fox, "The Culture of Liberal Protestant Progressivism," 650.

125. Catherine (Katie) Booth would marry Arthur Booth-Clibborn. Later they became deeply involved in faith healing and would leave the Salvation Army.

126. "The Salvation Army on Trial," *New York Times*, 13 December 1883, 1; *Chicago Tribune*, 15 May 1888, 8, reprinted in *AWC*, 2 June 1888, 7; Bosch, "The Salvation Army in Chicago," 22, 97.

127. *Chicago Tribune*, 28 August 1885, 4. "The Salvation Army," *North American*, 11 January 1884, quoted in Bob Bloom to Herbert Wisbey, 31 December 1949, Correspondence, Wisbey Research, Box 51/8, RG 20.53, SAA.

128. V. Foot, "Isn't It Unwomanly," *AWC*, 26 December 1885, 5.

129. "A Great Newspaper's Opinion on the Salvation Army," *New York Sun*, quoted in *AWC*, 16 March 1889, 9. See also "Statement by Ballington Booth," *AWC*, 13 August 1887. "[O]ver seven hundred self-sacrificing officers are leading

forward our work, receiving a salary which does not more than barely meet the necessaries of life."

130. Eleanor Kirk, "Practical Charity," Chicago *Citizen*, quoted in *AWC*, 1 March 1890, 10.

131. For more on the transformation of the Salvation Army at the turn of the century, see chapter 4.

Chapter Three

1. *LWC*, 4 April 1880, 4. Railton and the seven Hallelujah Lasses were the first "official" contingent sent to the United States from Britain. For more on the early history of the Salvation Army in the United States, see chapter 1. See also Commissioner Edward Carey, "Mission Flag Hoisted in Cleveland," *AWC*, 9 February, 1980, 11; St. John Ervine, *God's Soldier: General William Booth*, vol. 1 (New York: Macmillan, 1935), 481; and Robert Sandall, *The History of the Salvation Army*, vol. 2 (New York: The Salvation Army Supplies and Purchasing Department, 1950), 231.

2. James D. McCabe Jr., *Lights and Shadows of New York Life* (Philadelphia: National Publishing Company, 1872), 600–601; Elliott Gorn, *The Manly Art: Bare-Knuckle Prize Fighting in America* (Ithaca, N.Y.: Cornell University Press, 1986), 183.

3. "The Salvation Army," *New York Times*, 15 March 1880, 8.

4. *LWC*, 4 April 1880, 4.

5. "The Salvation Army," *New York World*, 15 March 1850, 5, quoted in Edward H. McKinley, *Marching to Glory: The History of the Salvation Army in the United States of America, 1880–1980* (San Francisco: Harper and Row, 1980), 13–14; *LWC*, 4 April 1880, 4; Sallie Chesham, *Born to Battle: The Salvation Army in America* (New York: The Salvation Army, 1965), 60.

6. In basic nineteenth-century minstrel format, all of the performers sat on stage in a semicircle which formed the setting for the various jokes, dances, and serious and comic songs that the players would perform. By the post–Civil War era, minstrelsy added features from other forms of entertainment, including tableaux vivants, or living pictures, in which "human figures [were] arranged to imitate paintings or statues." It should also be noted that for much of the nineteenth century, minstrel show audiences consisted of working- and lower-middle-class men. Robert C. Toll, *Blacking Up: The Minstrel Show in Nineteenth-Century America* (New York: Oxford University Press, 1974), 52, 137; Robert C. Allen, *Horrible Prettiness: Burlesque and American Culture* (Chapel Hill: University of North Carolina Press, 1991), 92, 163. Allen provides an excellent discussion of living pictures and other features of nineteenth-century burlesque.

7. In his recent book, R. Laurence Moore examined the commodification of religion and suggested that the "effort to create a demand for religion committed revivalism to a market logic and . . . market strategies." He argues that in the face of an expanding commercial culture in the nineteenth century that developed new forms of "worldliness," Americans also "developed new ways to be 'religious.'" These "new ways" included bringing theatricality to the pulpit. Although Moore did not explore this dynamic within working-class religion, the Salvation Army provides an excellent opportunity to examine how a working-class evangelical Christian organization helped to develop new ways to be religious by

employing working-class forms of popular culture. R. Laurence Moore, *Selling God: American Religion in the Marketplace of Culture* (New York: Oxford University Press, 1994), 6, 10.

8. Nathan Hatch, *The Democratization of American Christianity* (New Haven, Conn.: Yale University Press, 1989), 8 (quotation on p. 211).

9. Ibid., 10.

10. Roy Rosenzweig, *Eight Hours for What We Will: Workers and Leisure in an Industrial City, 1870–1920* (Cambridge: Cambridge University Press, 1983), 58–59. See also Jon M. Kingsdale, "The 'Poor Man's Club': Social Functions of the Urban Working-Class Saloon," *American Quarterly* 25, no. 4 (October 1973): 480; W. J. Rorabaugh, *The Alcoholic Republic* (New York: Oxford University Press, 1979), 151. For more on the democracy of the music hall and theater, see Toll, *Blacking Up*; and Lawrence W. Levine, *Highbrow/Lowbrow: The Emergence of Cultural Hierarchy in America* (Cambridge, Mass.: Harvard University Press, 1988).

11. Dickson D. Bruce Jr., *And They All Sang Hallelujah: Plain-Folk Camp-Meeting Religion, 1800–1845* (Knoxville: University of Tennessee Press, 1973), 4–5, 16, 19, 24, 34. "Mudsill" used by John Milsaps, John Milsaps Diary, vol. 3, Old Series, RG 20.54, SAA. See chapter 2 for more on violence and drink in the lives of Salvationists.

12. Bruce, *And They All Sang Hallelujah*, 84.

13. Dissociation, according to Taves, is not limited to religious experience but can happen with ordinary "overlearned" behaviors such as driving a car. Ann Taves, "Knowing through the Body: Dissociative Religious Experience in African- and British-American Methodist Traditions," *Journal of Religion* 73 (1993): 201–2. Taves argues that, while "enthusiasm" began to die out among European-American Methodists, "the greater openness of traditional African culture to dissociative religious experience and the crisis of enslavement, led African Americans to elaborate and institutionalize dissociative experience at the heart of their worship life." One of her sources, however, seems to suggest that some European-American groups also elaborated and institutionalized "enthusiasm." "James Monroe Buckley, a prominent late nineteenth-century Methodist (MEC) minister and editor, wrote that 'the cataleptic condition which occurred among Congregationalists in the time of Jonathan Edwards, certain Presbyterians and Baptists in the early part of this century in the South and West, and the early Methodists, . . . is still common among colored people, Second Adventists, and the *Salvation Army*, and not wholly unknown among others'" [my emphasis]. James Monroe Buckley, *Faith-Healing, Christian Science, and Kindred Phenomena* (New York: Century Co., 1898), 60, quoted in Taves, "Knowing," 208, 211, 213.

14. Sydney E. Alstrom, *A Religious History of the American People* (New Haven, Conn.: Yale University Press, 1972), 434–35; Catherine L. Albanese, "Savage, Sinner, and Saved: Davy Crockett, Camp Meetings, and the Wild Frontier" *American Quarterly* 33, no. 5 (1981): 495, 497.

15. According to Price, a "'Hallelujah wind-up' [was] a time of rejoicing following the service when a large number of converts came forward for prayers." James W. Price, "Random Reminiscences," 1889–99, 78, RG 20.27, SAA.

16. *National Baptist*, quoted in *LWC*, 10 July 1880, 4.

17. Charles Edwin Jones, *Perfectionist Persuasion: The Holiness Movement and American Methodism, 1867–1936* (Metuchen, N.J.: Scarecrow Press, 1974), 54.

18. Lt. Col. Arthur Jackson, "Reminiscences of Lt. Colonel Arthur Jackson," unpublished manuscript, 1939, SAA.

19. After years of training officers in the field, the Salvation Army began to organize "Training Garrisons" in various cities around the nation. As the Army became more bureaucratically centralized, training was shifted to three Territorial Training Colleges.

20. *AWC*, June 1, 1895, 6, quoted in Bosch, "The Salvation Army in Chicago," 55.

21. Price, "Random Reminiscences," 61–62.

22. Bruce, *And They All Sang Hallelujah*, 80–83; Damon Diaries, RG 20.38, passim, SAA.

23. Bruce, *And They All Sang Hallelujah*, 69, 96. In chapter 2, I have discussed this process using the terms "mortification" and "transcendence."

24. Jones, *Perfectionist Persuasion*, 20. Charles H. Lippy, "The Camp Meeting in Transition: The Character and Legacy of the Late Nineteenth Century," *Methodist History* 34 (1995): 6, 7 (critic's quotation on p. 3). See also Roger Robins, "Vernacular American Landscape: Methodists, Camp Meetings, and Social Respectability," *Religion and American Culture* 4, no. 2 (1994): 1065–109; Gregory D. Van Dussen, "The Bergen Camp Meeting in the American Holiness Movement," *Methodist History* 21 (1983): 69–89. Historians have also studied institutionalization of the late-nineteenth-century camp meeting into holiness and pentecostal churches. See Jones, *Perfectionist Persuasion*; Melvin Easterday Deiter, *The Holiness Revival of the Nineteenth Century* (Metuchen, N.J.: Scarecrow Press, 1980); and Timothy L. Smith, *Called unto Holiness: The Story of the Nazarenes: The Formative Years* (Kansas City, Mo.: Nazarene Publishing House, 1962).

25. Susan Davis, *Parades and Power: Street Theater in Nineteenth-Century Philadelphia* (Berkeley: University of California Press, 1986), 123.

26. *Chicago Blade*, reprinted in *AWC*, 14 July 1894, 16.

27. Kenneth Fones-Wolf, *Trade Union Gospel: Christianity and Labor in Industrial Philadelphia, 1865–1915* (Philadelphia: Temple University Press, 1989), 30–31.

28. "Capt. Daniel E. Smith of St. Paul 1, Minn. A Grand Life Record," *AWC*, 4 January 1890; on saloon culture, see Roy Rosenzweig, *Eight Hours for What We Will: Workers and Leisure in an Industrial City, 1870–1920* (Cambridge: Cambridge University Press, 1983), 52–53.

29. *The National Baptist*, reprinted in *LWC*, 10 July 1880, 4.

30. Commissioner Richard E. Holz, "Bringing Them to the Street Corner: Early Day Music of the S.A.," paper presented at The Salvation Army Historical Commission biennial meeting, 8 June 1984, 9; quotation in "Look Here!," *AWC*, 3 July 1884.

31. Ash-Barrel Jimmy, a.k.a. James Kemp, got his nickname when "he was found by a policeman dead drunk in a barrel, his hair frozen to the bottom, and was dragged thus embarrelled to the police court." McKinley, *Marching to Glory*, 14.

32. *AWC*, 26 December 1885, 5; other songs included religious lyrics set to "Them Golden Slippers" and "Grandfather's Clock." Norman H. Murdoch and Howard F. McMains, "The Salvation Army Disturbances of 1885," *Queen City Heritage* 45 (Summer 1987): 16.

33. The *Chicago Inter-Ocean* was "staunchly Republican, a real party organ, and

an influential paper during the late 1880s and the 1890s." H-SHGAPE (internet web page) message from Rebecca Edwards, Vassar College, 1996.

34. *Chicago Inter-Ocean*, reprinted in *AWC*, 25 April 1891, 8.

35. *Philadelphia News*, quoted in *LWC*, 31 January 1880, 1; "Salvation Army Methods," Paterson, *Daily Guardian*, quoted in *AWC*, 3 June 1881, 3.

36. "Glorious Times in Schenectady," *AWC*, 23 May 1885, 1.

37. "California San Jose," *AWC*, 13 November 1884, 2.

38. Until the late nineteenth century, all minstrel-show performers were men. In the 1870s, theatrical entrepreneurs created all-female minstrel shows that were quickly recognized as a separate form—burlesque. Allen, *Horrible Prettiness*, 163.

39. "The Hallelujah Octopus," *New York Times*, 20 March 1885, 2.

40. Jackson, "Reminiscences."

41. "Pickles," *AWC*, 17 July 1883, 4.

42. Captain Bayley and Cadet Alice Farrell, "Who Gets the Money?," *AWC*, 5 June 1884, 4.

43. "Hints for Testimony Meetings," *AWC*, 25 December 1886, 3.

44. The burning of effigies has a long tradition in both Europe and the United States. Most commonly effigy burnings have been used as a form of popular political expression, as in the burning in effigy of royal governors and traitors like Benedict Arnold in Revolutionary America or the traditional burning of the Guy on Guy Fawkes Day in Britain. Herbert Gutman also noted that in their failed 1877 campaign against a lockout, potters in Trenton, N.J., used "torchlight parades and effigy burnings" to protest the shift from preindustrial to industrial work cultures. Charles Royster, " 'The Nature of Treason': Revolutionary Virtue and American Reactions to Benedict Arnold," *William and Mary Quarterly* 36 (April 1979): 188; Lloyd I. Rudolph, "The Eighteenth-Century Mob in America and Europe," *American Quarterly* 11, no. 4 (Winter 1959): 451; "Work, Culture and Society in Industrializing America," *American Historical Review* 78 (June 1973): 559.

45. *AWC*, 22 September 1894, 12, quoted in Bosch, "The Salvation Army in Chicago," 71.

46. These special events brought in desperately needed funds which were shared between the national headquarters, divisions, and local corps.

47. McKinley, *Marching to Glory*, 23; Cresham, *Born to Battle*, 69. For more on dime museums, see Andrea Stulman Dennett, *Weird and Wonderful: The Dime Museum in America* (New York: New York University Press, 1997).

48. McKinley, *Marching to Glory*, 24.

49. *AWC*, 7 February 1891, 14, quoted in Bosch, "The Salvation Army in Chicago," 67–68.

50. Gunther Barth, *City People: The Rise of Modern City Culture in Nineteenth-Century America* (New York: Oxford University Press, 1980), 226; Cresham, *Born to Battle*, 69.

51. "Three Odd Salvation Soldiers," *Harper's Weekly*, 11 August 1894, 759.

52. See Notes attached to letter to Fannie Lawson from Charlie McAbee, 20 February 1889, McAbee Letters, SAWTM.

53. *AWC*, 25 April 1891, 8.

54. *Chicago Tribune*, 1 November 1886, 3, quoted in Bosch, "The Salvation Army in Chicago," 35–36.

55. *AWC*, 18 January 1890, 8.

56. Jackson, "Reminiscences."

57. James Gilbert *Perfect Cities: Chicago's Utopias of 1893* (Chicago: University of Chicago Press, 1991), 187, 189 (quotation re mastering popular culture on p. 205); Moore, *Selling God*, 188.

58. For more on the transformation of American culture in the nineteenth and twentieth centuries, especially the impact of urban middle-class commercial culture, see Allen, *Horrible Prettiness*; Levine, *Highbrow/Lowbrow*; John F. Kasson, *Rudeness and Civility: Manners in Nineteenth-Century Urban America* (New York: Hill and Wang, 1990); William Leach, *Land of Desire: Merchants, Power and the Rise of a New American Culture* (New York: Vintage Books, 1993); and Lary May, *Screening Out the Past* (Chicago: University of Chicago Press, 1980). Few works have explored the transformation of the sex-segregated world of working-class leisure culture. Only Kathy Peiss has looked at the way in which working-class women adjusted to the emerging heterosocial world of commerical amusements. Kathy Peiss, *Cheap Amusements: Working Women and Leisure in Turn-of-the-Century New York* (Philadelphia: Temple University Press, 1986). Although Roy Rosenzweig addressed the transformation of working-class culture, he paid little attention to the significance of heterosocial interaction. Rosenzweig, *Eight Hours for What We Will: Workers and Leisure in an Industrial City* (Cambridge: Cambridge University Press, 1983).

59. "Religion by Riot," *New York Times*, 22 March 1885, 8; "An Attack on the Outworks of Satan in Water-Street," *New York Times*, 19 March 1880, 8; "The Hallelujah Octopus," *New York Times*, 20 March 1885, 2. On the working-class nature of volunteer firemen, see Bruce Laurie, "Fire Companies and Gangs in Southwark: The 1840s," in *The Peoples of Philadelphia*, ed. Allen F. Davis and Mark H. Haller (Philadelphia: Temple University Press, 1973).

60. "Noisy Religious Work," *New York Times* 15 November 1886, 1; "The Salvationists," *New York Times*, 2 February 1892, 4; Virginia Lieson Brereton, *From Sin to Salvation: Stories of Women's Conversions, 1800 to the Present* (Bloomington: Indiana University Press, 1991), 68; Letter to the Editor by A.S.M.C., *Chicago Daily News*, 4 September 1885, 2, quoted in Bosch, "The Salvation Army in Chicago," 24.

61. *Chicago Tribune*, 28 August 1885, 4, quoted in Bosch, "The Salvation Army in Chicago," 22.

62. Ibid.; Editorial, *New York Times*, 16 July 1883, 8; "Noisy Tramps Arrested," *New York Times*, 24 December 1884, 2; *Chicago Tribune*, 1 May 1888, 9.

63. To "open fire" in Army discourse meant to attempt to open a corps or meeting hall. According to Allen Bosch, "Though individuals who were Roman Catholic actively defied the Salvation Army, there is no evidence of any organized Roman Catholic opposition." Bosch also cites articles published in the *Catholic World* that approved of the authoritarian structure of the Army and its bringing religion directly to the people. At the same time, however, the church disapproved of "the denial of the sacraments by the Salvation Army" and the more experiential aspects of their religious practice. " 'Their whole gospel is a whirl of natural excitement, with a determination to keep the mercury up to summer heat; and consequently there is no room for Christian dogma, any more than for quiet repentance and humility.' " A. F. Marshall, "The Salvation Army," *Catholic World* (September 1890): 738–46, and Gilbert Simmons, "The Salvation Army and Its Latest Project," *Catholic World* (February 1891), 633–46, both quoted in Bosch, "The Salvation Army in Chicago," 84.

64. *AWC*, 28 April 1888, 5; "Harassed the Salvationists," *New York Times*, 9 December 1892, 8; *AWC*, 10 November 1888, 10, quoted in Bosch, "The Salvation Army in Chicago," 87.

65. In 1880 the mayor of Newark, N.J., would not even allow "open air work." Wrote George Scott Railton, "The Mayor having been elected specially in the beer interest, of course forbade open-air work." *LWC*, 4 April 1880, 4.

66. "Sharps, Flats and Naturals," *AWC*, 23 January 1892, 2.

67. "A Salvation Ballet," *New York Times*, 10 February 1885, 8. For more on ballet as "leg business," see Allen, *Horrible Prettiness*, 124.

68. "Spared Yet a Little While," *New York Times*, 24 December 1883, 8; "Gen. Booth's Warriors," *New York Times*, 11 December 1886, 3.

69. "An Evangelist Locked Up," *New York Times*, 20 August 1885, 5.

70. "Disgracing the Salvationists," *New York Times*, 5 September 1884, 1; "A Salvation Army Captain," *New York Times*, 21 March 1885, 8.

71. *Chicago Herald*, reprinted in *AWC*, 16 September 1893, 7.

72. *Chicago Tribune*, 15 May 1888, 8, reprinted in *AWC*, 2 June 1888, 7; Bosch, "The Salvation Army in Chicago," 22, 97. It was not unusual for Salvation Army officers of the same sex to live together in the corps "barracks" or in nearby "quarters." Fannie Lawson to Charles McAbee, 29 October 1888, SAWTM. The Chicago middle classes may also have been responding to the opening of "training garrisons" in a number of cities, including Chicago. Here, larger numbers of cadets lived together in single-sex housing as they trained to be Salvation Army officers. I could find no support for accusations of widespread sexual misconduct. Indeed, the Army took great pains to regulate the romantic interaction between male and female officers with rules for courtship and swift dismissal if moral codes were violated.

73. See chapter 2.

74. Clarence W. Hall, *Samuel Logan Brengle: Portrait of a Prophet* (Chicago: The Salvation Army Supply and Purchasing Department, 1933), 46–51; "Mrs. Fannie McAbee," *AWC*, 6 July 1889, 3; Norman H. Murdoch, "Female Ministry in the Thought and Work of Catherine Booth," *Church History* 53 (September 1984): 357; "Adjutant Charles McAbee," *AWC*, 6 July 1889, 2; Susan Swift, "The Conversion of Susan Swift," RG 20.11, SAA.

75. Hall, *Samuel Logan Brengle*, 81–84.

76. Ibid.

77. *The Christian at Work*, 23 June 1883, reprinted in *AWC*, 19 July 1883, 1.

78. According to Norman Murdoch, in 1878 William Booth and his closest associates concluded that their Christian Mission was "a machine going about in bits." In response, these leaders rejected the "representative principle" by eliminating the annual conference which customarily met to make decisions on a variety of issues of importance to the mission. In its place, most observers agree, Booth institutionalized one-man rule in a "thoroughly military system" and called it the Salvation Army. For a painstakingly detailed account of this transition, see Norman H. Murdoch, "The Salvation Army: An Anglo-American Revivalist Social Mission" (Ph.D. diss., University of Cincinnati, 1985), 288–90.

79. Ibid., 305.

80. Wilkins-Booth, "What Is the Salvation Army?" 13 July 1912, 2.

81. *AWC*, 10 April 1886, 1.

82. Price, "Random Reminiscences," 84

83. Wisbey regarded the general's use of authority his "genius." Herbert A. Wisbey Jr., *Soldiers Without Swords* (New York: Macmillan, 1956), 30. Norman Murdoch stressed its long-term destructive impact suggesting that "[w]hile autocracy might have been the best way to produce efficient management and short term growth, Booth was already out of synch with the Anglo-American world." Murdoch, "The Salvation Army," 291; Edward H. McKinley also touches on Booth's autocratic tendencies (as well as that of his children), as does Roger Green in "The Theology of William Booth" (Ph.D. diss., Boston College, 1980), 64–66.

84. Quoted in Arthur Lipow, *Authoritarian Socialism in America: Edward Bellamy and the Nationalist Movement* (Berkeley: University of California Press, 1982), 85–87 (quotation on p. 22).

85. *Living Church*, 29 February 1896, 899, quoted in Bosch, "The Salvation Army in Chicago, 1885–1914," 131.

86. *Advance*, 12 March 1896, 368, quoted in Bosch, "The Salvation Army in Chicago," 132. See also "Protestant Jesuits," *New York Times*, 7 March 1883, 4.

87. Cmdr. Evangeline Booth had solicited contributions for the Salvation Army's building fund. Although Rockefeller agreed to donate $5,000 to the Salvation Army, he specified that the money should *not* "be used either for permanent endowment or for lands, buildings or other property which would constitute permanent assets of the organization," but rather should be used "toward the current expenses for the year." It seems that Rockefeller was loath to have his name associated with any permanent assets owned by the Salvation Army but was willing "to give tangible expression to his appreciation of the valuable work which the Army is now carrying on." By 1916, the Salvation Army was deeply engaged in social service work. With violent labor unrest still in recent memory, Rockefeller may have felt some reservations about the use to which the Salvation Army might put its authority over its working-class membership. Stan J. Murphy to Evangeline Booth, 24 April 1916, Damon Correspondence, RG 20.38, Box 235/5, SAA.

88. See chapter 1.

89. Unpublished letter from Captain Geo. Smith to Major R. E. Holz, Syracuse, N.Y., 1 September 1890, R. E. Holz Papers, RG 20.60, 62/5, SAA.

90. Between 1880 and 1885, National Headquarters was moved from New York City to Philadelphia, to St. Louis, to Brooklyn, and back to New York City. Between 1880 and 1904, the national leadership changed hands six times, from George Railton to Thomas Moore, Frank Smith, Ballington Booth, Emma and Frederick Booth-Tucker, and Evangeline Booth. While schisms ended the leadership of Thomas Moore and Ballington Booth, Emma Booth-Tucker died in 1903 and her husband Frederick Booth-Tucker left the United States soon after.

91. Damon Diaries, 1 July 1892, RG 20.38, Box 228/6, SAA.

92. "Attention Officers," 13 October 1881, 1. I found no evidence that Moore ever actually carried out his threat to publicly humiliate his field officers. Nevertheless, since this and similar requests were published repeatedly in *The War Cry*, it does not appear that Moore was successful in getting full compliance. The low educational level of many working-class officers may also have made it difficult for Salvation Army leaders to get accurate data from the field.

93. Capt. Eva Holden to Major Holz, 24 October 1887, R. E. Holz Papers, RG 20.60 62/5, SAA.

94. Murdoch, "The Salvation Army," 424; quotations in Price, "Random Reminiscences," 140.

95. Frank Smith, "Important," *AWC*, 6 December 1884, 4.

96. Murdoch, "The Salvation Army," 424.

97. Captain Seely, Binghamton, N.Y., to R. E. Holz, 24 November 1890, R. E. Holz Papers, RG 20.60, Box 62/5, SAA.

98. Lieutenant Mosher, Buffalo, N.Y., to R. E. Holz, 24 November 1890, R. E. Holz Papers, RG 20.60, 62/5, SAA.

99. Price, "Random Reminiscences," 140.

100. Col. Higgins, Chief Secretary, "Minutes by the Chief Secretary," 16 February 1898 and 1 October 1903, Field Activities, Series 20-2-2, SAA.

101. McKinley, *Marching to Glory*, 68; John Milsaps Diary, vol. 3, New Series, RG 20.54, SAA.

102. "To Our Comrades Communicating with Headquarters," *AWC*, 20 June 1885, 4.

103. "Important to Officers," *AWC*, 11 July 1885, 2. "Specials" were Salvationists who were not assigned to a particular corps but traveled around preaching at different locations.

104. William Eadie, Chief Secretary, unpublished memo, 6 August 1894, Field Activities, Series 20, SAA.

105. Price, "Random Reminiscences," 67.

106. McKinley, *Marching to Glory*, 12, 40.

107. "Re: Uniform Caps," 16 June 1891, National Headquarters, National Chief Secretary Field Notes, RG 1.17, Box 324/3, SAA.

108. Quotation in "A Question for You: When Should a Salvation Soldier Take Off the Uniform?," *AWC*, 25 July 1885, 1. I. B. Vint, "A Man Who Believed in a Quiet Religion," *AWC*, 18 September 1884, 4. "Why Should I Wear [the] Uniform?," *AWC*, 24 January 1885, 1.

109. "Re: Uniform," 25 March 1898, National Headquarters, National Chief Secretary Field Notes, RG 1.17, Box 324/3, SAA. By the late 1890s, the Salvation Army found itself contending with growing numbers of phony armies. The uniform was an important way in which it hoped to distinguish "authentic" Salvationists from the rest.

110. Price, "Random Reminiscences," 124.

111. The Salvation Army periodically held international and national "Congresses." At these meetings, officers gathered to tell of the work that was being carried on and to hear speeches and preaching by the leadership.

112. Lt. T. C. Morher, Buffalo, N.Y., to R. E. Holz, 18 November 1890, R. E. Holz Papers, RG 20.60, Box 62/5, SAA.

113. Charlie McAbee to Lieutenant Lawson, 16 October 1888, McAbee Letters, SAWTM. As noted elsewhere, field officers were responsible for organizing, financing, and preaching at each local corp.

114. Price, "Random Reminiscences," 98.

115. Many middle-class officers went to England for training before being sent back to the United States to take administrative positions. Until the turn of the century, when the Army had established more training facilities, many officers

were still being trained in the field. By the early twentieth century, a cadet, after completing the training-school course, undertook a series of uniform "probationary lessons" by correspondence. Phillip Gerringer, "Diary 1910–1911," unpublished manuscript, RG 20.22, Box 212/14, SAA.

116. By the turn of the century, all training courses included the doctrine, organization, and regulations "on which the Army is founded"; training in how to compose and deliver a sermon; the study of "Corps Bookkeeping," which, according to one officer, was "taught very thoroughly to the Cadets"; first aid ("A very useful subject"); Salvation Army literature; and "Mathematics, spelling and reading . . . for Cadets who need to brush up on these particular subjects." Anon., "A Day at the Training College," unpublished paper, 1904, VF-SFOT, East—History, SAA.

117. Jackson, "Reminiscences."

118. Wisbey, *Soldiers Without Swords*, 198.

Chapter Four

The remarks by General Booth in the epigraph are taken from an audiotape of a talk given by the General.

1. *Chicago Tribune*, 31 October 1886, 9, in Allan Whitworth Bosch, "The Salvation Army in Chicago, 1885–1914" (Ph.D. diss., University of Chicago, 1965), 33.

2. James W. Price, "Random Reminiscences," 154, RG 20.27, SAA.

3. Mary Ryan, "The American Parade: Representations of the Nineteenth-Century Social Order," in *The New Cultural History*, ed. Lynn Hunt (Berkeley: University of California Press, 1989), 148–49; Susan G. Davis, *Parades and Power: Street Theater in Nineteenth-Century Philadelphia* (Berkeley: University of California Press, 1986), 5. See also David Glassberg, "Public Ritual and Cultural Hierarchy: Philadelphia's Civic Celebrations at the Turn of the Twentieth Century," *Pennsylvania Magazine of History and Biography* 107 (1983): 421–48; Kenneth Moss, "St. Patrick's Day Celebrations and the Formation of Irish-American Identity, 1845–1875," *Journal of Social History* 29, no. 1 (Fall 1995): 125–48; Shane White, " 'It Was a Proud Day': African Americans, Festivals and Parades in the North, 17-41-1834," *Journal of American History* 81 (June 1984): 13–50; and Sean Wilentz, "Artisan Republican Festivals," in *Working-Class America*, ed. Michael H. Frisch and Daniel Walkowitz (Urbana: University of Illinois Press, 1983), 37–77. For parades as democratic legitimization, see Michael E. McGerr, *The Decline of Popular Politics: The American North, 1865–1928* (New York: Oxford University Press, 1986).

4. The prominent role women played in the public and private world of the Salvation Army stands in sharp contrast to other parts of American society in this period. Nineteenth-century parading, according to Mary Ryan, was largely "a male prerogative, offering women only a shadowy position in the line of march." Women might appear in parades as auxiliary contingents (e.g., the Masons) or as the "classic female symbol," the Goddess of Liberty. Generally, Ryan argues, "male marchers simply represented themselves, enacting a kind of cultural equivalent of descriptive representation," while women as "the Goddess . . . [or] the

female embodiment of the thirty-odd states of the Union evoked some abstract concept far removed from the women themselves — an overt expression, perhaps of their cultural utility." Ryan, "The American Parade," 148–49.

5. As Michael McGerr notes, political parades and rallies played a similar role in popular politics between the 1830s and 1890s. During that period, "American politics . . . demanded the legitimacy conferred by all classes of the people through parades and rallies and huge turnouts." McGerr, *The Decline of Popular Politics*, 5–6.

6. St. John Ervine, *God's Soldier: General William Booth*, vol. 2 (New York: Macmillan, 1935), 483.

7. Lt. Col. Arthur Jackson, "Reminiscences of Lt. Colonel Arthur Jackson," unpublished manuscript, 1939, SAA.

8. Anonymous, *The Bitter Cry of Outcast London: An Inquiry into the Condition of the Abject Poor*, quoted in Paul T. Phillips, *Kingdom on Earth: Anglo-American Social Christianity, 1880–1940* (University Park: Pennsylvania State University Press, 1996), 56. William Booth quoted in Norman H. Murdoch, "The Salvation Army: An Anglo-American Revivalist Social Mission" (Ph.D. diss., University of Cincinnati, 1984), 440. See also Victor Bailey, "In Darkest England and the Way Out: The Salvation Army, Social Reform and the Labour Movement, 1885–1910," *International Review of Social History* 29 (1984): 144.

9. Phillips, *Kingdom on Earth*, 48. Among the most famous of those studies was Charles Booth's *Life and Labor of the People* (1889); Charles Booth was not related to William Booth. See also Henry George, *Progress and Poverty* (London: C. K. Paul, 1881).

10. General William Booth, *In Darkest England and the Way Out* (London: International Headquarters of the Salvation Army, 1890), from caption on chart attached to flyleaf.

11. Smith had become involved in the early socialist movement. Murdoch, "The Salvation Army," 471; Bailey, "The Salvation Army, Social Reform," 147; Norman H. Murdoch, "Salvationist-Socialist Frank Smith, M.P.: Father of Salvation Army Social Work," paper presented at the Salvation Army Historical Conference, New York City, 1978, 7. Smith rejoined again in 1901 but resigned a second time a few years later and continued his secular political work, which culminated in his election as a Labor Party member of Parliament in 1929. Murdoch argues that Smith was able to help change the direction of the Salvation Army between 1887 and 1890 for several reasons. First, Smith encouraged Booth to find a role for the Army in the face of increasing trade union protest activity in Britain between 1889 and 1891. Second, Booth was very concerned about "a decline in The Army's appeal in London" and regarded social reform as simply another means to reach individual souls. Third, the death of Catherine Booth in 1890 and the declining influence of George Scott Railton removed the organization's chief advocates of a more traditional evangelical Christian approach to poverty. "Salvationist-Socialist," 3–5, 10.

12. Bailey, "The Salvation Army, Social Reform," 147, 148.

13. Bailey suggests that Stead introduced Booth to the works of W. L. Rees's *From Poverty to Plenty: Or, the Labor Question Solved* (1888) and Reverend Herbert Mills's *Poverty and the State or Work for the Unemployed* (1886). Bailey, "The Salvation Army, Social Reform," 150–51.

14. Booth, *In Darkest England*, 12; "The Salvation Army's Latest Problem," *Review of Reviews* 30, no. 4 (October 1904): 436.

15. Bailey, "The Salvation Army, Social Reform," 154.

16. Booth, *In Darkest England*, 48.

17. Booth, ibid., quoted in Bailey, "The Salvation Army, Social Reform," 154.

18. Bailey, "The Salvation Army, Social Reform," 154. See also St. John Ervine, *God's Soldier*, 696–97. Cab Horse Charter quotation in Booth, *In Darkest England*, 20.

19. Murdoch, "The Salvation Army," 300.

20. Joan M. Crouse, *The Homeless Transient in the Great Depression: New York State, 1929–1941* (New York: State University of New York Press, 1986), 82.

21. The book, said Ely, "has stirred the minds and hearts of millions on three continents. . . . [t]here is no great part of the world not reached by this remarkable man." Both quotations in Richard T. Ely, "Pauperism in the United States," *North American Review* 152 (1891): 395. As early as 1888, the British Salvation Army opened a food depot and the following year established three night shelters. As noted above, Frank Smith expanded the City Colony significantly during his eight-month tenure as leader of the "Social Reform Wing." After his resignation, Smith was replaced by Elijah Cadman who, according to Bailey, "if less eager than Smith to grapple with the root causes of poverty . . . worked energetically . . . for state assistance to help both the submerged and 'the respectable unemployed.' " Bailey, "The Salvation Army, Social Reform," 145 (quotation on p. 159). Herman Ausubel, "General Booth's Scheme of Social Salvation," *American Historical Review* 56 (April 1951): 525. See also Robert H. Bremner, *From the Depths: The Discovery of Poverty in the United States* (New York: New York University Press, 1956), 29.

22. As indicated in chapter 1, during their leadership of the Salvation Army in the United States, Maud and Ballington Booth chose to focus their energies on social rescue work. Scholarly discussion of the Salvation Army has historically emphasized its social service work in the United States to the exclusion of most other aspects of the group. Most often scholars accepted contemporary interpretations like Ely's and stressed the influence the Army had on evangelical work in the slums, the opening of institutional churches by mainline denominations, and the "awakening of interest in social reform." Indeed, Booth's entire social program is credited with popularizing the idea that moral improvement required economic amelioration. My interest in the Army's social service focuses on its effect upon the group's understanding of its mission, its expression of religious feeling, its relationship to members, and its impact on expressions of democracy and autonomy. Bremner, *From the Depths*, 28–29. See also Aaron I. Abell, *The Urban Impact on American Protestantism, 1865–1900* (Cambridge, Mass.: Harvard University Press, 1943); Sydney E. Ahlstrom, *A Religious History of the American People* (New Haven, Conn.: Yale University Press, 1972), 742; and Charles H. Hopkins, *The Rise of the Social Gospel in American Protestantism, 1865–1915* (New Haven, Conn.: Yale University Press, 1940), 155.

23. Chapter 5 will address the leaders' use of public performance to promote the social services and will also discuss changes in the organization's religious culture.

24. Organizationally, the Volunteers differed from the Salvation Army by com-

bining "military structure" with a "representative government." Furthermore, perhaps reflecting Ballington Booth's desire for acceptance among mainline churches, the new group incorporated observation of the sacraments and ordination of its clergy in the structure of the Volunteers. Warren C. Platt, "The Volunteers of America: The Origins and Development of Its Ideology," *Journal of Religious History* 16 (June 1990): 36–37.

25. Damon Diaries, 24 and 25 February 1896, RG 20.38, Box 228/10, SAA.

26. "Loyal to Old Leaders," *New York Times*, 23 February 1896, 4.

27. This theme resurfaced with a vengeance later in the Booth-Tuckers' administration.

28. "Loyal to Old Leaders," *New York Times*, 23 February 1896, 4. It seems likely that in the wake of William Booth's disastrous visit in 1894, when he complained about the Americanization of the Army in the United States, his chief-of-staff, Bramwell Booth, may have sent the very British Eadie to try to reassert the English way of administering the Army. Last quotation in Major John Milsaps Diary, vol. 9, New Series, SAA. Ironically, just a few years later, Milsaps would fulminate against what he regarded as the Booth-Tucker's favoritism of English officers and high-handed methods.

29. Herbert A. Wisbey Jr., "Religion in Action: A History of the Salvation Army in the United States" (Ph.D. diss., Columbia University, 1951), 253. Arch Wiggins, *The History of the Salvation Army*, vol. 4 (New York: The Salvation Army, 1964), 361.

30. Emma Booth-Tucker died in a train wreck on October 28, 1903.

31. Wisbey, "Religion in Action," 254–55. Booth-Tucker was also a distant relative of Virginia's Tucker family that included Henry St. George Tucker and John Randolph Tucker, both of whom had served in the U.S. Congress as representatives from the State of Virginia. Transcript, *The People of the State of New York v. Frederick de Lautour Booth-Tucker*, RG 20.100, Box 114/8, 128–29.

32. Damon Diaries, 7 April 1896, RG 20.38, Box 228/10, SAA. In a letter to his daughter Emma dated 22 April 1896, William Booth commented on a report he had received about the welcome meeting. Although Mr. Van Norden was reportedly "delighted with everything," he also indicated that "there was rather too much of the American Flagging." For Booth, Van Norden's criticisms confirmed his belief that "the real genuine American [presumably Van Norden] despises all the 'Yankee Doodleism' which so disgusted me when I was there. We accept the nation, we are loyal to it, when we are on its ground we are true Americans, but we belong to God and the world." General William Booth to Consul Booth-Tucker, 22 April 1896, RG 20.97, 89/9, SAA.

33. Damon Diaries, 8 April 1896. Alexander Damon was pleased that the Booth-Tuckers let officers return to the ranks. He wrote, "Major Glen has returned to the Army he couldn't stay away. God bless him he is to have his old rank of Major again." On the other hand, John Milsaps complained that by promoting so many "traitors" the Booth-Tuckers seemed to bribe officers by making a better offer than they could get with Ballington in the Volunteers of America. John Milsaps Diary, vol. 9, New Series, RG 20.54, SAA. William Booth to Emma Booth, 22 April 1896.

34. Damon Diaries, 22, 25, and 26 June 1896.

35. Frederick Booth-Tucker, "The Social Work in the United States," 1898,

Wisbey Papers, Record Group 20.53, Box 51/7, SAA. The report showed the following increases:

Program	1896	1897
Food and shelter depots	3	30
Rescue homes	5	12
Wood yards, etc.	4	10
Salvage brigades	—	5
Labor bureaus	—	5
Slum posts	13	16
Miscellaneous institutions	3	7
Total social institutions	28	85

36. Frederick Booth-Tucker, *The Relief of the Poor by the Salvation Army*, undated pamphlet, ARC 402, SAA; *Church of the Black Sheep: Annual Report of the Salvation Army in Cleveland, 1898–1899*, BB1128, SAA. See also Herbert A. Wisbey Jr., *Soldiers Without Swords* (New York: Macmillan, 1956), 129–39; Edward H. McKinley, *Marching to Glory: The History of the Salvation Army in the United States of America, 1880–1980* (San Francisco: Harper and Row, 1980), 88–93; and Clark C. Spence, *The Salvation Army Farm Colonies* (Tucson: University of Arizona Press, 1985). The Salvation Army's farm colonies, like so many others, failed due to the lack of farm skills, poor soil, drought, and insufficient land.

37. For more on settlement houses, see Allen F. Davis, *Spearheads for Reform: The Social Settlements and the Progressive Movement, 1890–1914* (New York: Oxford University Press, 1967); Mina Carson, *Settlement Folk: The Evolution of Social Welfare Ideology in the American Settlement Movement, 1883–1930* (Chicago: University of Chicago Press, 1990); Ruth Hutchinson Crocker, *Social Work and Social Order: The Settlement House Movement in Two Industrial Cities, 1889–1930* (Urbana: University of Illinois Press, 1992); and Judith Ann Trolander, *Professionalism and Social Change: From the Settlement House Movement to the Neighborhood Centers, 1886 to the Present* (New York: Columbia University Press, 1987). On African Americans and settlements, see Elizabeth Lasch-Quinn, *Black Neighbors: Race and the Limits of Reform in the American Settlement House Movement, 1890–1945* (Chapel Hill: University of North Carolina Press, 1993).

38. *Advance*, 6 November 1890, 819, quoted in Bosch, "The Salvation Army in Chicago," 105. Recent research has shown that advocates of social Christian thought "valued campaigns for conversion. . . . [w]hat they did was to add a social dimension to the prevailing emphasis on individual salvation, not deny it." Donald K. Gorrell, *The Age of Social Responsiblitiy: The Social Gospel in the Progressive Era, 1900–1820* (Macon, Ga.: Mercer University Press, 1988), ix.

39. Josiah Strong, *Religious Movements for Social Betterment* (New York: Baker and Taylor, 1900), 129–30. Charles Richmond Henderson, *The Social Spirit in America* (1897; reprint, Chicago: Scott, Foresman and Co., 1905), 319.

40. *Chicago Daily News*, 17 November 1890, 2, quoted in Bosch, "The Salvation Army in Chicago," 104–5.

41. "General Booth's Plan," *The Independent* 42 (1890): 1741–45, quoted in Wisbey Papers, RG 20.53, Box 51/5, SAA.

42. Ibid.; "The Salvation Army in America," *The Saturday Review* 81 (March 1896): 241; Phillips, *Kingdom on Earth*, 66.

43. "General Booth's Plan," quoted in Wisbey Papers.

44. Edwin D. Solenberger, "The Social Relief Work of the Salvation Army," reprinted from the Proceedings of the National Conference of Charities and Corrections, Philadelphia, 9–16 May 1906, SAA, 7, 10, 12, 14, 18–19, 23. See also Murdoch, "The Salvation Army," 500; and Josephine Shaw Lowell to Commander Booth-Tucker, quoted in William Rhinelander Stewart, *The Philanthropic Work of Josephine Shaw Lowell* (Montclair, N.J.: Patterson Smith, 1974), 449–50.

45. Stewart, *The Philanthropic Work*, 450 (italics in original); Frederick Booth-Tucker, "Our Future Pauper Policy in America: Being a Paper Read at the Monthly Meeting of the United Charities of New York" (New York: Salvation Army Publishing House, n.d.), ARC 402, SAA, 5.

46. Frederick Booth-Tucker, "Pauper Policy," 9.

47. A 1912 internal report on Salvation Army work in Massachusetts made note that the cause of the recent increased cost of living had "been placed upon the great Trusts." The report goes on to describe government action taken against the trusts. "Massachusetts Corporation," Field Secretary Papers, Series 29-1-1, 1912, SAA, 128.

48. Frederick Booth-Tucker, "Pauper Policy," 14, 18.

49. Ibid., 14–15, 22.

50. Booth-Tucker apparently did not support the notion that the West was closing. Of the four elements of this program, the settlement of the West received the least elaboration and discussion.

51. Frederick Booth-Tucker, "Pauper Policy," 23.

52. See letters of E. J. Parker to Eva Parker, 1900, Parker Papers, RG 20.12, SAA, passim. The nature and significance of these performances will be addressed in chapter 5.

53. Porter R. Lee and Walter W. Pettit, *Social Salvage: A Study of the Central Organization and Administration of the Salvation Army* (New York: National Information Bureau, 1924), 14.

54. Peter Steinfels, "Salvation Army Is More Than Christmas Kettles," *New York Times*, 18 December 1989, A10.

55. William Booth to Bramwell Booth, quoted in Phillips, *Kingdom on Earth*, 98–99.

56. Ibid.

57. Commander Frederick Booth-Tucker to Lt. Colonel Holz, 18 January 1899, RG 20.60, Box 62/9, SAA. "Samuri caste" quoted from Norman H. Murdoch, "Salvationist-Socialist Frank Smith," 11.

58. Rev. Henry R. Rose, B.D., quoted in Solenberger, "Social Relief Work," 23. See also Murdoch, "The Salvation Army," 500.

59. "Massachusetts Corporation," 116–17.

60. June Axinn and Herman Levin, *Social Welfare: A History of the American Response to Need* (New York: Longman Press, 1992), 151.

61. *Disposition of Forces*, March 1898 (New York: Salvation Army, 1888–1920), microfilm, SAA. Diane Winston suggests that this bureaucratization began during Evangline Booth's administration. I would argue, however, that she built upon the foundation laid by the Booth-Tuckers' efforts to establish the social scheme.

Diane Winston, *Red Hot and Righteous: The Urban Religion of the Salvation Army* (Cambridge, Mass.: Harvard University Press, 1999), 161.

62. At one point, the Reliance Trading Company even housed an insurance department through which Salvationists sold life insurance policies to members and friends for the Metropolitan Life Insurance Company. The Army had become involved in selling insurance as early as 1899 but in 1902 transferred that department to the Reliance Trading Company. The Army created Reliance by offering 6 percent preferred stock.

63. Industrial homes collected junk which was sorted for sale in Salvation Army Junk Stores. Army critics took a particularly dim view of the Industrial Homes Company expressing concern that Salvationists engaged in the work had a conflict of interest if they also owned stock in the company. They also argued that the Salvation Army competed unfairly with private junk dealers and made it more difficult for local charities to secure used clothing for the poor. Other critics claimed that the company deceived the public because it was "a commercial organization operating under the guise of charity." By 1912, the Army concluded that the Industrial Homes Company had become too great a liability and, having "served the purpose for which it was created," ought to be dissolved. "Massachusetts Corporation," 123; Solenberger, "Social Relief Work," 11.

64. R. E. Holz, "Brief Memoranda of National and Chief Divisional Staff Council Held in New York, May 16th–19th, 1899," ACC 82-75, SAA.

65. It will be remembered that the Moore schism in the 1880s had left Booth's international organization with no legal claim to property, insignia, and publications controlled by the Salvation Army in America. Letter of Frederick Booth-Tucker to Bramwell Booth, 18 January 1897, Frederick Booth-Tucker, RG 20.97, Box 89/33, SAA. The first schism was triggered in the 1880s, when Thomas E. Moore incorporated the Salvation Army in America. See chapter 1.

66. Booth-Tucker particularly stressed the potential benefits regarding "legacies," pointing out that most people make their bequests simply to the Salvation Army and leaving American courts to decide which Salvation Army would benefit: the local corps, national headquarters, or various imitation armies. While a portion of Thomas E. Moore's Salvation Army of America rejoined the Worldwide Salvation Army in 1889, others remained in the American Salvation Army. The Salvation Army was plagued by copycat organizations and, beginning with incorporation, maintained vigilance against organizations that encroached upon its symbols and methods. They ultimately brought suit against the American Salvation Army and forced that group to change its name and uniforms. Letter of Commander Evangeline Booth to Bramwell Booth, Chief of the Staff, 30 November 1906, RG 2.12, Box 96/2, SAA. In addition to the American Salvation Army, I also found evidence of several African American Salvation Armies, including an Afro-American Salvation Army in Philadelphia and a Colored Salvation Army in both Knoxville, Tenn., and Lexington, Ky. "Re Afro-American S.A." (memo), 20 November 1914, RG 2.12, Box 96/1, SAA; Letter to Colonel Peart from Field Secretary (no name), 3 September 1912, RG 2.12, Box 96/6, SAA. See also McKinley, *Marching to Glory*, 82–83. By 1920 the Salvation Army in the United States had been divided into three territories, each incorporated separately (New York, Chicago, and San Francisco). Lee and Pettit, *Social Salvage*, 33. Frederick Booth-Tucker to Bramwell Booth, Chief of the Staff, 18 January 1897, RG 20.97, Box 89/33, SAA. In the same letter Booth-Tucker pointed out the proposed form of

incorporation was modeled after others "already in existence for the holding of Property with a view to placing the power in the hands of the person who finds the capital." In a later communication he noted that similar acts had been passed for other Catholic and Protestant organizations. Frederick Booth-Tucker to Bramwell Booth, Chief of the Staff, 22 December 1898, RG 20.97, Box 89/33, SAA.

67. E. Fielding et al. to General Booth, 23 February 1896, Ballington Booth, Vertical File, SAA.

68. Songbooks also apparently represented an important source of income for NHQ. Said the Booth-Tuckers, "Great loss has been incurred by NHQ through the printing of Song Books in certain divisions." "Re: Song Books," 11 November 1896, National Headquarters, National Chief Secretary Field Notes, RG 1.17, SAA. It is interesting to note that a similar directive against local publication of songbooks appeared in 1911.

69. National Headquarters, Minutes, No. 1-151, Chief Secretary, May 1898, 17 March 1898, 8 August 1898, 20 February 1902, Series 20, Field Notes, Box 2, Fldr. 113, RG 1, Subgroup 4, SAA; John Milsaps Diary, vol. 11, New Series, RG 20.54, SAA.

70. "Re: Social Work," 1 March 1897, National Headquarters, National Chief Secretary Field Notes, RG 1.17, SAA.

71. Wisbey, *Soldiers*, 97; "Memorandum Re Social Work," 23 May 1906, Field Notes, National Headquarters, National Chief Secretary, RG 1.17, SAA. In Chicago during the 1893 depression and the following year during the Pullman Strike, the Salvation Army collected "donations of food, clothing, fuel, and money." Bosch, "The Salvation Army in Chicago," 121 (quotation on p. 123).

72. Colonel Higgins to Colonel French, 12 December 1904, Field Notes, National Headquarters, National Chief Secretary, RG 1.17, SAA. As with songbooks, it appears that some local corps continued to operate ad hoc social services. Evangeline Booth, who took over as national commander in 1904, continued to issue field orders addressing this issue. See Field Notes, passim.

73. Frederick Booth-Tucker, *Pauper Policy*, 17. Ironically, while the Associated Charities accused the Salvation Army of using funds raised for social services on behalf of their religious work, in the beginning just the opposite was the case. The Army purchased and outfitted its first Industrial Homes from the Army's General Fund, which included monies regularly sent to NHQ from corps collections and the "self-denial" efforts of individual soldiers. Lee and Pettit, *Social Salvage*, 39. As noted above, between 1903 and 1912 the Army also relied on the Salvation Army Industrial Homes Company to provide capital to expand that part of the City Colony.

74. Emma Booth-Tucker to Lt. Colonel Holz, 18 January 1898, Holz Correspondence, RG 20.60, Box 62/9, Ballington Booth Vertical File, SAA.

75. Memo from R. E. Holz to Commander Booth-Tucker, 26 January 1899, RG 20.60, Box 62/5, SAA. If a corps shared space with a shelter, they were admonished to make sure there was a separate entrance for people going to corps meetings. See also R. E. Holz, "Brief Memoranda of National and Chief Divisional Staff Council Held in New York, May 16th–19th, 1899," ACC 82-75, SAA. For salary cuts, see J. J. Keppel to Commander Booth-Tucker, 16 September 1898, Ballington Booth Vertical File, SAA.

76. They also ruled that the purpose of the meeting must be publicly disclosed and that the appeal for funds may last one-half hour. "Re Begging" (Booth-

Tuckers), n.d. National Headquarters National Chief Secretary Field Notes, RG 1.17, 324/8, SAA.

77. Holz, "Brief Memoranda."

78. If the "treasurer" was too busy to write the letters himself, some officer could do so, but the letter must be sent on his letterhead and signed by him. Holz, "Brief Memoranda."

79. John Milsaps Diary, vol. 6, New Series, RG 20.54, SAA. In contrast to Milsaps's implication that American officers were driven out of the Army and that many of these joined the Volunteers, Edward J. Parker, in an interview with Herbert Wisbey in 1948, suggested that most of the officers who went with Ballington Booth in 1896 were "English. The American officers almost to a man were loyal to the international army." Interviews, Wisbey Papers, RG 20.53, Box 51/19, SAA.

80. Wilber Gale to R. E. Holz, 7 May 1898; Staff Captain Joseph McFee to R. E. Holz, 3 April 1899; R. E. Holz to Colonel Higgins, 3 October 1898: all in R. E. Holz Papers, RG 20.60, Box 62/9, SAA.

81. Staff-Captain Joseph McFee to R. E. Holz, 9 March 1899, R. E. Holz Papers, RG 20.60, Box 62/9, SAA.

82. McFee to Holz, 3 April 1899, R. E. Holz Papers, RG 20.60 62/5, SAA. Ironically, in the following year National Headquarters increased its "centage" of all income that the divisions drew from social institutions. As Major Alexander Damon, general secretary of the Northwestern Division, recorded in his diary, "Letter from NHQ stating future the Social Institutions of the N West must pay 10% on all income we now pay $8.00 per week 10% will amount to about $40 per week quite a difference." Entry for 27 December 1900, Damon Diaries, RG 20.38, Box 229/7, SAA.

83. McFee to Holz, 13 May 1899, RG 20.60, R. E. Holz Papers, RG 20.60, 62/5, SAA.

84. R. E. Holz, National Social Secretary, to Colonel E. J. Higgins, 11 May 1899. R. E. Holz Papers, RG 20.60, Box 62/9, SAA.

85. R. E. Holz, National Social Secretary, to Staff-Captain McFee, 11 May 1899. R. E. Holz Correspondence, RG 20.60, Box 62/9, SAA.

86. From Colonel Higgins, Chief Secretary, to Colonel French, 12 December 1904, Field Notes, National Headquarters Minutes, No. 152, RG 1, Box 2/113, SAA.

87. At various times the Salvation Army divided itself into districts, divisions, provinces, and territories.

88. From Colonel French to Colonel Higgins, 17 December 1904, Field Notes, National Headquarters Minutes, No. 156, RG 1, Box 2/113, SAA.

89. Ibid.

90. "Re Financial Appeals," 15 January 1901, National Headquarters, National Chief Secretary, Field Notes, RG 1.17, Box 324/3, SAA.

91. Damon Diaries, 13 February 1906 and 1 March 1906, RG 20.38, Box 229/7, SAA.

92. Bosch, "The Salvation Army in Chicago," 142–43; McKinley, *Marching to Glory*, 84; Wisbey, *Soldiers Without Swords*, 132; *Disposition of Forces* (New York: The Salvation Army, 1888–1920), microfilm, SAA.

93. J. J. Keppel to Commander Booth-Tucker, 22 September 1898 and 16 September 1898, Ballington Booth Vertical File, SAA.

94. John Milsaps Diary, vol. 11, New Series, RG 20.54, SAA.

95. J. J. Keppel to Commander Booth-Tucker, 22 September 1898, Ballington Booth Vertical File, SAA.

96. Damon Diaries, 5 April 1906, RG 20.38, Box 229/8, SAA.

97. At one time NHQ even considered opening a real estate sales office in New York City. John Milsaps Diary, vol. 11, New Series, RG 20.54, SAA.

98. John Milsaps Diary, vols. 7, 11, New Series, RG 20.54, SAA; See also James W. Price, "Random Reminiscences," unpublished manuscript, 1889–1899, RG 20.27, SAA, 138, 183.

99. John Milsaps Diary, vol. 11, New Series, RG 20.54, SAA.

100. Damon Diaries, 13 June 1905, RG 20.38, Box 229/7, SAA.

101. Francis P. Lee to Colonel Thomas Holland, 16 September 1897, R. E. Holz Papers, RG 20.60, Box 62/5, SAA.

102. John Milsaps Diary, vols. 6, 11, New Series, RG 20.54, SAA.

103. Price, "Random Reminiscences," 137. It should be noted that Price's observation contradicts Milsaps's suggestion, noted earlier, that returning "traitors" were often given greater rewards than "loyal" officers.

104. Historically, the Salvation Army made very little headway in the South. John Milsaps Diary, vol. 7, New Series, RG 20.54, SAA.

105. Damon Diaries, 8 January 1900, RG 20.38, Box 229/7, SAA.

106. To "farewell" was to be transferred from an assignment. Damon Diaries, 16 February 1900, RG 20.38, Box 229/7, SAA.

107. Adjutant Wilber Gale to R. E. Holz, 10 May 1898, R. E. Holz Papers, RG 20.60, 62/5, SAA.

108. The Harvest Festival appeal began in the United States late in 1896. Each corps collected food or any salable items which were auctioned off or sold to Army institutions. "The money secured was used for the operations of the Army." Wisbey, *Soldiers Without Swords*, 134.

109. Damon Diaries, 31 October 1900, RG 20.38, Box 229/7, SAA.

110. R. E. Holz, "The Atlantic Coast Province," Holz Brief, RG 89-35, 1908, 115, SAA. It may be that her formidable fundraising skills allowed this officer to retain a considerable amount of individual and local autonomy.

111. Damon Diaries, 22 August 1905, RG 20.38, Box 229/7, SAA.

112. The phrase "woman's work for woman" emerged from the work of female evangelical societies that saw it as their duty to "bring the good news to other women." The Woman's Presbyterian Board of Missions used it as the title of the monthly publication. It was used to describe many different kinds of foreign and home missionary work financed by, carried out by, and aimed at women. Rosemary Skinner Keller, "Lay Women in the Protestant Tradition," in Rosemary Radford Ruether and Rosemary Skinner Keller, *Women and Religion in America*, vol. 1 (San Francisco: Harper and Row, 1981), 243–44.

113. According to Lee and Pettit the Eastern Territory included: 59 Industrial Homes, 45 Hotels, 1 Woodyard and 74 Labor Bureaus but only 14 Women's Homes and Hospitals, 3 Children's Homes, and 8 Settlements and Nurseries. There were 11 other institutions including Hospitals, Dispensaries and "Eventide Homes." Lee and Pettit, *Social Salvage*, 23.

114. Woodyards proved not to be a particularly good investment of Salvation Army social resources as the Army found it difficult to compete with machine-cut wood. In the Army's judgment the costs of the raw material as well as the means of

delivering the wood (teams and wagons) were far too high. R. E. Holz, "Brief Memoranda."

115. Wisbey, *Soldiers Without Swords*, 102–4. R. E. Holz, "Social Operations in the United States during 1898," unpublished manuscript, RG 20.60, Box 62/14, SAA. Men's social work also included cheap hotels and the Knights of Hope or work with prisons and jails.

116. Wisbey, *Soldiers Without Swords*, 103; quotation in R. E. Holz, "Social Operations in the United States during 1898."

117. Commissioner Frank Smith, *The Salvation War in America for 1885* (New York: Headquarters and Trade Department, 1885), RG 20.53, Box 51/15, SAA, 181; Lee and Pettit, *Social Salvage*, 25; see also Mrs. Colonel Higgins, "Rescue Brief," 1905, RG 2.7, Box 21.8, SAA. A 1906 annual report of this work referred to it as "The Women's and Children's Rescue Work." "Guests of Mercy: Review of the Women's and Children's Rescue Work during 1906" (New York: Headquarters of the Women's and Children's Rescue Work, 1906), BB312. For more on changes in these kinds of institutions, see Michael B. Katz, *Poverty and Policy in American History* (New York: Academic Press, 1983).

118. According to an annual report of Rescue Work in America, the contribution provided by "Home Industry" ranged from .04 percent in St. Louis to 35 percent at Beulah Home in Oakland, Calif. The average contribution was 12.5 percent. "Light and Shadow: Being the Annual Report of the Rescue Work of the Salvation Army in America," SAA, BB310.

119. In one city the PO provided a monthly grant "with the understanding that the officer in charge does no regular soliciting for money through the city." Mrs. Colonel Higgins, "Rescue Brief," 1905, RG 2.7, Box 21-8, SAA.

120. Relief consisted of the distribution of food and other supplies to families in need. Lee and Pettit, *Social Salvage*, 26.

121. Mrs. Colonel Higgins, "Slum Department," 1903, RG 2.7, Box 21-8, SAA.

122. Wrote the field secretary, "[W]herever Field Corps are within a reasonable distance of an Industrial Home, Army Soldiers employed at the Industrial Home should be enrolled in the Field Corps." Field Secretary to Lt. Colonel Parker, 19 September 1910, "Enrollment of Industrial Soldiers," National Head Quarters Chief Secretary Field Notes, RG 1.17, Box 324/13, SAA.

123. Lee and Pettit, *Social Salvage*, 7, 15. See also interview with Major Jane E. Wrieden, Superintendent of "Door of Hope," 2 February 1949, Wisbey Papers, Social Services, RG 20.53, Box 51/16, SAA.

124. "Octogram" represented the eight departments that made up the Men's Social. Parker, *My Fifty-Eight Years*, 162–63.

125. Wisbey, "Religion in Action," 288–90 (quotation on p. 289).

126. John Milsaps Diary, vol. 11, New Series, RG 20.54, SAA. In 1899 Milsaps wrote, "Should that policy [of only appointing Booth family members to leadership positions] be adhered to in coming years until the many junior Booth's come of age who are now growing up, we shall have the spectacle of a vast religious organization controlled and existing entirely for the members of one family" (vol. 9). Evangeline was William and Catherine Booth's seventh child. She was thirty-nine when she became national commander. Wisbey, "Religion in Action," 293.

127. McKinley, *Marching to Glory*, 94. Wisbey, "Religion in Action," 294–95.

128. McKinley, *Marching to Glory*, 111.

129. Ibid., 95. Earlier married leaders included George Scott Railton, Thomas E. Moore, Frank Smith, Ballington Booth, and Emma and Frederick Booth-Tucker. It should be pointed out, however, that Railton's wife did not accompany him to the United States.

130. Ibid., 103, 117–24. Diane Winston has a lengthy discussion of the Salvation Army Doughnut Girls. She argues that by World War I the Army had shifted its goals from sacralizing space to sacralizing action, for example, by mothering the troops. The Army had also learned to use nonreligious symbols, like the doughnut, to represent these sacred activities to the public. Winston, *Red Hot and Righteous*, 177–90. However, because Winston's work focuses so exclusively on the relationship between urban middle-class culture and the stories that the Army told about itself in its publications, she fails to recognize that many Salvationists found these nonreligious symbols troubling and sacralized social-service activity problematic. For example, in the course of preparing a display for the Sesquicentennial exhibit in Philadelphia, Salvationist Edward J. Parker asked a professional builder to help him design a thirty-foot-high tower on which would be "a globe with an illuminated hand reading, 'The World for God.' " When he returned the man had instead placed at the top of the tower, "a Salvation Army lassie standing like the Statue of Liberty, holding a doughnut high in her right hand." A horrified Parker claims to have spent the day disabusing the man of the notion that " 'the Army started by making doughnuts for the soldiers in France.' " Edward J. Parker, *My Fifty-Eight Years* (New York: National Headquarters, 1943), 176–77.

131. McKinley, *Marching to Glory*, 100, 128. For more on the Community Chest, see James Lieby, *A History of Social Welfare and Social Work in the United States* (New York: Columbia University Press, 1978).

132. Lee and Pettit, *Social Salvage*, 34. According to the report, the commander had the power to make all staff changes, to sanction all property sales, purchases, and construction, and held supreme control over the entire U.S. field. The governing board (established by incorporation in 1899) could only overrule the commander by a 4/5 vote. However, since there were only five members, including the commander, that meant that all four remaining members would have to vote against her. Still, even in the early twentieth century, Evangline Booth and NHQ's authority was not perfect. Field Orders issued in the early twentieth century indicate that corps continued to ignore orders. In this case they persisted in utilizing ex-officers or non-Salvationists to fill in as temporary officers or evangelists. Orders appear regularly warning corps not to do so unless they get permission from the provincial officer or from NHQ. By 1927, the American chief secretary issued orders that such appointees would not "be put on the payroll of the Army until a proposal has been submitted to the Field Department and written permission obtained." "Re: Revivalists," Richard E. Holz, 3 March 1927, National Headquarters National Chief Secretary Field Notes, RG 1.17, Box 324/6, SAA.

133. Margaret Troutt, *The General Was a Lady: The Story of Evangeline Booth* (Nashville: A. J. Holman, 1980), 127.

134. McKinley, *Marching to Glory*, 111.

135. Bramwell Booth to Chief of the Staff, Higgins, 26 April 1926, RG 20.111, Box 125/3, SAA; Bramwell Booth to Chief of the Staff, Higgins, 7 and 9 October 1926, RG 20.111, Box 125/5, SAA.

136. Bramwell Booth to Evangeline Booth, 4 February 1888, Evangeline Cory Booth, RG 20.40, Box 28/5, SAA.

137. Bramwell Booth to Evangeline Booth, 12 February 1896, Evangeline Cory Booth, RG 20.40, Box 28/5, SAA.

138. Wisbey, "Religion in Action," 359.

139. Ibid., 361; McKinley, *Marching to Glory*, 133. Most observers suggest that Evangeline Booth orchestrated the public outcry. Given her determination to retain her power, that seems quite likely.

140. McKinley, *Marching to Glory*, 133.

141. New York *World*, 6 December 1922, quoted in Wisbey, "Religion in Action," 362.

142. Wisbey, "Religion in Action," 362. While I would argue that Wisbey exaggerated the extent of William Booth's authority, the first general had successfully prevented his son Ballington from reversing IHQs order to relinquish the American national command twenty-six years before. In what appeared to be similar circumstances, Bramwell bowed to public pressure and reversed his decision to remove Eva.

143. Bramwell Booth to "My Dear Chief" (Higgins?), 30 September 1926, RG 20.111, Box 125/5, SAA.

144. McKinley, *Marching to Glory*, 133.

145. Ibid.

146. Theda Skocpol, *Protecting Soldiers and Mothers: The Political Origins of Social Policy in the United States* (Cambridge, Mass.: Harvard University Press, 1992), 5.

147. The notion of the semi-welfare state is drawn from Michael Katz, *In the Shadow of the Poor House: A Social History of Welfare in America* (New York: Basic Books, 1986), 111.

148. W. L. Atwood, Wichita Falls, Tex., to Commissioner Holz, 30 November 1927, and attached draft of a bulletin to be "sent to our officers in this country and abroad at an early date," R. E. Holz Correspondence, RG 20.60, Box 62/7, SAA. McKinley says that the Manifestos were "signed by 'W. L. Atwood,' supposedly a soldier at the Wichita Falls, Texas, corps, but apparently written by another hand." McKinley, *Marching to Glory*, 134.

149. Wisbey, "Religion in Action," 369.

150. It should be pointed out that in spite of his illness, Bramwell Booth fought back vigorously, probably through his family. To the horror of many Salvationists, he inaugurated litigation first because he claimed that he had not been given the opportunity to present his case to the council and later in an attempt to prevent Salvation Army governmental reforms from being implemented. Wisbey, "Religion in Action," 371.

151. The conference also attempted to establish seventy as a retirement age for generals and to set up an arbitration board to resolve conflicts between the general and high-ranking officers. For reasons not discussed in Salvation Army literature, the British Parliament struck down these two provisions when it passed the Salvation Army Act of 1931. Wisbey, "Religion in Action," 373.

152. Ibid., 384.

Chapter Five

1. *AWC*, 14 March 1896, 13, in Allan Whitworth Bosch, "The Salvation Army in Chicago, 1885–1914" (Ph.D. diss., University of Chicago, 1965) 191–92.

2. Lyell Rader, *Rediscovering the Open-Air Meeting: A Manual for Salvationist Soul*

Winning (New York: The Salvation Army, Eastern Territory, the Evangelism and Adult Services Department, 1983), edited by Capt. Lyell Rader Jr. from the 1953 edition, 18, 19, 24, 28, 36. A timbrel brigade was, according to Rader, "the Christian version of drum majorettes" (24).

3. Exceptions to this are the ubiquitous Christmas Kettles and in some areas Salvation Army bands that accompany them.

4. Lawrence W. Levine, *Highbrow/Lowbrow: The Emergence of Cultural Hierarchy in America* (Cambridge, Mass.: Harvard University Press, 1988), 177.

5. Ibid., passim; James Gilbert, *Perfect Cities: Chicago's Utopias of 1893* (Chicago: University of Chicago Press, 1991), 3; Robert C. Allen, *Horrible Prettiness: Burlesque and American Culture* (Chapel Hill: University of North Carolina Press, 1991), 192. See also John F. Kasson, *Amusing the Million: Coney Island at the Turn-of-the-Century* (New York: Hill and Wang, 1978).

6. John F. Kasson, *Rudeness and Civility: Manners in Nineteenth-Century Urban America* (New York: Hill and Wang, 1990), 123, 126, 147, 148, 251.

7. Letter to the editor of the *Inter-Ocean* signed "Justice," reprinted in *AWC*, 10 April 1886, 1.

8. "Explaining to the Pastors," *New York Times*, 19 March 1889, 9.

9. Kasson, *Rudeness and Civility*, 247.

10. For more discussion of attempts by college-educated Salvationists to curb expressive religion, see chapter 3. For more on the role of corporate holiness, see chapter 3.

11. For more on auxiliaries, see chapter 1.

12. For more on the expansion of this policy, see chapter 4.

13. These ideas are discussed in greater detail in chapter 4.

14. In his history of the Salvation Army in Canada, R. G. Moyles said that in the 1890s, "the Salvation Army's commitment to social work, with the large expenditure it involved, meant that the organization, more than ever dependent on public support, could no longer afford to antagonize other churches and local dignitaries." R. G. Moyles, *The Blood and Fire in Canada: A History of the Salvation Army in the Dominion, 1882–1976* (Toronto: Peter Martin Associates, 1977), 122.

15. The remaining witness, Harvey Correy was a policeman who testified that he went to the hall between 12:00 and 1:00 in the morning, and during the hour and a half that he was there the brass band finished (around 12:00) "and after that they had only singing and speaking." *The People of the City and County of New York v. Frederick De Lautour Booth-Tucker*, transcript, 43–46 (quotation on 45), RG 20.00, Box 114/18, SAA.

16. Among the witnesses for *The People*, two owned homes and/or engaged in real estate transactions in the area, six rented rooms in their houses to boarders, and four rented rooms in other houses on the street. One woman rented rooms to "gentlemen . . . businessmen" and the other rented rooms to 10–12 "trained nurses." Ten of *The People*'s witnesses mentioned being married and/or having between one and six children, and three indicated that they had live-in servants. *The People v. Frederick Booth-Tucker*, 6–118.

17. Ibid., 88, 79.

18. Ibid., 49.

19. Levine, *Highbrow/Lowbrow*, 198.

20. He repeated part of one song as an example: "No, no, we will never get

drunk again, for merry, merry, we will be tonight and tomorrow we will get sober again." *The People v. Frederick Booth-Tucker*, 13, 22, 42, 65, 68.

21. Ibid., 63, 65, 75.

22. William Marcy Tweed rose to power in New York City in 1851. By 1868 he not only served in the State Senate but also headed Tammeny Hall. A. Oakley Hall was one of the key members of the ring. Tweed and his machine fell from power after Thomas Nast and *Harper's Weekly* waged an editorial campaign against corruption in New York City. Tweed was convicted of embezzlement in 1871. Hall was also apparently prosecuted but not convicted. At Booth-Tucker's trial, Hall recalled, "Twenty-five years ago I stood where this man, my client, stands today. I was hounded into court by hungry reformers, who sought to convict me of crime. The jury did for me what I hope you will do for Booth-Tucker—they acquitted me." *New York World* quoted in Herbert A. Wisbey Jr., "Religion in Action: A History of the Salvation Army in the United States" (Ph.D. diss., Columbia University, 1951), 260. It is interesting to note that while Maud and Ballington cultivated the cream of New York society, the Booth-Tuckers apparently recognized that politicians could be more valuable allies. In addition to Tammeny Hall Democrats like A. Oakley Hall, the Salvation Army found a friend in Republican politicians like Senator Mark Hanna and William McKinley. McKinley, *Marching to Glory*, 91. For more on William Marcy Tweed, see Alexander B. Callow Jr., " 'What Are You Going to Do about It?': The Crusade against the Tweed Ring," *New York Historical Society Quarterly* 49, no. 2 (1965): 117–42; Seymour J. Mandelbaum, *Boss Tweed's New York* (1965; reprint, Chicago, I. R. Dee, 1990).

23. This is not the only time the Salvation Army relied on comparisons to earlier religious movements to justify its "methods." Throughout the 1880s and 1890s *The War Cry* published articles that compared the Army not only to the "Mosaic tradition" but also to the early Methodists. For example, one article reported, "Speaking of the Salvation Army, the other day, an old gentleman remarked that the methods of worship employed by the Army were exactly like those of the early Methodists. Why, said he, Peter Cartwright made more noise than twenty Salvation Army's like the one in Joliet." "The Poor Man's Church," *AWC*, 27 February 1886, 1. None of the Salvation Army's witnesses spoke to these arguments, however.

24. *The People v. Frederick Booth-Tucker*, 126, 127, 130, 131.

25. Ibid., 127, 129.

26. As indicated earlier, Frederick Booth-Tucker was related to John Randolph Tucker.

27. *The People v. Frederick Booth-Tucker*, 128.

28. Emma and Frederick Booth-Tucker were joint commanders, and Alice Lewis was a brigadier. Charles Anderson, Joseph John Stimpson, and Joseph C. Ludgate were cashier/bandmaster, drummer/printing department distributor, and headquarters corps leader respectively.

29. *People v. Frederick Booth-Tucker*, 143, 164.

30. I have been unable to find biographical information about Alice Lewis in the documents. Norman Murdoch includes her among the "middle-class women" who were attracted to the Salvation Army in the late nineteenth century. Norman Murdoch, "Female Ministry in the Thought and Work of Catherine Booth," *Church History* 53 (1984): 357.

31. Ibid., 188, 190.

32. The judge suspended Booth-Tucker's sentence. Madison Ferris, "Salvation Army Cases," unpublished typescript, RG 2.15, Box 143/6, SAA.

33. *New York Herald*, quoted in Wisbey, "Religion in Action," 261. By arguing that the decision reflected class bias, Booth-Tucker revealed differences with Maud and Ballington Booth. He seemed more inclined to court machine politicians and entrepreneurs than New York's upper classes.

34. J. W. Strine to Colonel Brewer, 22 March 1898, Property Department Eastern Territory, Legal Secretary's Correspondence, RG 2.15, Box 143/9, SAA.

35. The Salvation Army regularly referred to arrested officers as "jail-birds" for Jesus. See "Jail-Bird Smith of Iowa," *AWC*, 8 February 1890, 8.

36. "Our prison columns! Records of shame. More Arrests!" *AWC*, 6 June 1885, 1.

37. "Jail-Bird Smith of Iowa," *AWC*, 8 February 1890, 8.

38. "Our Jail Birds!" *AWC*, 21 December 1889, 4; "Imprisoned for Jesus," *AWC*, 21 December 1889, 1.

39. Ben Bengare [?] to Major Cousins, 6 September 1898; see also Captain Harrington to "My Dear Major," 1 April 1898: "I want my rights that is all. I ask your advise under the circumstances . . . I do not believe in breaking the law. But I do not want a few men to scare me"; both letters in Property Department Eastern Territory, Legal Secretary's Correspondence, RG 2.15, Box 143/9, SAA. As we have seen, Commander Booth-Tucker also used this argument when he suggested that the guilty verdict in his 1897 trial had been a blow against religious liberty.

40. Captain Waldron to Staff Captain Ferris, 12 November 1898; quotation in Captain Arthur Miles to Staff-Captain Ferris, 20 March 1899; both letters in Property Department Eastern Territory, Legal Secretary's Correspondence, RG 2.15, Box 143/9, SAA. The Legal Department was created in February 1897 from the combined Property, Legal and Janitorial Departments. From that time until August 1908, Madison J. H. Ferris (1846–1923) headed the Legal Department as attorney and counsel. See "Finding Aid," Legal Department, RG 2.10, SAA.

41. Captain Harrington to "My Dear Major," 1 April 1898, Potsdam, N.Y.; Madison Ferris to Major J. W. Cousins, 5 April 1898, both letters in Property Department Eastern Territory, Legal Secretary's Correspondence, RG 2.15, Box 143/9, SAA.

42. Staff Captain Ferris to Staff Captain Potter, 26 August 1898, Property Department Eastern Territory, Legal Secretary's Correspondence, RG 2.15, Box 143/7, SAA.

43. Staff Captain Ferris to Major McIntyre, 24 January 1899, Property Department Eastern Territory, Legal Secretary's Correspondence, RG 2.15, Box 143/7, SAA.

44. As the "Poor Man's Lawyer," Ferris's cases included helping widows get their husband's pensions (Civil War), helping people regain property lost to "unscrupulous lawyers," helping women regain their children who had been taken by the state, and assisting workers who had been injured on the job. His wife, Caroline Ferris, served as a probation officer for young girls. Property Department Eastern Territory Legal Secretary's Correspondence, RG 2/15, Box 1/1, SAA.

45. McKinley, *Marching to Glory*, 44; Staff Captain Ferris to Major J. W. Cousins,

5 April 1898, Property Department Eastern Territory, Legal Secretary's Correspondence, RG 2.15, Box 143/7, SAA.

46. J. B. Mugford, Ensign, 7 July 1898, Property Department Eastern Territory, Legal Secretary's Correspondence, RG 2.15, Box 143/7, SAA.

47. J. Barnett Mugford, Ensign, to Brigadier Gifford, 21 July 1898, Property Department Eastern Territory, Legal Secretary's Correspondence, RG 2.15, Box 143/7, SAA.

48. There is no indication that headquarters actually sent Joe. The corps must have contacted him directly or he heard about the situation from others. This is another example of headquarters' inability to stifle individual or local autonomy completely.

49. Staff Captain Ferris to Brigadier Gifford, 25 October 1898, Property Department Eastern Territory, Legal Secretary's Correspondence, RG 2.15, Box 143/7, SAA.

50. Brigadier J. C. Addie to Staff Captain Ferris, 15 September 1898, Property Department Eastern Territory, Legal Secretary's Correspondence, RG 2.15 Box 143/7, SAA.

51. Ferris to Staff Captain Potter, 12 August 1898; Ferris to Captain Harrison, 19 March 1898; both letters in Property Department Eastern Territory, Legal Secretary's Correspondence, RG 2.15, Box 143/6, SAA.

52. Kasson, *Rudeness and Civility*, 246–48. Frederick Booth-Tucker, *The Consul: A Memoir of Emma Moss Booth-Tucker* (London: Salvation Publishing and Supplies, 1928), 267. Even in its genteel form, Emma Booth-Tucker expressed some concern that the Army's use of these genteel versions of popular culture might arouse opposition " 'not only in our own ranks, but amongst the Christian public.' " Would Salvationists, she wondered, be able to remain free from " 'the ordinary dangers and worldliness attached to the stage,' " or would they " ' *cater to the worldling on worldly and forbidden ground?* ' " She went on to say that the danger would be minimized if clear guidelines were established. " 'I think a little Regulation Paper should be drawn up, which will in itself be a *great safeguard* ' " [italics in original].

53. Booth-Tucker, *The Consul*, 269.

54. McKinley, *Marching to Glory*, 224–25; Murdoch, "Female Ministry," 182; Booth-Tucker, *The Consul*, 269.

55. Booth-Tucker, *The Consul*, 269. Miraculously, the glass lantern slides from this program have survived virtually intact at the Salvation Army Archives and Research Center in Alexandria. I am very grateful to the staff for allowing me to examine them.

56. Edward Parker served as stage manager for *Love and Sorrow*, and his young son Paul played one of the children in the scene. In his autobiography Parker recalled the technical complexity of managing the program. In addition to setting up the stereopticon each night, he had to supervise the "hang[ing] and chang[ing of] five sets of scenery, instruct the stage hands concerning the colored lights, shift the stage properties . . . in time for the next pull-up, and light up for five of these shifts before the curtain came down on the final scene." Edward J. Parker, *My Fifty Eight Years* (New York: National Headquarters, 1943), 144, 146.

57. The "colonists cottage" refers to the Salvation Army's Farm Colony. For more discussion on this part of the social scheme, see chapter 4. Booth-Tucker, *The Consul*, 269–80.

58. Parker, *My Fifty Eight Years*, 172.

59. Clarence W. Hall, *Samuel Logan Brengle: Portrait of a Prophet* (Chicago: The Salvation Army Supply and Purchasing Department, 1933), 84, 104, 146–47.

60. McKinley, *Marching to Glory*, 86.

61. Moyles, *Blood and Fire*, 228–30.

62. Herbert Wisbey, *Soldiers Without Swords: A History of the Salvation Army in the United States* (New York: Macmillan, 1955), 195.

63. Edward and Eva Parker joined the Salvation Army in 1885 and 1890, respectively. They married in 1893. Edward Justus Parker Papers, RG 20.12, SAA. Nicki Tanner, "The Salvation Army Oral History Interview with Mrs. Brigadier John Fahey," unpublished typescript, 1987, RG 20.38, Box 81/15, SAA, 9–10, 14–15, 24. See also Mrs. Brigadier Marjorie G. Hartman, "The Salvation Army Oral History Interview with Colonel Rowland Hughes," unpublished typescript, 1989, RG 20.71, Box 80/15, SAA, 10 (for some discussion of education and "professionalism" among Salvation Army officers in the twentieth century).

64. Walter I. Trattner, *From Poor Law to Welfare State: A History of Social Welfare in America* (New York: The Free Press, 1989), 211–27. See also Michael B. Katz, *In the Shadow of the Poorhouse: A Social History of Welfare in America* (New York: Basic Books, 1986).

65. Hartman, "Interview with Colonel Rowland Hughes," 35.

66. Tanner, "Interview with Mrs. Brigadier John Fahey," 9–10. Mrs. Fahey was born in 1906 in Mount Vernon, N.Y.

67. *The Christian at Work*, quoted in *AWC*, 19 June 1883, 1.

68. Porter R. Lee and Walter W. Pettit, *Social Salvage: A Study of the Organization and Administration of the Salvation Army* (New York: National Information Bureau, 1924), 88. The female officers in this example probably also responded to the sexual implications of being a woman "rescued from sin."

69. Charles H. Lippy, "The Camp Meeting in Transition: The Character and Legacy of the Late Nineteenth Century," *Methodist History* 34 (October 1995): 7.

70. Moyles, *The Blood and Fire*, 229.

71. Bosch, "The Salvation Army in Chicago," 195.

72. Moyles, *The Blood and Fire*, 229.

73. Jobie Gilliam, "Salvation Army Theatricalities" (MA thesis, California State University, Long Beach, 1989), 150.

74. Nicki Tanner, "Interview with Lt. Colonel Lyell Rader," unpublished typescript, 1986, RG 20.82, SAA, 85. Rader was the author of *Rediscovering the Open-Air Meeting* cited above.

75. Similarly, according to Michael McGerr, spectacular political parades virtually disappeared in the first decade of the twentieth century because they "no longer reflected the patterns of Northern society." In the two generations since the Civil War, he said, "people lost the martial interest that was one facet of campaign spectacle"; parades now appeared "old fashioned." The most significant element in the decline of spectacular display, he argues, was its inability to compete with the entertainment offered by the emerging leisure and consumer culture. McGerr also points to the more antagonistic nature of class relations in the late nineteenth century that left the well-to-do with little appetite for public displays of mutual respect. Michael E. McGerr, *The Decline of Popular Politics: The American North, 1865–1928* (New York: Oxford University Press, 1986), 146–48.

76. Moyles, *Blood and Fire*, 239. Colonel McIntyre to Brigadier Ferris, 24 December 1912, RG 2.12, Box 109/3, SAA.

77. *AWC*, 12 September 1885, 2. See also "Talk with Captain Richard E. Holz," 16 July 1948, Interviews, Herbert Wisbey Jr., RG 20.53, Box 51/19, SAA. See chapter 3 for a discussion of the "musical" outcome of early Salvation Army efforts.

78. Kasson, *Rudeness and Civility*, 234; McKinley also calls this "the new era of professionalism" in his discussion of changes in Salvation Army bands. He points out that training began early for Salvationists with the opening of music or band camps beginning in 1920. McKinley also described an extreme case of professionalism in which a Salvation Army conductor/composer who was apparently a bit of a prima donna actually refused a request from Commander Evangeline Booth to end his carefully planned program with "an old-time chorus called, 'The Salvation Army Doxology.'" According to McKinley, the conductor was "always stiffly formal about such things. . . . [and felt that] after a superb, well-rehearsed, and brilliant evening: it would be a ruinous anticlimax." McKinley, *Marching to Glory*, 160, 169, 170.

79. "Armistice Day Parade," photograph, Dallas, 1922, PP3601, SAA. Interestingly, "1994 marked the Army's seventy-fifth appearance in the parade, earning it the distinction of being the longest running band in the parade." "The Salvation Army Tournament of Roses Band Celebrates a 75 Year Tradition," *AWC*, 29 January 1994, 10–11. Denise Lawrence, "Doo Dah Ladies and Tournament Gals," Paper delivered at a Women's Studies Seminar on "Gender and Public Ritual," 24 January 1998, Huntington Library, San Marino, Calif.

80. John Milsaps Diary, vol. 10, New Series, December 1899–April 1900, RG 20.54, M12910, SAA; Wisbey, "Talk with Holz"; Tanner, "Interview with Lyell Rader." Lieut.-Colonel Edward Justus Parker, "Problems of the Poor" (New York: The Salvation Army Social Department, 1908), Parker Papers, RG 20.12, Box 210/11, SAA.

81. Parker, *My Fifty Eight Years*, 168.

82. See chapter 3. See also Moyles, *Blood and Fire*, 230.

83. William Booth, handwritten memo, RG 20.97, Box 89/6, SAA.

84. Kasson, *Rudeness and Civility*, 215, 234–39, 242, 247.

85. Levine, *Highbrow/Lowbrow*, 195.

86. Tom Berg, "Salvation Army Has New Tune," *Orange County Register*, 1 December 1997, 1. Thanks to my colleague Stanley Burstein, for bringing this article to my attention. From its beginnings there has been a steady co-optation of rock music. Some performers of rock have always sought broad appeal, expressed mainstream values, and been easily adaptable to commercial culture. It is not surprising, then, that some rock music has become increasingly acceptable among evangelical Christian groups, particularly those in television ministries.

87. Lippy, "The Camp Meeting in Transition," 10.

88. For more on the bureaucratization and specialization of the Salvation Army, see chapter 4.

89. Between 1880 and 1896, the Salvation Army claimed 25,000 soldiers in the United States. By 1913, the number of soldiers had only grown by 6,700 to 31,703. Wisbey, *Soldiers Without Swords*, 122. Since the Army does not allow researchers to examine resignation statistics, it is not possible to say how many members resigned during those same years.

90. John Milsaps Diary, vol. 11, New Series, RG 20.54, SAA. Although the Salvation Army has always restricted publication of resignation statistics, many of the officers who lived through the period obviously found the rate of departure quite alarming.

91. "The Siege: Official Orders by Evangeline Booth Commander-in-Chief of U.S. Forces," AWC, 4 February 1905, 1, SAA.

92. As late as 1986, some older officers continued to lobby for inventive open-air evangelism, arguing that if officers developed the right techniques "for today's crowd," open-airs could still prove valuable as a way to bring salvation to sinners and new members to the organization. Eighty-four-year-old Lyell Rader told an interviewer that he'd "been barking about it a long time." It will be remembered that he wrote the book *Rediscovering the Open-Air Meeting* in 1953. In his interview Rader pointed out that of the two quartets that he used in neighborhood open-airs, seven members became officers and one became "a full-time independent evangelist. . . . Just being exposed to the fight." Tanner, "Interview with Lyell Rader," 84.

93. John Milsaps Diary, vol. 11, New Series, RG 20.54, SAA.

94. "The Siege: Official Orders by Evangeline Booth Commander-in-Chief of U.S. Forces," AWC, 4 February 1905, 1, SAA. As the numbers indicate, this model for raising soldiership was not particularly successful.

95. Price, "Random Reminiscences," 186. Price went on to join the Christian and Missionary Alliance, an evangelical Christian organization founded in 1881 by A. B. Simpson, "for the purpose of extending missionary work at home and abroad." Sydney E. Ahlstrom, *A Religious History of the American People* (New Haven, Conn.: Yale University Press, 1972), 812n.

96. Commander Evangeline Booth to Major Harris, Denver, Colo., 13 December 1906, 235/5, Damon Correspondence, RG 20.38, SAA.

97. Herbert Wisbey Jr., "Interview with Commissioner Edward J. Parker," 9 August 1948, Interviews, RG 20.53, 51/19, SAA.

98. Richard Niebuhr, *The Social Sources of Denominationalism* (New York: Henry Holt, 1929), 19. For other works that discuss the shift from sect to church, see Roger Finke and Rodney Stark, *The Churching of America, 1776–1990: Winners and Losers in Our Religious Economy* (New Brunswick, N.J.: Rutgers University Press, 1997).

99. Tanner, "Interview with Mrs. Brigadier John Fahey," 132. See also Wisbey, *Soldiers Without Swords*, 196.

100. Tanner, "Interview with Mrs. Fahey," 9.

101. At the Army's 1985 International Youth Congress at Western Illinois University, the group called on the special skills of two cheerleaders (one a former Rams' cheerleader, the other a cheerleader at Santa Ana College) to demonstrate through "simple choreography the beginning of birth and man by God's creation." Gilliam, "Salvation Army Theatricalities," 153, 155, 157 (quotation on p. 159).

102. Roy Rosenzweig, *Eight Hours for What We Will: Workers and Leisure in an Industrial City, 1870–1920* (Cambridge: Cambridge University Press, 1983), 191.

103. Ibid., 199–200.

104. Ibid., 210–11.

105. Levine, *Highbrow/Lowbrow*, 232; Allen, *Horrible Prettiness*, 192.

106. Edith Waldvogel Blumhofer, *Restoring the Faith: The Assemblies of God, Pen-

tecostalism, and American Culture (Urbana: University of Illinois Press, 1993), 56–58 (quotation on p. 57); Charles Fox Parham, "Baptism of the Holy Ghost," quoted in Blumhofer, 61, 101.

107. Price, "Random Reminiscences," 183.

Conclusion

The remarks in the epigraph are taken from an audiotape of a talk given by Evangeline Booth.

1. *The Salvation Army Year Book* (London: International Headquarters of the Salvation Army, 1988), 1, 7.

2. Sallie Tisdale, "Good Soldiers," *The New Republic* 3 (January 1994): 22. Tisdale reported that the Army claimed "more than 5 million members in ninety-nine countries." Moreover, in 1993 it had raised over $726 million from private donations in the United States alone. She also reported that the group provided a broad range of social services from homeless shelters to nursing care for AIDS patients.

3. Nicki Tanner, "The Salvation Army Oral History Interview with Mrs. Brigadier John Fahey," unpublished typescript, 1987, SAA, 9–10.

4. James R. Green, *The World of the Worker: Labor in Twentieth Century America* (New York: Hill and Wang, 1980), 159.

5. Ibid., 185.

{ INDEX }

"Slum Brigade," 41–43, 111, 118, 124, 128–30, 154

"Slum Settlements," 129

Slum Sisters, 42, 130

Smith, Frank, 34–39, 42, 47, 52, 83, 94, 214 (n. 11), 215 (n. 21)

Smith, Hannah Whitall, 68

Social Christianity, evangelical, 4, 6, 7, 71, 106, 108, 112, 217 (n. 38); W. Booth's version of, 106–7

Social gospel movements, 19

Social service, 102, 104–16, 108, 111, 120, 137, 155, 161, 166–67, 215 (n. 22); ambivalence toward, 115; W. Booth's attitude toward, 115–16; and gender, 128–29; symbols and rituals in, 130

Solenberger, Edwin R., 112–13

Stead, William T., 105–6

Strong, Josiah, 19, 47, 59, 179 (n. 8), 192 (n. 165)

Sunday school, 13

Swift, Susan, 49–50, 193 (n. 4)

Tableaux vivants, 74, 153, 205 (n. 6)

Taves, Ann, 76, 206 (n. 13)

Temperance, 17, 90, 137, 198 (n. 54)

Theology, 99, 181 (n. 25); and egalitarianism, 50, 65

Tompkins Square riots, 28, 187 (n. 101)

Training, 65; garrisons or colleges for, 77, 101–2, 119, 131, 142, 157, 207 (n. 19), 210 (n. 72), 212–13 (n. 115)

"Trophies of Grace," 67

Tweed, William Marcy, 147, 227 (n. 22)

Unions, trade, 27–28, 78–79

Upham, Nellie, 49, 58, 60

Volunteers of America, 2, 109, 119, 121, 216–17 (n. 24)

Walker, Pamela, 177 (n. 17), 181 (n. 31), 183 (n. 46)

Wanamaker, John, 131

Wanamaker, Mrs. John, 43

War Cry, The, 28, 43, 52, 66–67, 81–82, 91, 96–97, 99–100, 118–19, 121, 150, 161, 185 (n. 79); and Moore, 32–34, 36; and F. Smith, 38–39

"War Service," 132

Water Street Mission, 27

Wesley, John, 14

Westbrook, Emma, 25, 27

Winston, Diane, 7, 187 (n. 101), 218 (n. 61), 224 (n. 130)

Wollstonecraft, Mary, 182 (n. 45)

Working class, religion of, 4–5, 7, 13

World's Congress of Representative Women, 65